JAY PRAKASH NARAYAN

JAY PRAKASH NARAYAN

Edited by

M.K. SINGH

ANMOL PUBLICATIONS PVT. LTD.

NEW DELHI - 110 002 (INDIA)

ANMOL PUBLICATIONS PVT. LTD.
H.O.: 4374/4B, Ansari Road, Darya Ganj,
New Delhi-110 002 (India)
Ph.: 23278000, 23261597
B.O.: No. 1015, Ist Main Road, BSK IIIrd Stage
IIIrd Phase, IIIrd Block,
Bangalore - 560 085 (India)
Visit us at: www.anmolpublications.com

Jay Prakash Narayan

First Published, 2008

ISBN 978-81-261-3518-9

PRINTED IN INDIA

Printed at Mehra Offset Press, Delhi.

CONTENTS

PREFACE

Jay Prakash Narayan was one of the top ranking socialists of modern India. He significantly contributed to the Sarvodaya philosophy. Narayan along with Vinoba Bhave believed in a partyless democracy. He was a patriot who during first phase which spread between 1929-1953 thought in terms of socialism for solving India's socio-economic and political problems. He considered socialism as a way of reconstructing Indian economy. For him, the present socio-economic inequality in India was primarily because of disproportionate ownership and control of means of production. He has said that for country's development it was essential that institutions which create hurdles on the way of development of man, man should be removed.

The presented book comprises his life sketch, economic and political approach, concept of total revolution and overview etc.

The book is of greater importance for the researchers, teachers and students etc.

1

JAY PRAKASH NARAYAN : LIFE SKETCH

Jay Prakash Narayan was born on October 11, 1902, in Sitabdiara, a village on the border of Uttar Pradesh and Bihar. His father Harsudayal was a junior official in the canal department of the State government and was often touring the region. His mother Phulo Rani was a simple, religious-minded woman who cast a deep imprint on young Jay Prakash 's mind. Jay Prakash , called Baul affectionately, was left with his grandmother to study in Sitabdiara. Since there was no high school in the village, Jay Prakash was sent to Patna to study in the Collegiate School . While in school, Jay Prakash read magazines like Saraswati, Prabha and Pratap, books like Bharat-Bharati, and poems by Maithilsharan Gupta and Bharatendu Harishchandra which described the courage and valor of the Rajput kings. Jay Prakash also read the Bhagwad Gita. He excelled in school. His essay, "The present state of Hindi in Bihar" won a best essay award. He joined the Patna College on a Government scholarship.

Jay Prakash was married to Prabhavati, daughter of lawyer and nationalist Brij Kishore Prasad in October 1920. Prabhavati was very independent-minded and on Gandhiji's invitation, went to stay at his ashram while Jay Prakash continued his studies. Jay Prakash , along with some friends, went to listen to Maulana Abul Kalam Azad speak about the Non-cooperation movement launched by Gandhiji against the passing of the Rowlatt Act of 1919.

The Maulana was a brilliant orator and his call to give up English education "like leaves before a storm, (Jay Prakash was) swept away and momentarily lifted up to the skies. That brief experience of soaring up with the winds of a great idea left imprints on (his) inner being." Jay Prakash took the Maulana's words to heart and left Patna College with just 20 days remaining for his examinations. He joined the Bihar Vidyapeeth, a college run by the Congress. After the Chauri Chaura incident in eastern Uttar Pradesh, the Non-cooperation movement was suspended. Most students returned to their colleges. After exhausting the courses at the Vidyapeeth, Jay Prakash decided to go to America to pursue his studies. In May 1922 he obtained a scholarship from an association in Calcutta to study in the United States. At age 20, Jay Prakash sailed aboard the cargo ship Janus while Prabhavati remained at Sabarmati. Jay Prakash reached California on October 8, 1922 and gained admission to Berkeley in January 1923. To pay for his education, Jay Prakash picked grapes, set them out to dry, packed fruits at a canning factory, washed dishes, worked as a mechanic at a garage and at a slaughter house, sold lotions and accepted teaching jobs. All these jobs gave Jay Prakash insight regarding the difficulties the working class faced. Jay Prakash was forced to transfer to Iowa State when fees at Berkeley were doubled. He was forced to transfer to many universities thereafter. He pursued his favorite subject, Sociology and received much help from Professor Edward Ross, the father of Sociology. In Wisconsin, Jay Prakash was introduced to Karl Marx's "Das Capital". News of the success of the Russian revolution of 1917 made Jay Prakash conclude that Marxism was the way to alleviate the suffering masses. He delved himself into books by Indian intellectual and Communist theoretician M.N. Roy. His paper on Sociology, "Social Variation", was declared as the best of the year. Jay Prakash had to cut his doctorate short when news came that his mother was seriously ill. Jay Prakash returned to India in November 1929, "a mature young man with an enquiring mind, original in his thinking, and with the fierce, idealistic desire to devote himself to serve society."

For Jay Prakash it was not enough that the nation attain political freedom. To him, the definition of freedom was freedom from hunger, poverty and ignorance. While Jay Prakash became a believer of the Communist school of thought, Prabhavati became an ardent Gandhian. He respected Prabhavati's choice and did not force her to change her views. In 1929, both Jay Prakash and Prabhavati left for the Congress session at Lahore under Jawaharlal Nehru's presidentship. There Nehru invited Jay Prakash to join the Congress, an offer that Jay Prakash gladly accepted. He began work in the Labor Research Cell of the Congress at Allahabad. Following the 1930 Dandi March, most of the top Congress leaders were arrested.

Jay Prakash immediately set up an underground office at Bombay to continue Congress work. He traveled all over the nation, printing, distributing and organizing secret meetings. After an underground meeting of the Congress Working Committee in Banaras, Jay Prakash went to Madras where he was arrested. The next day the newspaper headlines screamed, "Congress Brain Arrested!" It was in the

States that Jay Prakash came in contact with radical socialist ideas. After his return to India Jay Prakash came in touch with Gandhiji. The failure of the Gandhi-Irwin talks led to the civil disobedience movement and Jay Prakash readily joined it. He was arrested shortly after and put in the Nasik Jail. Here he met Achyut Patwardhan and Minoo Masani, which reinforced his socialist leanings. Later, along with Acharya Narendra Dev, he organised the All India Congress Socialist Party, and in support of his cause, wrote in 1936 'Why Socialism'. In the Nasik jail, Jay Prakash had the opportunity to meet thinkers like Ram Manohar Lohia, Ashoka Mehta, Minoo Masani, P. Dantawala and Achyut Patwardhan. They all were impatient for freedom and agreed to steer the Congress toward the goal of socialism. Jay Prakash was released from jail in 1933. In 1934, Jay Prakash and his friends formed the Congress Socialist Party under the Presidentship of Acharya Narendra Deva and secretaryship of Jay Prakash himself. The group intended to function as the Socialist wing within the Congress party and aimed to make socialism the goal of the Congress. In a book "Why Socialism?" (1932), Jay Prakash explained why socialism would be right for India. He was adored by the youth for his idealism. Jay Prakash was arrested for speaking against Indian participation in the Second World War in February 1940 and sent to Deoli detention camp in Rajasthan. Jay Prakash was appalled at the conditions in Deoli. He organized a hunger strike to protest the conditions in 1941. The Government immediately released him. He was again arrested in 1942 for participating in the Quit India movement.

In November 1942, Diwali night, Jay Prakash along with five others escaped the prison by scaling the 17 feet high wall while the guards remained distracted by the festivities. A Rs. 10,000 reward was offered for Jay Prakash 's capture, dead or alive. Jay Prakash escaped to Nepal and organized a guerilla army called the "Azad Dasta". Jay Prakash and Ram Manohar Lohia were captured briefly but were rescued by the Azad Dasta members, who set fire to a hut to distract the guards. Both freedom fighters escaped to Bihar. Finally the British closed in on Jay Prakash in Amritsar when he was on his way to Rawalpindi to meet Khan Abdul Gaffar Khan. Jay Prakash was taken to Lahore Fort, notorious as a "Torture chamber" on September 18, 1943. 16 months of mental and physical torture followed. Jay Prakash was put in solitary confinement for the first month. Then came interrogations, physical torture and humiliation. Jay Prakash was released from jail on April 12, 1946. Jay Prakash believed in non-violence. However, during the Quit India Movement he supported violent measures against British atrocities. He criticised the War aims of Britain as imperialistic.

In the domain of socio-economic reforms Jay Prakash 's socialistic zeal prompted him to advocate the abolition of Zamindari, nationalisation of natural resources, peasant proprietorship of land, nationalisation of heavy and basic industries and such other measures. He also strongly championed the cause of rural upliftment. He believed that a nation, to be united and to remain strong, must bring the remotest village into the mainstream of its political, economic and cultural life. Jay Prakash returned to a nation he could barely recognize. Talk of partition and riots between Hindu and Muslims dominated the atmosphere. Jay Prakash rushed to Bihar to assist in curbing the riots. He pleaded with the Congress Working Committee not to accept the partition plan. Independence finally came on August 15, 1947. Within a year Gandhiji was assassinated. Prabhavati hid her sorrow behind the spinning wheel, but Jay Prakash 's mind "churned (with) grief and horror." He began to see the wisdom in Gandhiji's insistence on truth and non-violence. The Socialists lost to the Congress in the 1952 elections. Nehru invited Jay

Prakash to join the Cabinet. When Nehru could give no assurances on the implementation of Jay Prakash 's 14 point plan to reform the Constitution, the Administration and Judicial system, nationalize the banks, redistribute land to the landless, revive Swadeshi, and setup cooperatives, Jay Prakash refused the offer. Jay Prakash turned his attention to the trade unions he was President of. He, along with the unions was able to get a minimum wage, pension, medical relief and housing subsidy introduced.

At the same time, Jay Prakash was keenly watching events in Russia. The bloody purges and imprisonment convinced Jay Prakash that communism was not for India. He realized that Gandhiji's success in the freedom struggle had showed that it was possible to bring about change without sacrificing one's values. On April 19, 1954, at a meeting in Gaya, Jay Prakash made the dramatic announcement of dedicating his life (jeewan daan) to Vinoba Bhave's Sarvodaya movement. He renounced all self-interest, gave up his land in Sitabdiara, and withdrew from all personal activity to devote the rest of his life to the movement. Prabhavati was delighted at this declaration. Jay Prakash set up an ashram at Hazaribagh, a poor and backward village. He gave Gandhian concepts a new dimension by using modern technology to uplift the village. Jay Prakash believed that every village should be like a small republic-politically independent and capable of taking its own decisions. It was a marriage of Gandhian-Indian concepts and modern Western democracy. His thoughful, well-researched and brilliant book, "The Reconstruction of Indian Polity," won him the Ramon Magsaysay Award. In June 1971, Sarvodaya workers in Muzaffarpur, Bihar, received a letter threatening to kill them.

The area was continuously threatened by Naxalites, which was made up of young men. Jay Prakash walked into the heart of Naxal territory armed only with love and sympathy. He knew that the cause of the violence was that the youth were frustrated because of poverty and unemployment. He lived in Musahari block for many months and experimented to alleviate the problems of the Naxals. Jay Prakash was also a key person in acquiring the surrender of dacoits in the Chambal Valley. On April 15, 1973, Prabhavati died of cancer, leaving Jay Prakash alone. 1974 ushered in a year of high inflation, unemployment and lack of supplies and essential commodities. Jay Prakash was asked to lead a peaceful agitation by the Navanirman Andolan of Gujarat. On April 8, 1974, at the age of 72, he led a silent procession at Patna. The procession was lathi charged.

On June 5, 1974, Jay Prakash addressed a mammoth crowd at Gandhi Maidan in Patna. He declared, "This is a revolution, friends! We are not here merely to see the Vidhan Sabha dissolved. That is only one milestone on our journey. But we have a long way to go... After 27 years of freedom, people of this country are wracked by hunger, rising prices, corruption... oppressed by every kind of injustice... it is a Total Revolution we want, nothing less!" On June 12, 1975, the Allahabad High Court held the Prime Minister, Mrs. Indira Gandhi, guilty on charge of corrupt practices in the election. Jay Prakash advised her to resign until her name was cleared by the Supreme Court. Instead, she clamped Emergency on June 26. Jay Prakash was arrested and sent to Chandigarh where he was kept prisoner in a hospital. "My world lies in shambles around me," he cried. As his health worsened, he was moved to a hospital in Bombay. Finally in January 1977, Emergency was lifted. Fresh elections were declared. Under Jay Prakash 's guidance several parties united to form the Janata Party. The party incorporated all of Jay Prakash 's goals in its manifesto. Jay Prakash was weak and helpless by that time. He felt his work was done, but he had to sorrowfully witness the collapse of the Janata Party government. Jay Prakash died on October 8, 1979. People hailed him as "Lok Nayak" or leader of the people. Vinoba Bhave said after Jay Prakash 's death that Jay Prakash considered himself only a "Lok-sevak," or servant of the people.

Sarvodaya

On 19 April 1954, JP announced in Gaya that he was dedicating his life (Jeevandan) to Vinoba Bhave's Sarvodaya movement and its Bhoodan campaign, which promoted distributing land to Harijans (untouchables). He gave up his land, set up an ashram in Hazaribagh, and worked towards uplifting the village. In 1957, JP formally broke with the Praja Socialist Party in order to pursue lokniti [Polity of the people], as opposed to rajniti [Polity of the state]. By this time, JP had become convinced that lokniti should be non-partisan in order to build a consensus-based, classless, participatory democracy which he termed Sarvodaya.

JP became an important figure in the India-wide network of Gandhian Sarvodaya workers. In 1964, JP was vilified across the political spectrum for arguing in an article in the Hindustan Times that India had a responsibility to keep its promise to allow self-determination to the state of Jammu and Kashmir. He hit back at critics in a second article, dismissing the Indian version of the "domino theory" which held that the rest of India's states would disintegrate if Kashmir were allowed its promised freedom. In his graceful if old-fashioned style, JP ridiculed the premise that "the states of India are held together by force and not by the sentiment of a common nationality. It is an assumption that makes a mockery of the Indian Nation and a tyrant of the Indian State". JP returned to the prominence in State politics in the late 1960s. In 1974, he devoted himself to the peasants' struggle known as the Bihar movement, which demanded the resignation of the provincial government. He founded, together with V. M. Tarkunde, the Citizens for democracy in 1974 and the People's union for civil liberties in 1976, NGOs to uphold and defend civil liberties.

When Indira Gandhi was found guilty of violating electoral laws by the Allahabad High Court, JP called for Indira to resign, and advocated a program of social transformation which he termed Sampoorna kraanthi [Total Revolution]. Instead she proclaimed a national Emergency on the midnight of 25 June 1975, immediately after JP had called for the PM's resignation and had asked the military and the police to disregard unconstitutional and immoral orders; JP, opposition leaders, and dissenting members (the 'Young turks') of her own party were arrested on that day. JP was kept as detenu at Chandigarh even after he had asked for a month's parole for mobilising relief in areas of Bihar gravely affected by flood. His health suddenly deteriorated on 24 October, and he was released on 12 November; diagnosis at Jaslok Hospital, Bombay, revealed kidney failure; he would be on dialysis for the rest of his life. After Indira revoked the emergency on 18 January 1977 and announced elections, it was under JP's guidance that the socialist-leaning Janata Party was formed. Janata Party was voted into power, and became the first non-Congress party to form a government at the Centre. JP also wrote several books, notably Reconstruction of Indian Polity.

He promoted Hindu revivalism, but was deeply critical of the form of revivalism promoted by the Sangh Parivar. Not long before his death, it was in fact erroneously announced by the Indian prime minister, causing a brief wave of national mourning, including the suspension of parliament and regular radio broadcasting, and closure of schools and shops. In 1998, he was posthumously awarded the Bharat Ratna award in recognition of his social work. Other awards include the Magsaysay award for Public Service in 1965. JP is sometimes referred to with the honorific title Lok nayak or 'guide of the people'. A university (J P University in Chhapra, Bihar) and two Hospitals (L J N P Hospital in New Delhi and Jai Prabha Hospital in Patna) have been opened in his memory. October 2001 marks the beginning of Jay Prakash Narayan's (JP) centenary year. Long regarded as one of the tallest leaders of our freedom struggle, JP, founder of the Congress Socialist Party, took sanyas from politics soon after the first elections and dedicated himself to the Sarvodaya movement. Years later, deeply disturbed by the deteriorating trends in our democratic polity, he launched the Sampoorna Kranti (Total Revolution) movement, was imprisoned during the Emergency, and on his release help found the Janata Party. We reproduce below extracts from his seminal essay, 'A Plea for the Reconstruction of the Indian Polity', written for the Akhil Bharat Sarva Seva Sangh (Kashi) in 1959. Even four decades hence, its relevance for the ongoing discussion on electoral and political reforms remain undimmed.

2

Jay Prakash 's Outline of Polity

Jay Prakash says that the main outline of the polity which to my mind is not only most suited for us but also most rational and scientific, with a brief statement of the reasons for my views. I have pleaded for our present political institutions to be based on the principles that had been enunciated and practised in the ancient Indian polity because (a) I believe that would be in line with the natural course of social evolution and (b) those principles are more valid from the point of view of social science than any others. Present western polity is based upon an atomized society, the state being made up of an inorganic sum of individuals. This is both against the social nature of man and the scientific organization of society. Ancient Indian polity was much more consistent with both these. Let me make clear that this paper is not a treatise on democracy or government. I am dealing here with a practical and immediate question: what should be the principles and form of Indian polity at the present time. I have not looked at this question from the point of view of any readymade preconceptions and have avoided giving any label to the views expressed here. Even the phrase, communitarian, is reluctantly used, because a descriptive term sometimes becomes unavoidable. My search here has been for the forms of social life, particularly of political life, that would assure the preservation of human values about which there is hardly any dispute in the world today, and my approach has been non-partisan and non-sectarian. My colleagues in the Sarvodaya movement might miss the word 'Sarvodaya' in this paper.

But, I hope they will recognize that the goal of this enquiry is nothing else but the ultimate good and rise of all. At the same time, I should like to remind them that I am not concerned here with the ultimate state of things, but with the next immediate step towards a better way of life. Furthermore, my enquiry has been mainly confined to the political field. On the very portals of democracy irrespective of its form and structure are words written that can never be wiped off without wiping off democracy itself. No kind of democracy can exist without the democratic freedoms freedom of conscience, of association, of expression and the rule of law. Where these freedoms do not exist, nor the rule of law, there can be no democracy. For my enquiry here I take these words as axiomatic and inscribe them in bold letters on the doorway before entering the house of Indian democracy. If our present political institutions are to be soundly based, if they are to draw sustenance from Indian soil and, in turn, are to sustain, revive and strengthen the whole fabric of Indian society, they must be related to the social genius of India described above, and their texture must be woven again with an organically self determining, self developing communal life in which occupations, professions and functions are integrated with the community. This is not only a question of constitutional forms or political systems. It is a creative question in the widest sense of the term. It is a question of an ancient country finding its lost soul again. The old village communities have survived in nothing else than their physical existence. They are no longer living communities acting jointly for the solution of individual or communal problems and for the development of their moral and material life. It is not necessary here to go into the story of the destruction of the village communities. It would be enough to note that it was a result of the deliberate policy of an alien government that neither understood the character of a communitarian polity nor felt secure in the presence of such strong traditions of self government and self help.

Nevertheless, the very fact that the villages do exist physically provides us with a readymade foundation to build upon. A word that figures boldly on the ancient signpost is dharma. Indian polity held that the state was subject to the rule of dharma, which it was its duty to uphold and protect. The concept of dharma was of great importance in ancient India; it prescribed and regulated individual and group behaviour in all walks of life. This concept of dharma and its role in Indian polity and the wider life of society is another example of that synthetic, organic, communal organization of India society which has been discussed above.

Communities, territorial or functional, had developed laws and codes of behaviour to regulate the internal life of their communities and groups and their relations with the rest of society. There were in addition codes and laws that were common to and accepted by all of them and that made up the universal social ethics. The ensemble of these social ethics exercised a powerful influence over the state. Communal life having been completely destroyed, the roots of dharma have no soil from which to draw sustenance. Dharma has therefore declined and ceased to exercise any influence not only upon the present polity, which is a wholly foreign implantation and has no roots in the India soil, but upon all social activities such as commerce, education, labour, administration, priesthood. Unless life in India is again organized on the basis of self-determining and mutually coordinating and integrating communities, that organic self-regulation of society, which the concept of dharma represented, will not be possible.

To that extent democracy will remain distantly removed from the life of the people. Vinobaji is already speaking, for instance, of a gram dharma (the dharma of the village). But gram dharma will not arise, as he has stressed, unless the village becomes a community. Only then will it be possible for the village to adopt as its dharma the welfare of all the villagers so that none goes without food, clothing, a roof over his head, work to do; no child goes without a knowledge of the three R's; none goes without the benefit of a minimum health service. The ancient concept of dharma has to be revived and the appropriate dharma for a democracy has to be evolved. This, as of old, will not be brought about by a legislative process. It can be done only in an organic manner: dharma must arise from life itself life that is vital enough, real enough, organic enough to be able to throw up codes and laws for its internal regulation. The experience of recent social engineering may and should be drawn upon, but the main mould of life must be indigenous and consistent with the genius of Indian social organization. I believe it would be fair to say that even the most ardent defenders of parliamentary democracy agree that it has serious defects. But they console themselves with the thought (a) that there is no better alternative; and (b) that, within limits, it is possible to amend and improve it. No one will deny that the system is capable of much improvement and it is undergoing change all the time, though not always for the better. But no matter how much improved, its fundamental defects will yet remain because they are the very premises on which its entire structure has been raised. The fundamental defect, from which other serious defects arise, is that this form of democracy is based on the vote of the individual. We have already examined this situation and found that it is the atomization of society that is responsible for this kind of political system. But that does not alter the fact that the system is based on a false premise; the state cannot be an arithmetical sum of individuals. The people, the nation, the community can never be equated with the sum of individual voters. The partisans of parliamentary democracy claim that under it the government is at least representative of the majority of the voters, if not of the people. First of all, this is not true. More often than not it is commonly believed that governments elected under universal adult suffrage are minority governments, in the sense that they represent a minority of the voters.

Wherever there are more than two parties, this happens quite often, but even under two party systems it is not a rare phenomenon. At the last general election in this country, for instance, minority governments were established in a majority of the states, i.e., in seven out of the thirteen states, excluding Union Territories. It will not do to brush aside, as it has been done in this country, such serious anomalies and glaring defects in the parliamentary democratic system by the smug remark that such things are inevitable under a multi-party system. If such things are inevitable and if we are serious about democracy we must seriously set about to find a better type of democracy. The alternatives of plural constituencies, proportional representation, alternative vote cannot, even if there was general agreement about them, which there is not, take us far. The claim that parliamentary democratic governments at least represent a majority of the voters breaks down in a still more serious manner. Experience has shown that present-day mass elections, manipulated by powerful, centrally controlled parties, with the aid of high finance and diabolically clever methods and super media of communication, represent far less the electorate than the forces and interests behind the parties and the propaganda machines. It is not only in the totalitarian countries that the 'rape of the masses' happens. The basic difference is that in a democracy there is a competition between the violators while there is no competition in totalitarianism. Here we are face to face with another serious defect of parliamentary democracy demagoguery.

The need to 'catch' votes creates an unlimited opportunity for indulging in half-truths, even outright lies sometimes; for exciting the passions, more often than not, the base passions; for arousing false hopes by making dishonest; but pleasing promises. Hardly any issue of public policy is presented to the people in its true light; everything gets distorted by partisan demagoguery. The consequence of all this is that the real interests of the nation are sacrificed, more often than not, at the altar of demagoguery. Perhaps the most serious fault of parliamentary democracy, from the point of view of democracy itself, is its inherent tendency toward centralism. At one extreme of its political spectrum is the nation state and at the other the individual voter, with a blank in between. The local bodies that may exist have (a) little self-government powers, and (b) no direct or indirect influence on the nation state. Add to this the complexities of a highly industrialized civilization that are beyond even the understanding of the ordinary citizen, and you have a central state of overwhelming power and resources and the individual voter reduced to abject helplessness.

The 'sovereign people' being dispersed over the length and breadth of the country like particles of sand over the desert and having no other organized political force than the nation state itself to interpose between themselves and that state, the latter naturally becomes all powerful. The issue of power in such states is decided not by the fictitious 'people', but by a balance between political parties and such organized interests as industrialists and bankers and powerful labour unions. The people represent a wholeness, while the organized interests are sectional. Even a sum of the sections cannot make up the whole. Only their organic integration can do so. Such integration takes place only in the community at its various levels. In the communal or communitarian democracy that we are advocating there is natural decentralization and a multi-central pluralistic state. A natural outcome of centralization of power and administration is bureaucracy. The central executive or cabinet is so overburdened with work that it is compelled to leave more and more to, and depend more and more upon, the permanent officials, who in course of time gather more and more power for themselves. This soon leads to a dangerous autocracy, the autocracy of the bureaucrat, which is difficult to fight because it 'works in the shadows' and is hard to get at. The only answer to the problem of bureaucracy is more and more decentralization so that the people directly participate in the administration of their affairs and control the civil servants who owe their jobs and are directly responsible to them. This is exactly what will happen in the communitarian democracy outlined here.

The communal administrations might make mistakes and there might be inefficiency. But as they themselves will be the sufferers, they will learn and improve things. Moreover, during the British rule did we not say to ourselves repeatedly that good government was no substitute for self-government? Is that less true now? An inevitable concomitant of parliamentary democracy is the party system. So much has been written in criticism of this system that it seems unnecessary to dwell upon it here at any length. Some criticism of it has been implicit in what has been said above. It is clear that parliamentary democracy cannot work without parties. Parties of a sort will perhaps exist everywhere and at all times. Even in the family there may be 'parties'. In the ancient Indian republics, which were aristocratic democracies, parties and factions were a common feature. But the highly organized, centralized mass parties of modern times are a far cry from the factions of old, whether of the ancient Indian republics or the Greek city states. The old democracies were small and the factions and the people were not so far removed from one another. The people therefore could judge them and the issues that were raised with intimate understanding. The issues in those days were also simple enough. All this has changed now and parties have become a sort of state within the state. They are now the real arbiters of the people's fate, whose control over them is fictional. The citizens who cast their votes for the parties have nothing to do with the running of the parties: they are complete outsiders. Even the enrolled members of the parties have no say either in the policy-making or the inner administration of the parties. The parties are run by caucuses that are beyond democratic control. Party rivalries, we have seen above, give birth to demagoguery, depress political ethics, put a premium on unscrupulousness and aptitude for manipulation and intrigue. Parties create dissensions where unity is called for, exaggerate differences where they should be minimized. Parties often put party interests over the national interests because centralization of power prevents the citizen from participating in government; the parties, that is to say, small caucuses of politicians, rule in the name of the people and create the illusion of democracy and self-government. No doubt the party system has its good points and because parliamentary democracy cannot work without it, those who swear by that type of democracy and see no alternative to it, are prepared to accept the evils of the party system as inevitable and satisfy themselves by pointing out their virtues. For my part, it is not the party system that is the main culprit, but parliamentary democracy itself, which gives rise to it. In the communitarian democracy that I have proposed here, there may conceivably be parties, but they are likely to be local factions, and, in any case, their role in the state will not be as commanding as that of the parties in the parliamentary system. Another serious fault of parliamentary democracy is the system of elections that it fosters and requires for its proper functioning. First of all, the system is very expensive and appallingly wasteful.

The fabulous expenses involved have the effect of mortgaging democracy to moneyed interests or large sectional organizations like trade unions. As compared with this, elections in the communitarian system would cost practically nothing. It would have been a matter of some consolation if the huge expenditure had resulted in any public good. In fact, the result is just the contrary. A general election, as noted above, creates unnecessary passion and excitement; instead of educating and enlightening the people it befogs their mind; instead of resulting in the election of able and good men, it tends to favour demagoguery. Serious political and economic issues and other questions of policy, it is obvious, should be considered calmly and dispassionately and not in the heat of partisan warfare. That is why I hold that the practice of general elections should be abolished. The elected houses should be continuous in nature, with a part of them being renewed periodically. It is time now to gather all the threads of the argument and tie them together. Ancient Indian thought and tradition; social nature of man; social science; ethical and spiritual goals of civilization; the demand of democracy that the citizen should participate in the ordering and running of his life; the need of saving man from himself and from the fate of robotism; the requirement that the state and other institutions of society be reduced to a human scale; the ideal, above all, that man should become the centre of civilization all these point in the same direction: to a communal or communitarian way of life; communitarian ethics and education; communitarian social, economic and political organization. In this paper I have been mainly interested in the political aspect of the matter: the shape of the political organization, or polity, most desirable for our country. The foundation of this polity, as I have pointed out, must necessarily be self-governing, self-sufficient, agro-industrial, urbo-rural local communities. The existing villages and townships provide the physical base for such reconstruction.

A laudable beginning has been made in this connection by establishing gram panchayats and instituting such programmes as community development, 'intensive area' development (of the Khadi and Village Industries Commission), and co-operativization of the rural economy. But from the point of view propounded in this paper these programmes suffer from several serious defects: (a) they lack an integrated social philosophy; (b) they have no clear concept of community; (c) they do not aim to create a balance within the community between agriculture and industry; (d) even though the aim is to create communities (no matter how vaguely understood) at the bottom level, the concept of social organization at the higher levels remains the same as that of the atomized industrial society of the West (which for our purpose here includes Russia). Let me return now to the foundation of our polity. The foundation, as stated already, must be self governing, self sufficient, agro-industrial, urbo-rural local communities. The highest political institution of the local community should be the General Assembly the gram sabha of which all the adults should be considered members. The selection of the Executive the panchayat should be by general consensus of opinion in the sabha. There should be no 'candidates', i.e. no one should 'stand' for any post. There should be clear-cut qualifications, as in ancient times, laid down for all selective posts. No individual should hold the same post for more than a defined period of time.

The panchayat should function through subcommittees charged with different responsibilities. There should be no official or member appointed or nominated by the state government in the panchayat or its sub-committees. It may be questioned if there can ever be a general consensus of opinion amongst villagers who are divided into castes and factions and have conflicting interests. We have seen already how for thousands of years the villages of India elected their executive councils by general agreement. Those villages were by no means homogeneous and ideal communities. Therefore, there is no reason to believe that the experience of centuries cannot be repeated again. We may also recall that the only alternative method of election of village councils or panchayats was that of drawing lots. There is nothing undemocratic in selection by general agreement or by drawing lots; alternatively, it might be provided that the villages first try the former method, and failing therein take recourse to the latter. Something similar happens in the Bhoodan movement. When the landless families are unable to agree about the distribution of bhoodan lands between themselves, the issue is decided by drawing lots. It is not our experience that there has been in any case dissatisfaction with decisions reached in this manner. The question may also be asked if the village panchayats, as they are today, would be able to function in the manner visualized above. There is no better way to teach the young except by giving them responsibility. In the same manner the only way to make the villages self-governing, self-reliant and self-sufficient is to throw upon them real responsibilities. There was a time when the Indian village republics were self-created, like the Swiss communes, and their powers and functions were not given to them from above. But in the present conditions they have to be recreated by a deliberate and bold process of devolution and decentralization if Indian democracy is to have a firm base and living reality. I believe that the responsibility given to the gram sabha and the panchayat should be in things that really do matter. For instance, it should be the responsibility of the gram sabha and its panchayat to ensure that no one in the village goes without food, clothing and shelter; no child without primary education; every one receives primary medical care.

The sabha and panchayat should see that the village becomes self-sufficient in the matter of food and clothing as soon as possible. Further, they should so plan that within five years, let us say, there is no unemployment in the village and every family reaches a minimum standard of living. Self-government, to be real, should be about essential problems of life. It would be necessary for some time to help the village from above, but the responsibility must be clearly defined and the demand for help must come from the village in specific terms, meant to supplement what has been or is proposed to be done by the collective effort of the village. No help should be given until the village has proved that it has done that and is prepared to do its best to help itself. Eventually such help will have to come from the next larger communal organization, the regional community, but at the beginning it will have to come from the state government. Social and political workers must go in large numbers to the villages, not to make promises but to preach self-reliance and to help them to practice it. The development of the rest of the polity need not wait till the villages and townships become real communities as visualized here. Our work must begin at all levels simultaneously, otherwise it will not succeed at any level. The next level of the political structure would obviously be that of the regional community. Here, as already indicated, the gram panchayats will have to be integrated into the panchayat samiti, as recommended by the Balvantrai Mehta team, with this difference that the nature and functions of the samiti should be those of an autonomous self-governing community as discussed in the previous section: the samiti should have powers and obligations to do all that may be within its competence. As suggested already, the panchayat samiti, comprising the optimum community as defined above, would play a key role in the political and economic life of the country, particularly in the processes of planning and development. There is one important point which I wish to emphasize in connection with the formation of the panchayat samiti.

The samiti should be elected by the gram panchayats and not by their members. This at first might appear to be a distinction between six and half-a-dozen. But that is not so. We have here a major principle of communal life involved. It is the gram panchayat as a body that represents the village community and not its members. The panchayat samiti, in its turn, is a representative of the gram panchayats, and it is the latter that should be represented as such and not their members. Following the pattern of social organization described in the previous section, the political structure would rise storey by storey from the foundation. The next storey above the panchayat samiti would be that of the district council (or whatever name given to it), which will be formed by the integration of the panchayat samitis of the district again the samitis as such electing their representatives and not their members. The district councils, in their turn, should have all the powers and obligations necessary to do everything that may be within their competence. In a similar manner all the district councils of a state would come together to create the state assembly. The state assemblies, in like manner, would bring into being the Lok Sabha. Thus the political institution at each level is an integration of all the institutions at the lower level. The picture drawn here of the polity of India, and of social organization in general, might perhaps appear to be idealistic. If so, I would not consider that to be a disqualification. An ideal cannot but be idealistic. The question is if the ideal is impractical, unscientific or otherwise ill-conceived. I have tried in the preceding pages to show that all relevant considerations lead irresistibly towards it. The achievement of this ideal would, however, be a colossal task. Thousands, perhaps hundreds of thousands, of voluntary workers would be needed over a number of years to accomplish it. The governments should lend their full support; but it is necessary to remember that the main burden of the task would have to be borne by voluntary political and social workers and institutions.

The heart of the problem is to create the 'spirit of community', without which the whole body politic would be without life and soul. This is a task of moral regeneration to be brought about by example, service, sacrifice and love. Those who occupy high places in society in politics, business, the professions bear the heavy responsibility of leading the people by personal example. The task also is one of social engineering, needing the help of the state; of scientists, experts, educationists, businessmen, experimenters; of men and women; of young and old. It is a task of dedication; of creation; of self-discovery. It is a task that defines India's destiny. It spells a challenge to India's sons and daughters. Will they accept the challenge? At the root of all-pervasive problem of the crisis of character is the decline of religion. I wish to voice my serious concern over the state of Hinduism as it is found in practice. For the educated class, and more so for the young, it has no meaning except for certain ceremonies which are performed without faith to conform to social customs.

For some important sections of the Hindu community, piety or religiosity is only a means to obtain divine sanction for unethical behaviour, such as black-marketing, tax-evasion, profiteering, etc. For the mass of Hindus, religion means nothing more than a few mythological tales, crass superstition, some taboos and empty observances. Religion as a formative, humanizing, ennobling force hardly seems to have survived. The great movements of religious reform of the nineteenth and early twentieth centuries have spent their driving force. The outer dead shell of Karma kanda is all that seems to be left of Hindu religion, and nothing or little of the inner core. In its outward form our religion still sanctions the hierarchy of castes, even the crime of untouchability. Between word and deed there are contradictions that balk the imagination. It is not uncommon to meet the catholicity of Vedantism in words accompanied with the most narrow-minded caste observances in deeds. We talk glibly about the tolerance of Hindu religion, yet do not raise an eyebrow when men, women and children are butchered for belonging to another religion. Only recently, no less than a hundred murders were committed because, to begin with, a non-Hindu student, while protesting deep reverence for one of our departed national leaders, refused to garland his bust on the ground that his religion forbade every form of idol worship. There is a good deal of current talk about Hindu revivalism. I believe firmly that for Hindu society, revival is essential if it is to put forth its best and reach its height of achievement. But the revivalism now taking place will push Hindu society further backward, and may incidentally destroy even what we have of the unity of our nation. The Hindu religion is a strange mixture of good and bad, sublime and low, the most emancipated thought and bigoted obscurantism. What happens to the future of Hindu society depends upon which of these strains are to be selected, nourished and propagated.

During Presentation of Magsaysay Award in 1965 he said :

> I feel greatly honored to be here today, a great day for the people of the Philippines, a day of remembrance and dedication remembrance of a great leader of men and dedication to his great ideals of freedom and fulfillment of the human spirit. This Award and this day make it possible for peoples beyond these islands, which Ramon Magsaysay was privileged to serve and lead, to participate in this inspiring ceremony of remembrance and dedication. I should like to express my gratitude to the Trustees of the Magsaysay Award Foundation that they found me deserving of this honor, and for their generous citation. In this I find not a personal recognition but recognition of the ideas that I have been pursuing and trying to translate into action. In that sense this Award will be a source of much encouragement to me and my colleagues in the work that we are doing to build a new India. As an Indian I feel proud that since their inception, one of these Awards has gone every year, except for one, to my country. This indeed is an indication of the high regard in which the people of these islands hold India. Let me on my part assure you that the people of India reciprocate in full measure this feeling of friendship and hold you in great affection

and regard. I hope these Awards will be a powerful bond to bring our countries closer than they happen to be today. All the countries of the world of Asia, Africa and South America that have won their freedom in recent times and whose natural growth had been retarded on account of the bonds of colonialism, are trying to catch up with the advanced countries and build their societies as fast as possible. In this the model many have before them is that of the highly industrialized and affluent West. A few countries have set up before them the Eastern model presented by successful communism, whether Russian or Chinese.

There is much in both the Western and Eastern models that is of abiding value and that the developing countries should accept and assimilate. The ideals of individual liberty, of government by consent and of the rule of law that the Western model has, by and large, emphasized as the true foundations of society's political organization, are undoubtedly ideals that should be adopted and assimilated by the developing peoples. In the same manner, the concern of communism for the toiler and its drive toward greater economic equality are values that must also inspire and guide them. But there are in both models essential characteristics that, to my mind, should be rejected. In the Western model, the ruling ethic is that of individualism and competition, it being assumed that in the process the weaker will be driven to the wall. There is also an excessive emphasis on the satisfaction of material needs and their consequent multiplication, leading to serious imbalances. Western life is also unbalanced for the reason that sufficient attention is not paid, on account of the predominance of certain utilitarian and commercial values, to the interrelationship between man's work, leisure, habitat and happiness.

The drive towards urbanization, resulting in the monster of the megalopolis, has destroyed the community, divorced the urban from the rural and forcibly alienated man from nature. The result is a distorted growth of man and society. On the other hand, the communist model also presents a distorted picture of human and social development. It strikes at the very root of man, by denying the primacy of his spirit and by deliberately suppressing it. By glorifying power and authority, as represented by the party and the state, and by making everyone and every thing subservient to them, it makes of society a vast prison house for the human spirit. The new countries, therefore, while rejecting in totality both these models, must take from them what is of value and conducive to balanced spiritual and material growth of man and society.

Happily, in the advanced countries themselves, particularly of the West, much thought is being given to this problem, and there is also some experimentation. These should be of great value to the new countries. Development of science, both physical and social, has made it possible for the first time in history for human societies consciously to shape their future. But in no society, not even those where the sciences have developed farthest, are men prepared to be guided by science. They have their narrow interests, their prejudices and predilections, their concern with immediate things, their myths and ideologies all these make the voice of science a cry in the wilderness. As far as the new countries are concerned, even though they have an almost clean slate to write upon and a wonderful opportunity to select the best from the extant models and reject the rest, two circumstances make it almost impossible for them to do so. Firstly, vast numbers of the peoples of these countries are too uneducated to be able to draw upon the teachings and techniques of science; and secondly, they are economically so backward and poor that their single overpowering anxiety is to secure before all else their economic development. This is understandable. But there was no reason to believe that economic development would have suffered if equal attention had been paid to the task of achieving a balanced human and social development. Indeed, if economic development had been thought of in terms of economic well-being of the mass of the people and not in terms of providing a base for industrial and military power, there should have been every reason to believe that the rate of development might have been faster. Many of the new countries, it hardly needs to be pointed out, present such unstable societies due either to their having become arenas of the power-struggle that rages between the mighty nations or to their internal situation that they will be unable for a long time consciously to build their future. Nonetheless, it needs to be stressed that even those new countries that are in some position consciously to direct their future course, have no clear picture of their goals apart from such cliches as democracy, socialism, communalism, industrialism, modernism and the like. The central point to be stressed in this connection, and with that I wish to conclude, is that the question posed here is a question of values. Looked at from that standpoint it should not be difficult, not only to chalk out the course for the future, but also to achieve a consensus of public opinion behind the endeavor to reconstruct a new society. Jay Prakash Narayan (1902-1979), Indian nationalist and social reform leader, was India's leading indigenous critic after Mohandas Gandhi. A disciple of Mohandas Gandhi and leader of India's independence movement, Jay Prakash Narayan remained a rebel in his native land until the end of his life. Born of middle-caste Hindu parents in a small village in Bihar on Oct. 11, 1902, he became politically active in high school. Just before his graduation, he followed the call of Indian nationalists to quit British-assisted institutions. In 1922, he went to the United States, where he studied political science and economics at the universities of California, Iowa, Wisconsin and Ohio State. During his seven years in the United States, Narayan paid his tuition by working as a fruit picker, jam packer, waiter, mechanic and salesman. His nationalist and anti-imperialist convictions developed into Marxist beliefs and participation in Communist activities. But Narayan was opposed to policies of the Soviet Union and rejected organized communism upon returning to India in 1929. Narayan became secretary of the Congress party, whose leader was Jawaharlal Nehru, later to become the first independent Indian prime minister.

When all other party leaders were arrested, Narayan carried on the campaign against the British; then he, too, was arrested. In 1934, Narayan led other Marxists in the formation of a Socialist group in the Congress party. During World War II, Narayan became a national hero by leading violent opposition to the British. Embracing the resistance movement led by Mohandas Gandhi, Narayan repudiated its commitment to nonviolence, engineering strikes, train wrecks and riots. He was repeatedly jailed by the British, and his escapes and heroic activities captured the public's imagination. After India gained independence, violence and Marxism waned in Narayan. He led his socialist group out of the Congress party in 1948 and later merged it with a Gandhian-oriented party to form the People's Socialist party. Narayan was considered Nehru's heir apparent, but in 1954 he renounced party politics to follow the teachings of Vinoba Bhave, an ascetic who called for voluntary redistribution of land. He embraced a Gandhian type of revolutionary action in which he sought to change the minds and hearts of people.

An advocate of "saintly politics," he urged Nehru and other leaders to resign and live with the impoverished masses. Narayan never held a formal position in the government, but remained a leading political personality operating outside party politics. Late in his life, he regained prominence as an active critic of the increasingly authoritarian policies of Prime Minister Indira Gandhi, Jawarhalal Nehru's daughter. His reform movement called for "partyless democracy," decentralization of power, village autonomy and a more representative legislature. Despite ill health, Narayan led student agitators in Bihar in a fight against government corruption, and under his leadership, a People's Front took power in western Gujarat state.

Indira Gandhi responded by branding Narayan a reactionary fascist. In 1975, when Gandhi was convicted of corrupt practices, Narayan called for her resignation and a massive movement of pacifist noncooperation with the government. Gandhi declared a national emergency, jailed Narayan and 600 other opposition leaders and imposed censorship of the press. In prison, Narayan's health collapsed. After five months, he was released. In 1977, thanks largely to Narayan's uniting of opposition forces, Gandhi was defeated in an election. Narayan died at his home in Patna on Oct. 8, 1979, from the effects of diabetes and a heart ailment. Fifty thousand mourners gathered outside his home, and thousands followed as his casket was carried through the streets. Calling Narayan "the conscience of the nation," Prime Minister Charan Singh declared seven days of mourning. Narayan was remembered as the last of Mohandas Gandhi's colleagues in the independence movement. "I did a mistake. I thought Niraahaara-Deeksha is the best shiksha, praayashchittam" replied the adhyaksha (head) of Post and Telegraph workers when asked why he was fasting. Once when the Post & Telegraph workers went on a strike in June 1952, this person talked with the Communications Minister and fixed a deal.

The Minister also agreed to pay the workers for the time they did strike. Since Bhaarateeyas never leave Satyam, the adhyaksha believed the words of the Minister and left without taking any written agreement. However the Minister cheated them and didn't pay the workers. Since the adhyaksha was the representative of the workers, the adhyaksha felt he was responsible for the mistake. If he had been more careful, the Minister wouldn‘t have cheated them. Hence as Praayashchittam for his mistake he was doing Niraahaara-deeksha! He did this for 21 days!! He is none other than “Jay Prakash Narayan“, well known as “Lokanaayak”. It was the summer of 1959. I was working as secretary of an organisation of which the late Shri Jay Prakash Narayan was the president.

One day an RSS leader walked into my office. I had known him for a number of years. After some small talk, he suggested that I should request J.P. to visit an RSS camp which was being held in New Delhi at that time. J.P. also happened to be in town. I was diffident about the proposition. Having worked with J.P. for more than an year, I had sensed his preferences and prejudices. But I promised to the RSS leader that I would do my best. I broached the subject to J.P. next day, as soon as I found him alone, which was a rare event. J.P. seemed to be stunned as if I had uttered an obscenity. There was an expression of displeasure on his face which made me too feel uncomfortable. He was a gentle person who seldom lost his temper. But now he seemed to be on the verge of exploding. The atmosphere became tense. For a moment none of us could find words to break the spell of silence. At last J.P. controlled himself and said : “Do you know what you are talking, and to whom ?” There was a touch of temper in his voice. By now I had also managed to collect my wits to a certain extent. I said: “ I knew that the suggestion would be annoying to you. Even so, I took a chance." He relaxed. I also heaved a sigh of relief. He said: "You know that I have a certain standing in the country and a certain reputation in public life. You should not expect me to get mixed up with an organisation which is known for its communal, reactionary and revivalist character." I said: " It is exactly because of your standing in the country and your reputation in public life that i have conveyed their invitation to you." He said: " I do not understand. Could you make yourself a little more clear ?" I explained: " Your standing in the country is that of a man of reason and your reputation rests upon the keenness of your moral sense. I am sure you will live upto that standard in this instance as well." He said: " I try to do my best according to my understanding and strength of will. Tell me where and how I have failed." This encouraged me and I said: " You have been practising untouchability towards a section of your own people. You have never met the RSS people face to face. You have never listened to their side of the story. Yet you have formed an unsavoury opinion about them. This does not sound reasonable to me, nor just." He became thoughful. I continued: " Your status today is not that of a party politician seeking power and fomenting partisan strife. You have become a father figure for the nation as a whole, almost the conscience-keeper of your people. You raise your voice whenever and wherever you feel that an injustice has been done or that justice is being denied. That is why people of all persuasions Congressmen, Socialists, Communists, Akalis, National Conference men and so on-come to you for consultation, for registering their complaints, for presenting their point of view, and for seeking your advice. You do not always agree with them. Yet you listen to them patiently and give them your advice. They do not always agree with your view of men and matters, nor always follow your advice. The points is that you are always accessible to them. You always go out and meet them whenever they invite you. It is only the RSS and allied people whom you avoid, so much so that one of their leaders could not come to you directly and had to convey an invitation through a small fry like myself. Tell me if this is not tantamount to practising untouchability." He closed his eyes and shook his head several times. He seemed to be engaged in some inner struggle. I pressed the point: " I am not inviting you to get mixed up with the RSS. Nor is it their intention to spread some snare for you. What they expect from a man like you is that you should try to know them first-hand rather than depend upon hearsay and political gossip in a partisan press controlled almost entirely by people who are hostile to them. May be you find that you have been mistaken about them. May be they benefit from the advice that you give them. But all this can happen only when you meet them, listen to what they have to say, tell them frankly what you feel about them and thus open the door for a fruitful dialogue in days to come. In any case, the heavens are not going to fall because you go and visit one of their camps. That is all I have to say. Rest is for you to decide." He opened his eyes, smiled somewhat sadly and said: " You have put me in a rather awkward position. But I can see the point in what you have said. I cannot easily refute your accusation. I can really be held guilty of practising untouchability." I kept quiet and waited for him to make up his mind. He did it in a moment and said: " Okay, you win. I am willing to visit the RSS camp. Make an appointment with them and let me know. I hope tomorrow evening will suit them. Day after I am leaving Delhi." Next day he spent nearly two horse in the RSS camp, witnessing their mass drill, moved by their prayer of devotion to the motherland, meeting and talking to their leaders asking all sorts of questions and offering his own comments. Finally, he sat on a chair facing a group of about a hundred RSS workers from several parts of the country. The workers who sat on the ground in row after row stood up one by one to introduce themselves to their honoured guest of the evening. Each one of them told his name without mentioning any surname indicative of caste or community, his educational qualifications, the province from which he came and the years he had spent as a swayam sevaka. I could see that J.P. was highly impressed. His face which had been grim so far softened suddenly and visibly. Most of the Swayam sevakas held graduate and postgraduate degrees in arts or commerce or science. All of them were between the ages of 20 and 35. Finally, J.P. was requested to say a few words and bless the young men. That he politely refused. He whispered to me that he was quite confused and did not really know what to say. I conveyed his feelings to the RSS leader who showed immediate understanding and did not press him any more. As he was taking leave, J.P. looked at the Bhagwa dhwaja and observed: "That I suppose is the Maratha flag." The RSS leader explained: "The Marathas did not invent it. They borrowed it from an older national tradition. The saffron colour has always been the colour par excellence of Indian spirituality as well as of Indian nationalism." J.P. saids, "I do not know. I have not been a student of history. But that is what a well-known historian told me." The RSS leader smiled and remained silent. The parting was very warm on both sides. On our way back J.P. muttered as if he was talking to himself: "They have a lot of young and very disciplined workers. Their workers are also highly educated. I never knew that. In our socialist movement most of our workers are not even matriculates." I kept quiet and waited for him to say something more. He made one more comment as we got out of the car at the end of our journey. He said: "Sitaramji, I am grateful to you for helping me to break down what looked like an insurmountable wall. But I am not at all satisfied that it is not an attempt to revive the Maratha empire." I could have asked him as to what was wrong with Maratha the empire. I could have also told him that the Maratha empire represented the triumph of a tough and long-drawn-out struggle against Islamic imperialism. But I was not prepared for some more frowns on his face. My version cf Indian history was after all not the version which was being taught in school and college text-books all over the country. J.P. was repeating what most of our historians were saying from their august seats in universities and research institutes. According to the professors, the Mughal empire was a many-splendoured national mansion, while the Maratha confederacy was a congregation of self-seeking marauders.

What was my locus standi for raising a controversy about what had come to be universally accepted in the world of learning? I was not even a school teacher. I have told this story not as a part of my autobiography but in order to point out the gulf which divided a national leader from a national movement. Here was a leader who had fought for national freedom and who was actively thinking and experimenting with methods of national reconstruction. And here was a national movement which took its birth at a critical juncture in the same fight for national freedom and which was now concentrating on training our youth for the same task of national revitalization. Yet the two of them--the national leader and the national movement-stood apart and could not see eye to eye on matters of major importance. Nor have I chosen J.P. simply because I happened to see him functioning from close quarters at one time. I have chosen him because he was a leader who had continued to grow out of closed ideologies, who had shed prejudices and who was sincerely in search of a wider vision. He was not like Pandit Nehru and many others whose thought-processes became fossilized in the `thirties or the `forties and who had subsequently failed to have a fresh look at national or international affairs. It was all right for J.P. to disown, even denounce the RSS so long as he was an orthodox socialist with his moorings in

Marxist thought. But the event I have described took place several years after he had publicly renounced Marxism and affirmed his faith in the path shown by Mahatma Gandhi. Nor yet is it my intention to build a case for the RSS which is quite capable of looking after itself. I have chosen the RSS as the symbol of an ancient society and culture which have suffered for a long time and in no small measure from successive waves of aggressive imperialism let loose by Islam and Christianity, now joined by Communism. The aggression from all these dark forces is still continuing. There are many people like myself who have never been a part of the RSS but who nevertheless feel strongly that this aggression should stop, that our people should come into their own in their ancestral homeland, and that our culture should flower and contribute to the greater good of mankind. J. P. had at last visited an RSS camp. He had been positively impressed by the quality of the workers whom the RSS had mobilized in the service of the nation.

And yet he had retained his earlier reservations about the RSS. He could not visualise that the RSS was not a miracle which had materialized out of the blue. He could not see that there must be something in a society and a culture and historical tradition which had created such a splendid band of selfless workers without the benefit of any patronage from the powers that be and in the face of much malicious propaganda in the national and international press. These were some of the thoughts which rose in my mind at that time. I felt very strongly that there was something seriously wrong somewhere. But I could not resolve the contradictions. I failed to lay my finger on the sore spot in that sorry situation. Ever since I have pondered over the subject. And I have at last come to a conclusion which I can now present with some confidence. To my mind the key to an understanding of the whole situation is to be found in the political parlance which has been prevalent in this country for more than five decades. Over the years, this parlance has been parodying the RSS as a "rightist, reactionary and revivalist movement of militant Hindu communalism." Over the years this parlance has been pillorying Hindu society as a "crowd of caste-ridden, cow-worshipping and superstitious primitives." Over the years, this parlance has been regarding Hindu culture as a "close preserve of obnoxious obscurantism." Most of this mud has got stuck to the RSS as well as to Hindu society because neither the RSS nor Hindu society has thought it fit to put up a defence not to speak of turning the tables on their adversaries. J.P. was not the only one who had swallowed heavy doses of this political parlance in his younger days in India and abroad. There are so many others who have done the same in schools and colleges, in seminars and conferences, in discussions and debates. For, this pernicious parlance has been and is still being doled out on a large-scale in most of the media and other avenues of education, all over the country. J.P. had at least tried to disgorge this poison and succeeded to a large extent in the later years of his life. There are many others who do not even suspect that they are being fed on poison, not to speak of making an effort to disgorge the doses which they have already imbibed. I am not referring to those who have consciously chosen to be inspired by Christianity or Islam or Communism and who have made it a profession to be hostile towards every effort at strengthening Hindu society and culture as a means to strengthening the nation.

They are the hawkers of this poison and find the profession very profitable. My reference here is to that vast intelligentsia who see a lot that is valuable in Hindu culture but who run away when it comes to the defence of the society which serves as the vehicle of that culture or who join the hawkers of poison whenever they find that this society is not going to take it any more. I have done some investigation into the history and role of this political parlance which has by now become petrified into a series of stereotyped slogans. Today everyone is shouting these slogans, back and forth. But I fear that there are not many people, not at least in the political field, who have tried to find out the source of these slogans and the nature of causes they serve.

3

Jay Prakash : His Economic and Political Approaches

Political Ideology

After a long stay in the United States, J.P. found himself academically and politically well-equipped to face any challenge that might come in his way as a complex problem. As mentioned earlier, he was greatly influenced by the socialistic thought effecting Europe as well as Asian countries. Thus he had in mind a big change-a revolution which should support the upliftment of the economically weaker sections.

Where are Congress Going?

Where are we going? Where do we want to go?' These questions are not idle questions of merely debating, academic or non-practical value. On their answer, indeed, depends the future of our country and of the millions of the humble people whom every Congressman claims to represent. The Constituent Assembly is no longer a dream of the future. It is the next political step in our march towards freedom and progress. The demand for it has reference not to some distant date at which most of us do not expect to be living, but to the immediate present about the disposition of which every one of us wishes to have a say. And what will the Constituent Assemble do? It will endeavour to answer precisely those very questions with which we have started. It will lay down the principles on which a free Indian society shall be reared; it will fashion the foundations of the liberty, prosperity and happiness of the future generations.

Work of Constituent Assembly's Performer

But who will be the actors on the stage of the Constituent Assembly? We believe, and rightly so, that the Congress occupies the first place in the affections of an overwhelmingly large section of the people.

Naturally, therefore, it would be the voice of the Congress that, at any rate, would preponderate in the Assembly (except, it should be added, in matters concerning the minorities which shall have the main voice in determining such questions as concern them as minorities). If it be so, and is it possible to disagree with it, should not Congressmen turn their attention to these serious questions and seek their answer? It is not our intention to appeal to the ranks over the heads of the leaders.

Our appeal is as much directed to Congress readers as to the humblest Congress worker. In seeking to answer these questions here, first, let me state the principles that are already explicitly set forth in the declarations of the Congress. The first and foremost of these is, of course the principle of complete independence. It is the creed of the Congress, being the first article of its faith.

Declaration of Rights

Beyond the basic principle there are certain others that are explicitly stated. The second great principle is that of economic freedom. The Swaraj that the Congress wishes to fashion (see the famous Karachi Declaration of Rights) is conceived above all as a Swaraj for the masses. This Swaraj, it is stated, has no reality unless economic freedom is added to political freedom. But, beyond the clear enunciation of the goal of economic freedom there is little light shed on the means of securing such freedom. Yet, it is necessary to keep in mind the indubitable aim of economic freedom explicitly enunciated by the Congress-an aim that is second in importance only to the aim of political freedom. We will return later to a consideration of economic freedom. Among other great principles enunciated by the Congress are complete freedom of conscience, full protection of the rights, faiths and cultures of the minority peoples, absence of all racial or sex discrimination, peace between nations and peaceful means to settle all social disputes. The list is not exhausting nor mention has been made of many noble principles that are implicit in the position of the Congress. These are great principles and they have rightly raised the Congress in the estimation of the people of India and the world. But they are not enough, or not clearly enough stated, to enable the people of this country to choose their future path and to avoid the fatal dangers in the way. Let me come directly to the point. It would be trite to say that the basic problem of India is poverty. Yet, that is the profoundest truth of our social life, challenging our utmost wisdom and resource. The Congress is deeply conscious of this problem and it is out of that consciousness that the idea of economic freedom has grown.

The difficulty, however, is that no concrete shape has been given to this freedom. As a vague generalisation it is more than useless, nay, it is dangerous. Because, on the one hand, it might lull the poor people with the faith that Congress will end their poverty, and, on the other, it might fail on account of its vagueness (as it is bound to) to solve the actual problem. Hard-headed, clear, concrete measures and not slushy sentimentality would be necessary to tackle the question. What may these hard-headed, concrete measures be?

Encountering Economic Salvation

The first difficulty we encounter in our search for economic salvation is our fixed, performed notions that have unconsciously laid hold of our thinking. We are living in a capitalist age and we have been closely associated, through its language, educational system, juridical, political and economic institutions, with the classic capitalist country of the world-England. The ideas and thoughts of capitalist England and also generally of capitalist Europe and America, have seeped into the very pores of out thinking till they have begun to appear to be as sound and unalterable as the laws of nature.

In other words, without any conscious attempt, we have imbibed capitalist ideals and have come to look upon capitalist institutions as embodying eternal truths of social organisations. The result of this unconscious conditioning of our social thought is that whenever we seek to reconstruct our own-society, all our plans run into capitalist moulds and we find ourselves reproducing the well-known institutions of capitalism. The attitude of the Congress ministries towards large-scale industry is an instance in point. In considering labour legislation, wages, price of sugarcane and other similar matters, the ministries were over-anxious about the "flight" of capital-from their provinces. They felt compelled to give encouragement to capitalist industrial enterprises. Within the limits of their social thinking it was not unnatural for them to do so. But, this only proves our case anew. It requires no effort to show what should happen if we were to approach the task of national reconstruction with the kind of outlook described above. Capitalist industry, capitalist finance, capitalist commerce would rapidly develop and take firm grip over the economic and political life of the country. The next thing we would find after that would be that poverty was still prevalent, unemployment still rampant, the violence of capitalist exploitation fully functioning.

No one should have any difficulty in coming to the conclusion that such would be the state of affairs. For, we live in a curious paradoxical mental state. On the one hand, while we are a prey to capitalist modes of thought, on the other, the present collapse of capitalist civilization has exposed to us the ineffectualness, the brutality, the misery of capitalism. Thus while we hug the thought-complexes of capitalism, we also clearly see its hollowness and futility. We cannot help seeing them, unless we are blind, for they are writ large across the very face, of capitalism. Therefore, in our unthinking drift towards, national reconstruction we are heading straight to a terrible social abyss. There is another circumstance which multiplies the danger towards which we are drifting.

Among Congressmen while the larger section is an unconscious prey to capitalist ideals of social organisation, there is not an inconsiderable number of Congressmen who hold those ideals consciously, because they are personally interested in the industries, banks, insurance companies, in short, in all manner of capitalist undertakings and in their profits. The main interest of these Congressmen in Swaraj is that it would free native capital from the bondage of British Capital and thus enable it to foliate in all its magnificence.

The leading cadres of the Congress are recruited from the educated middle class. Now, the chief characteristic of this class is that its dominating outlook is that of a social climber. The middle class man desires nothing more than to lift himself' to the level of higher classes. Therefore, the pull of these classes towards the profits of capitalism would be a potent driving force towards the abyss of which we-have spoken. We have therefore to be doubly vigilant.

Sense of Security

In discussing this matter with Congressmen one comes across all kinds of mental twists which, no doubt, give them the sense of security for the future and make them complacent. One of these mental outfits is that the ship of state would succeed in avoiding all dangers because it would be captained by men possessing the highest ideals of social justice and of the common good. Such men would surely avoid the dangers of capitalism by keeping it in check and "holding the balance" between all classes. Those who seek solace in such thoughts hardly appreciate the nature of the problem before us. The problem is not to eradicate or bring under control this or that evil in society, but to determine the very basis and character of society. Politics are the expression of economic issues. The national parliament and the national government as soon as they come into existence, will be faced with such questions as taxation, tariffs, currency, exchange and banking, the public debt, railway freights, foreign and internal commerce, resolution of wages, hours, agrarian matters, industrial manners, etc. These questions admit of no temporising. They require immediate, straight, clear-cut answers. Idealist captains of the ship of state in answering these would be laying the foundations of Indian, society.

One type of answer would Jay the basis of a capitalist society, another type of another kind of society. They will not be called upon to hold the balance between the classes, but to decide which classes would rule. If their basic economic policies (in answering the above questions) are such as to give scope to capitalism to develop, they will be caught in the grip of the laws of capitalism which are inexorable and which will take them step by step to a goal which might not have been before their eyes at the beginning. Once the course towards capitalism has been fixed it will be not so much a question of "controlling" capitalism, but of developing and protecting it, that is, of being controlled by it. In fact, the interest of the whole nation would soon appear to have become bound up with capitalism itself. If the capitalist, system suffers, wages fall, unemployment shoots up, agriculture declines. In short, successors of the idealist captains of the ship of state would be reduced to nothing more than the highest executives of the capitalist class seeking to bend all national energies into the service of that class. The efforts of the class-conscious Congressmen, mentioned earlier, would hasten this process. Furthermore, the rise of corruption, the swarming up of job-hunters and office-hunters within the Congress will hasten this process. A glimpse of this development (in a lower key) could be had during the days when the Congress ministries were in office. The question may be asked why should only the capitalists, be able to capture the machine and not the masses? We are not suggesting that they would do so in every case. We are pointing out the danger that is inherent in current mode of thought and making an appeal for clear thinking on these issues. The problem may be restated thus.

The masses will capture political power; but how will they retain that power and use it in their interest and for their prosperity and happiness and progress? We have shown that they will not be able to do so if we on their behalf make a present of this power to the capitalist class, as we surely would do if we nurtured it and developed its economic power.

Success of Congress

Before proceeding with this analysis it is necessary to point out that in supposing that the success of the Congress would mean the success of the masses, we are idealising the situation and taking it at its best. In actuality it will not be such an unalloyed victory of the masses. We have shown that there is a considerable section in the Congress which represents materially, or in spirit, the interests of the upper class. These Congressmen due to their social position, education, etc., are nearer the top of the Congress than the bottom and therefore, they influence its policies to an extent out of all proportion to their numbers. Therefore the success of the Congress will also largely be the success of the upper classes. We have to decide who would be successful in the next contest that will ensue the masses or the classes? There is another complacement solution of the difficulty we have raised. India being preponderatingly an agrarian country and most of us having our roots in the primitive village, it is natural that many of us call up to our minds and idyllic picture of village civilization. The self-sufficient village with its crafts is the answer of these people to the problems of poverty and capitalism.

Unfortunately, there is little clear thinking on this question, and most people use the argument without conviction in political thinking. Let us admit without any ado that the village crafts should be revived and the economy of the village set upon its legs. Even after that is admitted a good chunk, the larger chunk to our mind, of the problem still remains unsolved. No sane man, can deny that a modern state cannot be organised on a handicraft basis alone. It has to have large-scale machine production in many spheres in order to provide a decent standard of living to its citizens, modern amenities of life, security and the means of progress.

Economic Organisation

No one has given more serious thought to the economic organisation of the country from the point of view of their village and the elimination of poverty and exploitation than Professor J.C. Kumarappa, Secretary of the All-India Village Industries' Association. After much thought, Professor Kumarappa reached the conclusion that industries could be divided, into two classes : One, those which in their very nature can be carried on in a decentralised manner; two, those which in, their very nature must be centralised. Among the latter mentioned are iron and steel, mining, transport (railway, shipping and motoring) electricity, aviation, defence, machine manufacture, etc. Thus it should be clearly understood by our agrarian politicians that their idyllic picture of rural life must be considerably overlaid by a good bit of industrialisation and urbanisation.

The question remains, what shall be done with the large-scale industries that must remain or be created? Who shall own them and who shall ran them? Private individuals driven by the quest of profits or the people in the quest of an ample life?, Professor Kumarappa, it gives us pleasure to state, has no hesitation in answering that the people, that is the state should own them and run them in their own interest. The reason why he comes to this conclusion is not far to seek. If the necessary large-scale industries are left in capitalist hands, not only would exploitation and poverty remain in-those spheres, but the capitalists would grow in power and would soon destroy the handicrafts and capture the balance of power.

Self-Sufficient Village

In passing it may be added that the ideal of a wholly self-sufficient village economy, apart from its impracticability, is not a desirable basis of political organisation as it is the mother of fissiparous political life. The political disunity of India throughout history, in spite of a remarkable cultural unity has been due in the main to the self-sufficiency of the villages. A nation to be united and to be enduring must bind the remotest village in a common political, economic and cultural life. Now we come to the third solution of the questions we have raised. It is said that truth and non-violence will solve everything. Let us admit for the sake of argument that they will do so, but yet it is necessary to ask in what measure? Truth and non-violence are not mantras that their chanting would work miracles. They are a social methodology.

The question how non-violence would solve the problem of poverty 'is not answered by saying that non-violence would solve it. Yet, this is the manner in which the question is answered by those who mouth non-violence but do not understand it. Whenever the question of the abolition of the Zamindari system, or of capitalism is raised, we are solemnly reminded that it is against non-violence to talk of abolition. We are told that landlords and capitalists may live side by side with tenants and workers and that both the rich and poor may live happily. Such talk, we regret to have to say, is indulged in only by those who either wish to exploit Gandhism or wish to avoid the pain of thinking.

Social Property of Gandhiji

We have given the views of Professor Kumarappa, who may be considered to be an expert on these matters from the point of view of Gandhism. The views of Gandhiji himself about them are no less clear. Gandhiji rejects capitalism. He believes in social property. He believes in the elimination or private profit from large-scale industry and in its social ownership. Perhaps the clearest expression of his views regarding these questions is contained in his recent note on the draft resolution of Shri Jay Prakash Narayan enunciating basic political, social and economic principles of a free India. We shall request the readers to turn to that note and ponder over its importance. Gandhiji has put the seal of his approval over far-reaching economic measures, such as socialisation of transport, shipping, mining, heaving industries, abolition of all forms of landlordism and resettlement of land so that no peasant has more land than he requires for a decent living. Gandhians make a virtue of the fact that they are blind followers of Gandhiji. Will they accept these views as expressed in Shri Jay Prakash 's resolution and endorsed by Gandhiji? It-they do; a new chapter may open up in the history of the Congress.

Security of People's Consent

Many people who may be opposed to Shri Jay Prakash 's socialistic programme may take shelter behind Gandhiji's caution against baste in carrying it out. But, before we-begin to quarrel about the speed of executing a programme, let us first agree about the programme itself. Regarding the speed, there is not much that has to be said. It is rather difficult to persuade people to concur in the disappearance of their economic privileges and profits. Nor, is it always possible to secure their concurrence before action is taken. It is necessary to remember that we are considering these questions in the context of Congress assuming state power. We have pointed out above that immediately after taking the reins of government, the Congress will be faced with basic tasks of reconstruction. They will have to be immediately tackled and while harmful haste might be avoided the foundation stones must be laid forthwith, otherwise no structure would rise. No one can construct without foundations. The opposition of vested interests-cannot delay our action, nor the latter be made to wait upon their pleasure. It is very doubtful that we would ever succeed in winning them over. Let us take the experience of the ministries. Did the Bombay ministry give up prohibition in Bombay because of the opposition of the interests affected? Should the ministry have waited till it had converted at least a majority of the liquor dealers to its side? No believer in nonviolence would answer in the affirmative.

Again, should the Madras ministry have waited till it had got the money lending interests to its side before enacting its debt legislation? Should the U.P. ministry have dropped the tenancy legislation because, the taluqdars vehemently opposed it? Should the Bihar ministry have not levied income-tax on agricultural incomes because the big landlords opposed it? These instances show that a government must carry out the mandate it has received from the people and disregard the opposition of the interests adversely affected. Can there be any doubt that the Congress will get an overwhelming mandate from the Indian people in favour of the programme that Shri Jay Prakash has proposed or any similar programme? If the Congress then fails to carry out that mandate, it would be guilty of having betrayed the people. Today when we stand on the threshold of the Constituent Assembly, it is our duty to tell the people where we are going and where we wish them to accompany us. It is likely that before the final decision to launch civil disobedience is taken, the A.I.C.C. shall be called. That will be opportune occasion for a declaration of our aims and objectives. The suggestions that Shri Jay Prakash has made may serve as a basis for such a declaration now that they have received the general approval of Gandhiji. Will the great leaders of the Congress who are proud of being guided by Gandhiji give need to his guidance in this matter too? He propounds his views which is as under :

> I have been charged with trying to impede the production of munitions and other supplies essential to the efficient prosecution of the war, and with trying to influence the conduct and attitude of the public in a manner prejudicial to the defence of

> British India and the efficient prosecution of the war. I plead guilty to these charges. These charges, however, do not constitute a guilt for me but a duty which I discharge regardless of the consequence. That they also constitute an offence under certain laws of the foreign Government, established by force in this country, does not concern me. The object of these laws is diametrically opposed to the object of nationalist India of which I am but an humble representative. That we should come in conflict is only natural. My country is not a party to this war in any manner, for it regards both German Nazism and British imperialism as evils and enemies. It finds that both the sides in this war are driven by selfish ends of conquest and domination, exploitation and oppression. Great Britain is fighting not to destroy Nazism, which it has natured, but to curb a rival whose might can no longer be allowed to grow unchallenged. It is fighting to maintain its dominant place in the world and to preserve its imperial power and glory.

As far as India is concerned, Great Britain is fighting to perpetuate the Indian Empire. Plainly, India can have no truck with such a war. No Indian can permit the resources of his country to be utilized to bourtrees up imperialism, and to be converted through the processes of the war into the chains of his country's slavery. The Congress, the only representative voice of nationalist India, has already pointed out this sacred duty to the people of this country. I, as an humble servant of the Congress, have only tried to fulfil this duty.

The British Government on the other hand, in utter disregard for Indian opinion, has declared India a belligerent power and is utilizing Indian men, money and materials for a war to which we have pledged our uncompromising opposition. This is in the nature of an aggression against India, no less serious in the circumstances than German aggression against Poland. India cannot but assist this aggression. It therefore becomes the patriotic duty of every Indian to oppose the attempt of the British Government to use the country's resources for its imperialist ends. Thus the charge framed against me of trying to impede the efficient prosecution of the war is only the fulfilment of a patriotic duty. That the British Government should consider what is a duty for patriotic India to be an offence, only proves further its imperialist character. Regarding the speech for which I am being prosecuted, I cannot say how far it succeeded in achieving its ends. But nothing would please me more than to learn that it did save some success in impeding the effective prosecution of the war. I shall deem the beavest punishment well earned if I am found to have succeeded in this. As for the charge of endangering the defence of British India, I think the irony of it cannot be lost upon us. A slave has no obligation to defend his slavery.

His only obligation is to destroy his bondage. I hope we shall know how to defend ourselves when we have achieved our freedom. I consider it fortunate that I have been prosecuted for a Jamshedpur speech. This important industrial centre, which I consider the most important in the country, is peculiarly backward politically and from the point of view of the labour movement. I shall drive some satisfaction in prison, where I expect incredibly to find myself, from he thought that my arrest and incarceration for a speech delivered there has attracted to that city the notice of the political and labour leaders of my country. It seems scandalous to me that the country's most vital resources should be so wasted in a war to which we are so imply opposed. And it seems no less scandalous to me that while labour throughout the country should be reacting vigorously to the conditions created by the war, Jamshedpur labour should carry on as if nothing extraordinary has happened.

May, at least, the demand for a war bonus gain some momentum from this prosecution. Before concluding I should like to add that, lest as an Englishman you should misunderstanding one. I should make in clear that in impeding the prosecution of the ward have no desire to help Germany or to see Germany victorious. I desire the victory neither of Imperialism nor of Nazism. Yet, as a Congressman... socialist I have nothing but goodwill for the British and German people. If India's opposition to Britain's imperialist war ensures a Nazi victory, at is for the British people to decide whether they would have Nazi hegemony or 'victory with real democracy at home and in India. If the people of Great Britain remove their present rule and renounce imperialism with its capitalist rulers, not only India but the freedom-loving people of the whole world exert themselves-to see the defeat of Nazism and the victory of freedom and-democracy. In the present circumstances, however, India has no alternative but to fight and end British imperialism. Only in that manner can it contribute to the peace and progress of the world. I am conscious, Sir, that I have made your task easier by-this statement. I do not regret it. In the end I thank you for your courtesy and consideration during the trial. We have been accused of attempting to import a foreign-system into India, which has its own peculiar problems and solutions thereof. I wish to make it clear that we have no desire to disregard either the peculiar problems of India or its history-cultural background. We have, in fact, examined to the best of our ability the so-called "Indian" solutions : and we are satisfied that where present conditions they cannot take the place of Socialism. This is no refection on the genius of social philosophers of ancient India.

Unfortunately for them Indian Society has changed so drastically, its problems have been transformed so radically, that their ideas hardly bear any relation to present facts. There are certain broad principles which hold good in all ages and climes. But broad principles are of little value when concrete means are sought for the removal of concrete evils. And it is here-act in their conception of general social and individual good-the old systems and the new reflections break own completely. The old principles were laid down when civilization was much simpler that at present.

Neither industry nor agriculture had developed far enough to make it possible for men to exploit the labour of others to any considerable extent. All production was on a small individual scale. Population was low and Nature kind and bountiful. It was possible for any able-bodied man to clear the jungle and settle down with his family on the reclaimed land. From this it is a far cry to our present agrarian and industrial problems. Landlordism is an un-Indian institution, mills and factories are also new to the country. New likewise are all the problems that have been created by the imperialist domination. The basic economic problem of our society-the problem of exploitation of the many by the few-which arises, from the monopoly of land and other instruments of production-did not exist in its present universal form at the time of Manu. This problem, which we find has no relation with India's, ancient past, has, on the other hand, a basic unity with the problems of the modern world. In China, Japan, England, France, Germany, the United States of America cast majority of the people has to face essentially the same problem.

The development of the powers of production, in order words, the invention of steam and electrical power, has given birth to, and reared, the most extensive, and thorough system of human exploitation ever known-the system of capitalist production and distribution. Socialism, which is an inevitable reaction to this system, is, therefore, not bound by national frontiers. Its home is as much in England as in Japan, as much in Germany as in China in the United States of America as in India. Wherever conditions of capitalist exploitation exist, Socialism too will spread, to the four corners of the globe. India can be, and events are showing, is no exception. The existence of feudalistic relics in India modifies its problems to some extent, but it does not change its essential nature. The balance of power between the various sections of the-exploited masses would be somewhat different here, and their-transition to Socialism slower-otherwise their goal as well as their initial task of overthrowing the system of capitalist-cum-feudal exploitation and rule, work remain essentially the same as in the developed capitalist countries. It is for those who accuse us of imitating the West, to produce a truly "Indian" solution of the problems that face us. But though there has been a good deal of talk about India's peculiarities and its unique recipes for its ills, no one seems to have taken the trouble of formulating them in intelligible language-with perhaps only one honourable exception. As far as I am aware, Dr. Bhagwan Das is the only one among the leaders of the country, who has given serious though to this problem, and laid before the public what he considers are Indian solutions of Indian problems.

To us what is of greater value and importance than the solutions that the neared Doctor advocates, is his bold insistence on the view ;that the nature of Swaraj is a subject of paramount importance and calls for urgent and earnest inquiry and discussion. But, apart from the socialists, the Doctor stands..... alone in holding this view. As far as most other lovers of Indian culture are concerned their task is finished after they have tarred us with the brush of

"Foreignism" and prated some nonsense about the folly of troubling about matters that concern the remote future "Let us win Swaraj first" they say. One wonders if they see the inconsistency of their position when they.... and oppose 'Socialism. By that action they make it... that whatever "ism" they might accept after they have won Swaraj, they would, at least, be opposed to Socialism. Apart from being a breach of the neutrality they assume, this gives a clear indication of their sympathies. Before proceeding to consider some of the alternatives, I should like to point out the curious fact that these Indian culture enthusiasts, when they are faced with Socialism, fail to show at the least interest in the Manu-ite solution presented to them by Dr. Bhagwan Das.

The fate of the Das-Das Swaraj Scheme is well-known. And now his Ancient vs. Modern, Scientific Socialism has fallen again, it seems, on deaf ears. To take a concrete instance. It will be recalled that at the time of the last Assembly elections, of 1934 the learned Doctor had pointed out that according to Indian traditions it was for the people to seek out their leader and ask him to legislate for them and not for "candidates" for leadership to go running about begging the people for their "votes".

At that time it was not noticed that the lovers of Indian tradition welcomed Dr. Das suggestion with any visible enthusiasm. I suspect, on the other hand, that he was looked upon by most of these gentlemen as a mere Manu-crank. The greater part of this talk of "Indianism" is, to my mind a mere cloak for reaction to conservatism. If the leaders of the country (with one or two exceptions) seat down today to forge out a Constitution for India, I have not the least doubt that, in spite of all this condemnation of Socialism as un-Indian, that Constitution would be an utter imitation of the democratic constitutions of the West. It is often said that India's conditions are peculiar; that India's traditions are different; that India is industrially a backward country; and that, therefore, Socialism has no applicability here. If by this it is meant that the basic principles of Socialism, have no validity in India, it would be difficult to imagine a greater fallacy. The laws by which wealth accumulates hold as true in India as elsewhere and the manner in which the accumulation can be stopped is the same here as anywhere else. The peculiarity of Indian conditions may influence and determine the manner and the stages in which the principles of Socialism may be applied here, out never alter those principles. If social, ownership of the means of production is essential for stopping exploitation and unequal distribution of wealth in other parts of the world, it is equally essential in India. As for Indian traditions, as far as I know them, they are not averse to the sharing of life and its privileges. It is said that individualism has always been the dominant feature of Indian civilization and therefore the latter is opposed to Socialism. To put the problem in this manner is not to understand either of the ideals and to get lost in words.

Individualism has been the prominent motif in our culture only in the sense that perfection of the individual has been its ideal; never in the sense of narrow, self-seeking individualism, which is the motif of capitalist society. And, if individual perfection is the goal, the socialist has not the least difficulty in showing that such perfection can come about only by aiming at the utmost common good. Does not Trotsky say somewhere that only in a socialist society can the average of humanity rise to the level of Plato or a Marx? Finally, India's industrial backwardness need not discourage us. If anything, this backwardness would be helpful to us because it means a much weaker opposition. As for the practicability of applying Socialism to a region of industrial backwardness, it is enough to remind the reader of what the Russians are doing in some of the most backward parts of the globe. It is for these reasons that the Party has set for itself the object of establishing a socialist society in India after independence has been won.

Extract from a Report of 1948

From time immemorial there have been politicians who have preached that there is no such thing as ethics in politics. In the old times, however, this moralism did not spread its corrupting influence beyond a small class that played at politics, and the mass of the people were left uncorrupted by what the leaders and ministers of State did. But since the rise of totalitarianism, which includes both Fascism-Nazism and Stalinism, this principle has been applied on a mass scale and every individual in society has been affected by it. This has resulted in such an eclipse of moral values from social life that not only its political sector has been darkened but every sector of human life, including even family life. Since the victory of Stalinist methods in Russia, it has been commonly believed that there is no room for moral values in Marxism, and it is usual for a socialist who talks of such matters to be branded as a renegade or, at the least, a deviationist. I should, therefore, like to state before you in the clearest possible terms that I for one have come to believe that for the achievement of socialism a strict regard for means is of the highest importance.

Socialism means different things to different persons, but if by socialism we mean a form of society in which the material needs of every individual are satisfied and also in which the individual is a cultured and civilized being, is free and brave, kind and generous, then I am absolutely clear that we will never reach this goal except by strict adherence to certain human values and standards of conduct. It is too often believed that all would be well only if there were no exploitation in society and everyone was well fed and clothed and housed. But a society of well fed and clothed and housed brutes is a far cry from socialism. There were many things that Mahatma Gandhi taught us. But the greatest thing he taught us was that means are ends, that evil means can never lead to good ends and that fair ends require fair means. Some of us may have been sceptical of this truth, but recent world events and events at home have convinced me that nothing but good means will enable us to reach the goal of a good society, which is socialism. When, in a statement the other day, I talked of the need of spiritual regeneration, some of you might have thought perhaps that I had been so deeply shaken by recent happenings that I was trying to escape from the hard realities of life. Those of you who might have thought so are completely mistaken. I have no knowledge of matters spiritual, if the term is understood in a religious or metaphysical sense. I have not suddenly come to acquire faith in something called the spirit or the soul or Brahma. Such philosophy as I have is earthy and human. I am concerned merely with the problem of the type of men I should like to live with in society. Clearly, I do not like to live in society of liars and murderers, of men who have no kindness in them, no tolerance, no fellow-feeling. No one can say what human nature is; but this much can be said that it is what you make of it. A good man is not born. He becomes good by training.

Therefore, if the aim of our Party is not only to produce well-fed, well-clothed and well-housed animals, but also to produce good men, then I say that all our political work must be inspired by certain ethical values. I hope that you will give this viewpoint the consideration it deserves. I crave your indulgence again to permit me to examine another problem from a somewhat unorthodox point of view.

There is a view held by some that all politics, are power politics. I consider this to be a disastrous point of view. I shall examine here two important aspects of this way of thinking. First, let us see how it affects Party organization. Those who hold this view should logically make every attempt—I do not say that they are actually doing so-to secure power within the Party itself. And power, according to this view, being the quintessence of politics, the use of every kind of means may be considered justified to secure it, including means such as lying, scandal-mongering and cheating at Party elections. Clearly-and I hope all of us would agree-such means could only result in the complete disintegration of the Party. I, therefore, hope and pray that every one of us will reject all-such means and eschew all quest for power within the Party. It is human to yearn for recognition and aspire for positions of influence and leadership. But one should be content to, reach these positions by virtue of one's work and service done to the cause. The second aspect of this view which I wish to examine here has a far deeper and wider significance. The theory that all politics are power politics has the necessary underlying basis-though this may not be obvious to the protagonists of this theory-that the State is the only instrument of social good. In other words, those who subscribe to this theory believe-unless they are mere self-seekers, in which case unworthy of notice-that they must capture the State in order to, be able to serve society and bring about the social transformation they desire. I reject this view completely.

The Congress today has captured the State, but every thinking Congressman will agree that the Congress would completely undermine itself if it depended on the State for every effort at social change and development. In fact the view is growing among the constructive workers in the Congress that they must cut themselves off from the parliamentary machine and function independently so as to serve both society and the State. The experience of totalitarian countries, whether fascist or communist, has shown that if the State is looked upon as the sole agent of social reconstruction, we get nothing but a regimented society in which the State is all-powerful and popular initiative is extinct and the individual is made a cog in a vast un-human machine.

Such a society is surely not the objective of our Party; nor could a society of this nature ever be an intermediate stage in the evolution of the democratic socialist society that is our aim. Democracy requires that the people should depend as little as possible on the State. And, both according to Mahatma Gandhi and Karl Marx, the highest stage of democracy is that in which the State has withered away. Totalitarianism, as distinct from a transitional 'dictatorship' of millions of toilers. Over a small defeated class of vested interests, can hardly be a half-way house to full democracy.

It is necessary for the growth of full democracy that popular effort has the freest possible chance and that the people, through varied kinds of economic and cultural organizations and institutions, are enabled and encouraged to improve their condition and manage their affairs. Accordingly, the type of mind that I should like to see develop within the Party is one that would make every one of us indifferent to whether one is Prime Minister of the Republic or a trade union or other field worker. I believe that whether or not we have the government in our hands, if we succeed by constructive work in creating a sound trade union movement capable of running industry; in educating the working class in the arts of citizenship; in creating co-operative communities in the villages; in mobilising the youth and children as voluntary servants of the nation; in creating cultural influences that go down even to the most backward sections of the people; if we succeed in eradicating caste, superstition and bigotry; if we succeed in enlisting the cooperation of hundreds of thousands of selfless workers to whom the seats of power offer no, attraction-if we succeed in all this, we shall also succeed in, building up a socialist society.

In this event, the State will inevitably become a socialist State and will play its inevitable and appointed role, which would go little beyond the imprimatur of the law on what has already been accomplished, or on what cannot be prevented from happening. The State in this manner will only be an instrument in the hands of a popular socialist movement i.e. of the people organized independently of the State for a socialist way of living, rather than the source and fountain-head of all authority and will.

Concept of Socialist Economy

Socialism is not merely anti-capitalism, nor statism. Nationalization of industry and collectivization of agriculture are important aspects of socialist economy; but in themselves. They are not socialism. Under socialism there is no exploitation Of man by man, no injustice and oppression, no insecurity and an equitable distribution of wealth and services and opportunities Now, even in a nationalised and collectivised economy there may be exploitation, injustice, oppression, insecurity and glaring inequalities. If under such an economy, all political and economic power is concentrated in the hands of a party oligarchy, irreplaceable and self-perpetuating, there can be no socialism but its suppression, no revolution but reaction. The Communist in as much as he believes in and Works for just such an oligarchical society is a reactionary rather than a revolutionary. The Party, therefore, felt that unless the goals of socialism were clearly defined and steadfastly adhered to, there was danger again of the revolution being betrayed.

The aims of the socialist movement which needed to be emphasized were not mere overthrow of the capitalist order and establishment of a party dictatorship, but the creation of a society of free and equal peoples, a society based on certain values of human and social life, values which could never be sacrificed in the name of theory or the Party line or expedience of any sort. In the noble words of Ignazio Silone : 'On a group of theories one can found a school; but on a group of values one can found a culture, a civilization, a new way of living together among men.' Socialism in not just a school of thought, but a new culture a new civilization.

The Party's Policy Statement clearly says that there are two roads to the social revolution :

(1) the road of armed mass rising or the insurrectionary method;

(2) the peaceful or democratic method. The Policy Statement elucidates these terms further and distinguishes the insurrectionary method from mere violence or terrorism or putschism, and the democratic method from mere constitutionalism. The Statement goes further and declares categorically that in the present conditions of India, and future anticipated conditions, the democratic method is the 'only' right method to work for socialism.

There is thus no ambiguity in Party polity on this score. Yet, there are complaints that our policy is not clearly defined in this regard. The confusion, no doubt, is in the minds of the critics, for they do not fully understand the implications of the democratic method. There are other critics whose complaint is not that our Policy is ambiguous, but that it is wrong. According to, them, to say that it is possible to establish socialism without bloodshed is to dupe the workers. For them there is only one road to socialism : that of a blood-soaked revolution. They quote Marx's authority for this dogmatic assertion. Let me therefore quote Marx. This is what Marx said in the course of a notable speech on tactics at The Hague Convention of the International Workingmen's Association (the 'First International') in 1872 : The worker must one day capture political power in order to found the new Organisation of labour. He must reverse the old Policy, which the old institutions maintain if he, will not, like the Christians of old who despised and neglected such things, renounce the things of this world. But we do not assert that the way to reach this goal is the same everywhere.

We know that the institutions, the manners, and the customs of the various countries must be considered, and we do not deny that there are countries like England and America, and, if I understand your arrangements better, I might even add Holland, where the worker may attain his object by peaceful means. But not in all countries is this the case. If the critics do not hold that Marx was temporarily demented when he delivered his famous inaugural address, they will see that they had completely misunderstood him. Let it, therefore, be clearly understood that it is as un-Marxian to hold that only an armed revolution can lead to socialism as to assert that only a peaceful method can do so. The correct Marxian position is that either method can be used, but that which of the two is suitable to a particular situation can be determined only by the relevant historical and objective conditions. In a given situation only one method is the right method but only the facts of the situation, and no 'a priori' dogmatizing, can decide which method is right. To this the critics reply that the situation today is not what it was in Marx's days, and that in the existing world conditions socialism can never be achieved by peaceful methods! It is a healthy sign to try to correct Marx, but if the process of rethinking does not follow the scientific method of Marx, it is likely to degenerate into mere rationalisation of preconceived notions. When Marx spoke at The Hague Convention, reaction was reigning supreme in Continental Europe and even in England and Holland political democracy had not fully developed. Today, one-sixth of the world is under Soviet-communism and China and the whole of Eastern Europe and part of Central Europe are communist.

In Scandinavia and Great Britain there are socialist governments and strong cooperative movements. In other countries of Western Europe there is at least full political democracy and, as a result of the last war, European capitalism lies shattered. Imperialism is also on the decline and India, Pakistan, Burma and Ceylon are already independent countries. Elsewhere also the chains of imperialism are loosened. In America the New Deal initiated a progress towards the welfare state which has not yet been checked and there has been, since the war years, a tremendous resurgence of labour. Elsewhere in the world too the forces of democracy are to the fore more than ever before. Therefore, while it is true that the situation today is different from what it was in the days of Marx, the difference is all in favour of a peaceful evolution of socialism.

Socialism and Its Problems

Jay Prakash says that, I should like to start by saying that socialism is ninety per cent practice and ten per cent theory. I am afraid socialists are often inclined to forget this rather simple axiom. If we always remember that after all the test of theory is in practice, there would not be in the socialist movement so much controversy, so much hair-splitting. Practice and theory must obviously be interrelated, for, as I have said, the test of every theory must lie in the practice. If we look at the ideological problems of socialism from this point of view, we will also have to examine the practical tasks which are facing the socialists throughout the worlds.

The field is too wide to be covered in a short address. I shall, therefore, confine myself to a few problems which have arisen out of certain practical objective situations. I propose to deal only with five such problems, the first of which is' the problem of socialist axioms. I have placed this problem in the first place, because I am convinced that unless a solution is found to this problem, all our attempts a socialist reconstruction of society are bound to fail. How has this problem arisen? It has arisen in many ways, but let me point out only two sources from which it has appeared. We have before us the very vast experiment of socialist building in the U.S.S.R. It was assumed, I believe, by the architects of socialism in Russia that if they proceeded with certain changes in the society, in the social environment, in the foundation of the social structure and in the structure itself, it would be possible for them to build up a socialist society of which they had dreamed for years and for which they had struggled through perhaps an equal number of years. But while we find that the economic basis of socialist has been laid down : industry has been nationalised, agriculture has been collectivised, the motive of private profit has been removed from the economic system, the social structure or superstructure that has been built up on this foundation does not answer to the description of socialism. I doubt whether there would be any delegate or any comrade here who would describe the society in Soviet Russia as a socialist society. He would perhaps describe it more as state capitalism than socialism. Now, there must be certain reasons why all these things happen. It you go back to the ideological formulations of Marx, if you go back to dialectical or historical materialism, as, it is called, for an answer, I am afraid you will be disappointed.

The means of production are supposed to govern the relations of production, and the changes in the means of production are supposed to govern the changes in the relations of production. You have, as far as the productive technique is concerned, a highly industrialised technique based on electricity and large machines. You have mechanisation of agriculture. You have a technique, which looked at purely from the technical point of view, is not different from the technique of production found in the U.S.A.; but whereas that technique in the U.S.A. gives you an capitalist society, in Soviet Russia it gives you an entirely different system. Therefore, you will have to go deeper into the problem. Let me also at this stage point out that as far as the old ideological formulations are concerned, somehow their development has been arrested. The interpretation of history which was started by Marx, I am afraid, has more or less stayed at the stage where Marx had brought it. It was hoped that after the socialist government had been established in such a large country as Russia, we would have further development of the science of socialism, of its philosophy, of its historical interpretation and so on, but we find that in Russia instead of interpreting history, they are busy distorting history : and if you start distorting history, you cannot interpret history. If you begin to deny facts, historical facts, if you shut your eyes to events that have taken place, there cannot be any scientific interpretation. However, this was by way of digression. Going back to Russia, we find that after the achievement of power there began a very bitter struggle for power inside the ruling party itself. That struggle for power, knew absolutely no bounds. Every means was used in that game of power. We have found a repetition of the same process in other countries which have come under the domination of Stalinist communism We had for instance the recent trials in Czechoslovakia and the execution of Slanaki and the rest of them. Now, here you are faced with a very serious problem.

A party comes to power. It starts with very noble ideals. It aims at the creation, ultimately, of a society in which even the State has ceased to exist; there are no classes, there is no money, no wages-that is the ultimate picture of communist society which the Communist Party of Soviet Russia always had before it. But in the achievement of that objective they failed dismally. And you may have found that they are now claiming in Soviet Russia to have more or less completed the socialist stage of their task.

They claim that they are now beginning with the building up of a communist society, that is, a society in which there will not be institutions, social and economic, which I have just referred to. Every socialist Party throughout the world must be constantly aware of this serious problem of the demoralisation of the party and the corruption of the ideals in the midst of this struggle for power, and answers will have to be found for this very serious problem. I am afraid that the commonly accepted philosophy of Marxism, a philosophy accepted by many socialists, including the Stalinists, is based on a moralism, a philosophy that does not take into account the question of good or evil, a philosophy that regards this question as relative and relative to such an extent that these considerations can completely be disregarded, if the immediate purpose were to be served in that manner. There is another source from which this problem arises and that is a universal source, that is, the weakness of human nature, the weakness of individual man everywhere, his ambition, his selfishness, his stupidity, his hate, his fear. Now, if you are engaged only in shaping the environment in which the individual man lives-the social, economic and political environment-and if you are neglecting the individual, I am sure you will find that all these elements that go to constitute the nature of man as he is today will vitiate all your efforts, all your attempts at social reconstruction. We have in history attempts made to improve the individual by forgetting the environment in which the individual lives. For instance, we had Buddha.

Looking at the problem of human misery and arriving at the conclusion that human misery can be traced to human desire, he developed a system of self culture, a system for the culture of the individual, for the making, moulding and shaping of individual human nature so that he may be free from misery by controlling his passion, his desire. That was a very noble effort, but it was, if you forgive me for so saying, a one-sided effort. Today many socialists are again making the mistake of making another one-sided effort, namely, that of changing society alone and forgetting the individual. When Lord Buddha said that misery came from desire, he did not consider the misery that was the product of social institutions, of social environment. Supposing there are two babies born in this world, one in a very poor home, the other in a very wealthy home. The miseries of these two human personalities would not depend merely on their own nature, but also on their social circumstances, Similarly today, as I have already told you, if we merely create a socialist environment and leave the question of the individual alone, we will again find that it is a very partial effort at constructing a new social order, because the same individual will be functioning in that social environment and, if he is not a disciplined individual, if he is not an individual who is in tune with the aims of that society, who has not been trained, who has not learned to subdue and subjugate his personal desires and ambitions to the social good, we will find that the experiment of social engineering would miscarry. I therefore place this before you as one of the fundamental problems of the socialist movement today. We are seeing before us experiments that are being shipwrecked on the question of a moralism.

Therefore I hope you will agree with me that whatever be our conception of the path to socialism, whatever be our interpretation of theories, we in the socialist movement must subscribe to certain values, values which we will not consider relative in the sense that we could sacrifice them in order to achieve an immediate end. The communist started with this noble idea of a new society, a classless, stateless-society, a society of free and equal individuals, but he believed that no matter what he did today, no matter what were the means that he employed today, as long as he was successful he would ultimately arrive at these goals. So we see that his objective is noble but instead of progressing towards it he has been going astray. He has taken a different path which will never take him to the goal of communism, and therefore, if I may refer to a very brilliant thesis of my friend Dr. Ram Manohar Lohia, we should in our movement apply what he calls the test of immediacy, that is, we must see that what we are doing immediately squares up with what we intend to do in the ultimate stage. If our present action is in consonance with the ideals that we have before us, there is no reason to doubt where we would ultimately land ourselves.

For there is some rational ground for assuming that if our present action squares up with the noble ideals that we have before us, then-ultimately it is bound to take us there. If on the other hand we indulge in activities which contradict these ideals, these values, on which the new society will ultimately be based, if our present values contradict ultimate values, there is no rational ground for supposing that we will by some dialectical-contrivance ultimately arrive at that goal. Therefore, friends, I should emphasize that the socialist movement along with the economic and political and social programmes must also have a programme which includes this question of values. I should now turn to the next problem which I wish to place before you, that is the problem of creating a proper political-framework for the development of a socialist society. Here, I am afraid, we are still grouping. Various experiments have been made. If you go back to the classics of socialism, you will not get much light, because neither Marx nor Engels, nor Kautsky nor Lenin described in detail the political characteristics of a socialist society. Marx and Engels, as you know, were mostly concerned with analysing the capitalist society and finding out the dynamic of that society which would help the socialists to create out of capitalism a socialist society. Now as far as the political expressions of socialism are concerned, the first one that, historically speaking, arose was the Russian political system. The Russian political system, as you know, has gone through a long process of evolution. Some of us believe that if the original concept of the political structure had been adhered to then, possibly, Russia would not have socialism or communism, but it would also have not landed itself in the morass in which it finds itself today. We have today there a structure which is a one party dictatorship.

At the same time we have there a party which has a restricted membership, which goes periodically through purges, a party in which democracy does not seem to exist any longer; and in this one party dictatorship we have a completely bureaucratic State, which cannot in any way be described as a worker's State, as a people's State. Obviously for the socialist movement of the world the Russian picture of political organisation would be found wanting and unacceptable. We would have to devise a different structure. We have in certain Western countries such as Sweden or Finland, socialist governments trying to build up a socialist society. This task in these countries is being fulfilled within the framework of formal parliamentary democracy. It is possible in such countries, as it happened in Great Britain, for instance, that the socialist party should come to power for a number of years and then again lose that power as a result of the popular vote. To many socialists in Asia, and I have heard it being discussed in socialist circles, this could be a failure of socialism. Obviously those who consider this to be a failure of socialism believe that once a socialist party comes to power, every attempts should be made by that party by whatever means possible not to let that power slip out of its hands.

Well, obviously that cannot happen within the confines of formal political democracy; there socialist reconstruction will have to take chances. It may be that in course of time socialism comes to be so entrenched in the heart of the people that the socialist party is perpetually in power and has got unrivalled opportunities for socialist reconstruction. Then in that country the question would arise whether the political structure that was evolved through the age of bourgeois liberalism should be preserved or there should be drastic changes made. I believe it is felt in this country also that representative government is not enough, that it is necessary in the political sphere as well as in the economic sphere to give power of self-government to the people at large. I think socialists in the West too are becoming aware of the problem of decentralisation of political power, so that the people themselves may participate in the management of their affairs.

It is not enough for a socialist parliament through a socialist cabinet to rule over a country, it must be supplemented by the people's participation at the lower levels of the administration also. Socialism today has to give the answer to the question whether even in those countries which have a tradition of democratic, representative government, the political structure of socialist society should be the same as it is now. Would it be enough if the economy of the country has been socialised? Would it be-enough if a socialist party has come to power, if all these conditions have been fulfilled? Would we be satisfied or would we have to go forward and evolve a technique of political living and government in consonance with the ideals of socialism? We have another example of a socialist political system that is in the process of evolution. It is very rapidly evolving and it is difficult for anyone to say at any period of time whether 'he is up-to-date with the developments that are taking place. I refer you to Yugoslavia.

Yugoslavia is a country which till-recently was ruled by the Communist Party. Yugoslavia too was and to a very large extent is today a one party state. But the Yugoslav Communists are anxious to bring to an end as speedily as possible this one party rule; and I hope you are aware of some of the most unorthodox steps that these Communists of Yugoslavia have taken. When I say unorthodox I have in mind the orthodoxy that is preached and practised at Moscow. Somehow or other they claim to be the true interpreters of Marxism-Leninism which some of us, I am sure, would question, It is an axiom with all of us that socialism cannot exist without democracy, nor democracy be complete without socialism. The Yugoslav Communists are aware of this axiom of socialism which, I may say, is also the axiom of Marxism as I understand it. Being aware of this axiom the Yugoslav Communist Party has decided that it is for the people themselves to rule over themselves through Peoples' Committees, Workers' Councils, and the representative institutions of the peasants. It should be these that should come forward and take the responsibility of administering the country, and therefore they are bringing to the forefront what was known as people's front and which they have now renamed as the Socialist Alliance of the working people of Yugoslavia. The Yugoslav friends believe that in a society in which socialism has universally been accepted as the goal, the responsibility of ruling should be given to the people. They believe that a multi-party system does not answer to the needs of socialist politics, and that the problem is to create a new political framework for socialist society. According to them once the goal of socialism has been popularly accepted, there is no nee& even for one party, much less many parties. Instead of a multiparty State, they are driving at a no-party State.

That is a, problem which all of us must seriously consider, namely, creation of a no-party State. That is why they have converted the Communist Party of Yugoslavia into the League of Communists which is going to perform the functions of political education, and all education in general, civic education included. I am sure they are going to give their attention to the education of the individual also. I do not know what will be the outcome of this development, but it is a very interesting development. If the State is to melt away, to wither away, the party must also wither away. The aims of the party should become so broadcast, so popularised, so universally accepted that the party becomes superfluous. Now, I have my reservations about this development. It seems to me that if in a particular society at a particular period of time certain aims are universally accepted, it does not mean that there should necessarily be a single party in existence. For instance, in the age of liberalism, in the age in which capitalism was performing a revolutionary function and playing a progressive role in Europe, the ideals of free enterprise and of individual liberty as conceived by liberal capitalism were commonly accepted by the people; nevertheless we had in these countries different parties owing allegiance to capitalism and still functioning in opposition to one another. The Conservative Party of Great Britain and the Liberal Party of Great Britain have accepted the foundations of capitalist society and still there are two parties.

In America you have the Democratic Party and the Republic Party. Both believe in free enterprise. Both accept the ideals of capitalist society and yet you have these two different parties. So I am not quite sure that when socialism comes to be generally accepted by most of the people there should be or there would be only a single party in existence.

Socialists themselves might differ as to how to carry on their task from day to day and those differences might lead to the formation of different socialist parties. Therefore I am not quite convinced that at least at this stage it would be possible to do away with the multiplicity of parties. Some of us may not be very happy at the multiplication of socialism and multiplicity of parties in the world, but we have to adjust ourselves to the needs of the situation. It seems to me that the Yugoslav Communists are trying to create a democracy within a one party dictatorship and therefore, perhaps, it is possible for them to go forward in the manner in which they are doing. But if we were, functioning under democratic conditions and through the vote of the people a socialist party comes to power it cannot wish all the parties off the map, as it were. It will have to reckon with them if it does not wish to give up its faith in democracy, its faith in socialism itself. If we believe that socialism is for the good of the people, if we believe that only under socialism the people will come into their own, then there should be no reason for us to deny democracy, because only through democracy can we go to the people, and therefore if we come to power democratically it does not seem possible for you to do away with the multiplicity of parties and the multi-party system might remain a feature of socialist society. How permanent a feature, it is not possible for me to say now, but in the foreseeable future, I am quite sure, that in a democratic socialist set-up other parties, even other socialist parties, are bound to exist.

The socialist parties might act concertedly up to a point, but they may have their differences also. Now, whether there is this no-party structure, or whether there is a multi-party structure, that fundamental problem of the self-government of the people is always before you. All of us are apt to talk about the common man, but when we think of socialist reconstruction we think of ourselves. When we come to power we will do this, that and other things, and we will do it, if necessary, by force. But if we were to give the common people a place that is rightfully theirs in the political system, I am quite sure that you will have to evolve a decentralised State. I need not go into all the details of this question, but I should like you to keep it in view as the only possible means of translating socialism into people's rule at the lowest level. The third problem is an allied problem, and that is the problem of the economic structure that would be necessary for a socialism society. Now according to Marxism, step by step as you go to examine the superstructure you begin with the means of production, relations of production the relations of production determining the economic structure. If in Russia we do not have socialism but some kind of state capitalism, there must be something wrong vitally with the economic structure there.

All of us know what is wrong with the economic system there. Centralisation, bureaucratisation, lack of industrial democracy, lack of workers' participation in the management of industry, in short, lack of popular control over the economic processes. We are apt to take over these ideals from Russia, the economic pattern that exists in Russia, in the hope of avoiding the defects that have grown out of it in Russia and grafting on it a democratic, decentralised political superstructure. Now one of the most important items of the economic programme of socialism is nationalisation of industries. Well, the industries in Soviet Russia have been nationalised, but they have not produced socialism; they have produced something else. Therefore there must be something wrong in this system of nationalisation, in this system of the management of nationalised industries. I do not know if in all the Asian countries the transport system has been nationalised, but speaking for India let me give you one example. In India our railways are a nationalised concern. They are not owned by private companies but by the State. We have a Railway Board which administers the railways and the railway administration is responsible to parliament. Now, supposing in India all the other industries or big industries were nationalised and we had the same kind of administrative structure to run these industries as we have for the railways, then, even after complete nationalisation, there will be no socialism. There would be bureaucratism, there would be exploitation, there would be no equal distribution of surplus value, as is the case with the railway system in India.

The only difference between privately-managed railways and these State managed railways is that whereas in the former there used to be a management board responsible to the shareholders, here you have a management board officered by the bureaucracy and responsible to the central government. The railway men have no voice from bottom upwards to the level of the railway board. They have no voice in the running of the railways. The wage structure is an entirely capitalist structure where the difference between the lowest wage and the highest wage is so great that we cannot imagine that difference being excelled even in a capitalist system. Now, we know that in Russia in the economic sphere these defects do exist. There is no hand either of the consumer or of the producer in the management and control of industry and in the distribution of profits. It is the bureaucracy, the hierarchy of the party, of industry, of army, of collectivised agriculture that decides this question. Therefore, we in the socialist movement must think concretely of steps that will eliminate bureaucracism and centralism, give to the producer and to the consumer a hand in the management, and also ensure that the fruits of labour are equitably distributed. We will have to give our attention to this problem. I believe that one solution of this problem would be the dispersal of the ownership at different levels, instead of concentrated ownership in the hands of the central government dispersed ownership at various levels down to the cooperative, down to the village organisation or municipal corporation. That would be one way of ensuring, that too much economic lower is not concentrated in too few hands, and we do not have an economic dictatorship along with the political dictatorship. We in Asia must also be conscious of our other limitations and in the light of those limitations approach this problem of economic structure. In most countries of Asia we have very meagre capital resources. The rate of capital formation is very slow because productivity is very low, even though the rate of consumption is low. The level of consumption is very low although the rate of saving is insignificant. Now, if we were to build up our economy under a dictatorship, it would be possible for that dictatorship to extract as much surplus value as possible from the producer, from the primary producer. Take the peasants, for instance. For industrialisation you require raw materials and good grains. Now whatever is available of these is not enough, because they have also to, serve the individual needs of the primary producers, as well as the needs of socialist reconstruction. Now supposing we have a dictatorship, under that dictatorship it may be possible for the State to expropriate the produce of the peasant and let him starve. It would be possible to engineer a famine and blame the starvation on the famine; and with your censorship, and your propaganda you can always make it out that it is not a State-made famine, but it is due to the nefarious activities of the foreign agent and various other circumstances, and in this manner, if over a period of time you went on forcing the people to deny themselves, to deny their present needs, you, could possibly industrialise at a rapid rate and on a large scale. Even then your limitations will not leave you, but if you function democratically and if you rely on the votes of the peasantry, on the votes of the workers, it will not be possible for you to go beyond certain limits in trying to force the savings necessary for economic development. Therefore, the structure of socialist economy in most of the Asian countries is, necessarily going to be a dispersed structure, a structure based not on concentrated, mass producing manufacture but on dispersed, decentralised manufacture beginning with the homes of the producers to small townships etc.; that again gives you a guarantee that economic power will not be concentrated in the bands of a small number of people, that you will be saved from economic dictatorship. Decentralisation would more or less arise out of the limitations of the situation in which you find yourselves. In connection with this problem of economic structure we will have also to take into account the relationship of socialism to the worker, to the peasant, to the trade unions and the peasant unions and so on.

In Russia the unions of the workers, as you know, are merely to perform the function of what the Americans have called 'papboys', that is, to goad the people to produce more, to work harder. Now we have to consider, in a socialist society, the relationship of the party, of the State to the peasants and to the workers. We have in Asia trade union movements of sorts largely manned at their managerial level and at the level of leadership by middle class people. In that sense it is not a genuine trade union movement which draws up leaders from its ranks and grows up as a result of the efforts of that leadership.

The relationship of such trade unions to political parties is a very vexed question throughout Asia. There are many trade unions and there are many socialist parties or leftist parties or Marxist parties, and there is a race between them for the soul of the workers. But I should like to emphasize, as one of the fundamental ideological problems of socialism, at least in the East, that if we rely here on the working class and on the trade union movement to the same extent to which socialists in the West do, we will find that we will never be able to establish socialism. In the East it is not possible only with the support of the working class to establish socialism. It will become possible only if we have the support of the peasantry. If you wish to have the support of the peasantry, naturally you must satisfy their elemental urges. You have to give them land by abolishing feudalism and redistributing the land holdings. Now if you go about re-distributing the land, what you do is to create a new class proprietary owners, peasant proprietors. These millions of peasant proprietors are your constituencies, the constituencies of the socialist movement in the East. You must get their support in whatever you are trying to do; whether it is an armed insurrection you are engineering or whether it is an election you are fighting, you must have the support of this peasant mass. If we understand this fully, then our conception of the economic organisation of socialist society is bound to be drastically different from what it is elsewhere. Many socialists, I am afraid, talk to the peasants with their tongue in the check. They think the peasant is a fool and we would cheat him, in the first instance, by giving him land and thus get his support, and after we have got his support we will deal with him properly and put him in his right place, expropriate him again and bring him into our collective farms. I shall very humbly beg to submit that if we follow that course of action, whatever we may be able to achieve, we will not achieve socialism. It may be a new pattern of dictatorship, but it will certainly not be socialism. Therefore you have to take peasant with his small holding, living in his village, very-emotionally attached to that plot of land which belongs to him, and yet make him a socialist and create a socialist society in which he plays his part. I do not know the rural community in the rest of Asia, but in India we have villages, hundreds and-thousands of villages. I believe that in a country like India the objective should be to pool their holdings, so that we might have, instead of collectivisation or nationalisation what I should call villagisation of land : an economic structure which seems to me to be ideally suited to the rural community and in which the ownership of the land is transferred to the village community, not to an abstract entity known as the State or the nation, but to the concrete entity with which the peasant is acquainted and of which he is a part. Collectivisation in Soviet Russia has become a tool in the hands of the bureaucracy for exploiting the peasants. I am sure that you are aware that the rulers of Russia were not satisfied even with this-weapon that they have in their hands of ruling over the peasantry through the collectivised farm, and therefore a proposal was made which has presently been given up but may be revived again, a proposal to create what was called 'aggregate', agricultural cities into which collectivised farms-five, six or a dozen of them-were to be amalgamated and the population of the villages were to be shifted to a town, so that the intimate human and personal relationship that exists in a village might cease and an impersonal relationship of a town come to, take its place, so that it could become easy for the party bureaucrat to rule over the peasants who become workers of the 'aggregate' or agricultural factories, if you wish to call them so. That is the course of development that naturally comes out of the Russian system. Having dealt with the economic structure that we need to fashion in order to sustain a decentralised political system, I shall now refer to two other problems and close my remarks.

The technique of struggle is also a part of the socialist ideology and there is a great deal of controversy in the ranks of socialism on this question. I hope that all of you will agree that if we are going to establish a democratic society, we should follow the democratic means, of course, if those means are available to us. But democratic means are not always available. They are not available in dictatorships. They are not available in a country where there is a civil war going on. However, if democratic opportunities do exist, it should be our concern to see that we function democratically. We have at the back of our mind, many of us, a lurking suspicion that democratic methods might take us forward to a certain extent, but at the last stage violence will be necessary, that without violence the socialist revolution would not be complete.

Friends, I wish most earnestly to impress upon you the wrong assumptions on which this belief, that in the ultimate stage violence would be necessary, is founded. For the Western socialists this is an axiomatic truth, but in Asia where we have been used to feudalism, imperialism, civil war, the idea that it is possible through democratic means to establish socialism appears to be a reformist proposition. When I speak of democratic methods, let me make it clear that I am not speaking only of parliamentary methods, of constitutional methods. I am also thinking in terms of vital, large, mass movements, mass action of a non-violent character, unconstitutional but at the same time peaceful. If we are working with the sanction of the people behind us, if we have achieved contact with the hearts of the people, if we have got their backing, there is no reason why it should not be possible for us to move the masses into such peaceful activity.

For instance, there is the problem of redistribution of land. The problem can be solved in three ways : by the socialist party coming to power and legislating in that behalf; by a violent action by the peasantry or by the landless workers for the occupation of the, land, that may or may not succeed; by a peaceful mass action by the peasantry for the occupation of those lands. Where the socialists are in power, the other two questions do not arise; but where they are not in power and where they have the opportunity to function democratically, where there are civil liberties, where there is scope for organisation and propaganda, there, if we are able to move hundreds and thousands of landless people and make them peacefully squat-on the lands which are owned by landlords but which are tilled by the landless labourers and which should rightfully belong to them and thereby offer resistance to the powers that be, no matter whether there are arrests, baton charges and shootings, then there is reason to believe that no power would be able to overcome that force. Even violent action will not succeed unless it is a real mass action.

The action of fully armed insurgents will not help the landless people in forcibly occupying the lands. There also has to be a mass movement which will end up in the revolutionary capture of power by the socialists. Now this technique of peaceful action was experimented upon in India by Mahatma Gandhi in the course of our national struggle. And it proved successful. I for one am convinced, that under proper conditions and under proper leadership, this technique can succeed in the matter of land and social change also. Therefore, I do commend this technique of peaceful struggle against the State, the capitalists and other exploiters as a method of achieving socialism. I should like to refer here to a very interesting movement that has been started in India recently. When the Socialist Party in India thought of redistribution of land, we thought of it in terms of a movement which I have just now explained to you. But now has come forward a great Indian, therefore most follower of Mahatma Gandhi, called Vinoba Bhave. He said 'Yes, land must be redistributed, land must belong to the tiller, landlordism must go. But let us do this by the method of love.' Now, this is not an Evangelist platform. I am aware that I am speaking from a socialist platform, but still I feel that this method is vital enough. Vinoba Bhave started going from village to village on foot and asking those who have land to give part of it for the benefit of those who do not. Just as simple as that; in fact so simple that it sounds nonsensical, foolish, but it seems to be working. We are all human beings, the landlord is a human being, the capitalist is a human being; there is something in all of us to which this man is appealing and there is good response : hundreds and thousands of acres of land have already been given to him. When he started this movement he was alone, assisted by a handful of Ashramites, inmates of the 'Ashram' of Mahatma Gandhi.

But now there are thousands of people who work with him. Many in the Indian Socialist Party are working under him, going from village to village, asking people to give away land for the benefit of the landless people, making a moral appeal to them, saying that no one should have exclusive rights in land. For land is not created by man. Every one who lives by land should have a share in it. As a result of this campaign a climate has been created practically in the whole country in favour of redistribution of land. Even those who were at one time opposed to this idea are coming round. They have begun to advocate redistribution of land as the immediate programme after which all other development projects can come or should come.

Now, I do not know why socialists in the world should close their eyes to a phenomenon of this kind, to this new approach to economic problems. As a matter of fact, I was very reluctant to come here, because I was in the midst of this land gift movement, Bhoodan movement. I was also going from village to village and I intend, as soon as I return from Rangoon, to go back to this work in the state where Bhave is at present conducting this movement.

Everyone who has land, big landlords, small landlords, everyone is now convinced that he will not be very long in possession of all the land that he owns today. Everyone is convinced that this movement has created a new climate, a new atmosphere. Those who do not have land, will have land given to them. The test of immediacy of which I spoke to you in a different context is somehow proving very useful here. And so in the next movement when we start an action of this nature people will be attracted because they get immediate benefits. Whatever happens immediately you collect land, you collect 10,000 acres of land, 50,000 acres of land, 100,000 acres of land; you collect here and now and redistribute them. True, there are millions of people who are to be given land and by merely giving it to a few thousand people you do not solve the problem; but a hope is generated in the hearts of the people that something is going to be done here and now, that we shall have our rights fulfilled. That is the tremendous advantage in this type of movement.

Even if you have a peaceful resistance movement for the occupation of land, it might end in absolute failure. Not an inch of land may come under the occupation of the squatters if the resistance is beaten down. But here that question does not arise and even if we have ultimately to go forward to that state, the atmosphere, the consciousness, the hope and even the organisation required for getting response of that kind is thereby created. I do not know if a similar technique can be evolved in other spheres for the redistribution of capitalist wealth, for the peaceful transformation of the capitalist system. This technique did not come out of my head, but I had humility enough to accept it when I saw it work. Therefore, friends, I would submit that in the sphere of technique, as in other spheres, the last word has not been said. We are all going through the stage of experimentation and it is worthwhile that we experiment in this sphere of technique also. Yet another question that confronts the socialist movement is the question of relationship between socialist countries. Marx will not help us here nor will Lenin help us here, except in the sense of giving us general direction. Here also we have to go back to Soviet Russia. We find that when a number of Communist States came into existence, the relationship of these states to Soviet Russia was not much different from the relationship of the metropolitan States to their colonial empire. The relation of Soviet Russia with Poland, or Hungary or Baltic States which have ceased to exist, or Yugoslavia was not based on the principle of equality and mutual aid. You are all aware of the main issue on which the break between Yugoslavia and Soviet Russia came about. It was this issue of what the relationship between Yugoslavia and Soviet Russia should be. 'Are we equals', asked the Yugoslavs, are we going to co-operate on the basis of equality? Or is Yugoslavia going to become an economic colony? Are the resources of Yugoslavia going to be used for the development of the Russian economy at the cost of the Yugoslav economy? I think that the Yugoslav Communist Party has made a great contribution to socialist ideology by bringing this problem to the forefront and emphatically stating this principle of equality between socialist States.

There are not enough socialist States established today for us to concretely discuss the issue but theoretically the issue has to be discussed, and I am, sure that all of us will agree that no matter what the difference be in the development of the socialist countries, the relationship among them must be that of equality, of mutual aid. As a matter of fact, if there is any tilting of the balance it should be in favour of backward and weaker countries and not in favour of the stronger and more developed ones as is unfortunately the case with the Communist bloc. 'If there is a highly developed country which has become socialist it should be its responsibility to remove the unbalance that exists in the world today. There are a few, as some one used the phrase, super developed countries, some well developed countries, some backward countries, and just as it is the task of socialism in a given country to equalise opportunities within, to redistribute the wealth that has been produced, and the power, economic and political, that has been concentrated in the hands of a small class, likewise, in the international sphere, it should be the task of socialism to remove this discrepancy, to help, through some kind of world development pool, world development organisation, raise the level of the backward countries. The domestic task should be extended to the foreign sphere. What we are trying to do in our own country we should try to do on the international level.

This undoubtedly is a very difficult task. I have found that in our own country there are certain states which are, in the matter of food, surplus states, and some deficit. We have found it very difficult to persuade the surplus states to part with some of their food so that the deficit states might be able to feed themselves adequately. Even within a country this kind of provincial and regional selfishness exists, much so on the international plane; but if we were to keep this in mind and at least accept this as a basis and make an honest attempt to implement it, I am quite sure that the socialist movement which is represented here will give a new direction to the world socialist movement. Socialism has placed before mankind noble ideals of equality, freedom and fellowship of peace and international brotherhood. But these ideals are yet distant dreams. The assumption of earlier days that once the socialists were in power, all the dreams would come true has proved to be too facile. And a real danger has arisen of the ideals and principles being forgotten or being given a back seat and the means or the doctrines being mistaken for the former. The reason seems to me to be a wrong approach to these ideals. All of us agree that socialism is a way of life, an attitude of mind, a certain ethical behaviour. What is not so universally recognised is that such a way of life, attitude, behaviour, cannot be imposed from above by dictates of the government or by merely nationalising industry and abolishing capitalism. Construction of a socialist society is fundamentally construction of a new type of human being. The importance of such human reconstruction is admitted on all sides, but I am afraid no sooner the admission is made than it is forgotten and every one joins the race to get on the State wagon. Clearly if human reconstruction is the key to socialist reconstruction, and if that is beyond the scope of the State, the emphasis in the socialist movement must change from political action to such work of reconstruction. The question is and I think it is the most important question for socialism how is such human reconstruction passible? By education, some may reply. Education, no doubt, can play a valuable part, but it is not an adequate answer to the question. What is needed is a socialist movement, a mass movement of human reconstruction.

Such a movement, to my mind, would be the real socialist movement. Such a movement, obviously, will be non-political in the sense that its aim will not be the capture of the State, because the State will be irrelevant to its purpose, namely, the remaking of man. What will be the dynamics of such a movement? So far the dynamics of social change has been the conflict of self-interests The self-interest of labour has been juxtaposed to the self-interest of capital, the intermediary interests choosing their side according to their own view of the main conflict. Labour actuated by self-interest wishes to create a different social order in which it is assumed selfishness will not rule the lives of men. Here you have a fundamental contradiction. As the Hindi proverb says you cannot plant a thorn-tree and expect it to bear mangoes. I think, therefore, that a now dynamics has to be found in consonance with the ultimate values of socialism. The reason the ideals of socialism are eluding the 'socialist movement is that the approach to them is faulty. Socialism has been defined in various ways. I would like to define a socialist society as one in which the individual prepared voluntarily to subordinate his own interest to the larger interest of society.

The key world in this definition is the word voluntary. Men may be forced in various ways to subordinate their interest to the interest of others, but as there is force needed to do so, socialism would be limited, even distorted, may be even denied. Equality freedom and fellowship can never become realities unless the moral evolution of the individual has been such that he is voluntarily prepared to limit his wants and his freedom in the interest of his fellow human beings. A socialist society cannot be built up if every individual wants and hankers after more and more for himself. Unless the individual learns the lesson of self-control and adopts a way of life based on such control, strife between man and man and between his groups, classes and nations, is bound to continue. Science has placed in the hands of man the means of an ample life. In the midst of this possibility of universal happiness there is universal misery because of man's covetousness, his greed, his selfishness. The world is plagued by wars-cold and shooting wars and threatened with total destruction, not because there is not enough for everyone, but because everyone wants the most for himself. I fear that unless the moral development of man caught up with his scientific and technological development, his fate is pretty tightly sealed.

Therefore, what is needed is not a system of dynamics based on a conflict of interests, but one that is based on the values of the society that we all wish to create. What is need is not so much a movement for the capture of power, but a movement that required that those who participated in it should begin, here and now to live the new way of life. Let those who believe in the ideals and values of socialism begin to live them now. If we believe in equality, for instance, let us begin to practise it.

Real equality is not possible, to my mind, unless members of society live according to the noble Marxian ideal, 'from each according to his capacity and to each according to his needs.' No State can force the individual to live in accordance with this ideal. It can be put into practice only if it is willingly accepted by the community. Therefore, let those who believe in equality proceed to live accordingly. Equality does not consist in taking from the rich and distributing to the poor. If the poor tried to establish equality by merely distributing the wealth of the wealthy amongst themselves, without accepting the philosophy of life behind it, they would soon recreate different forms of inequality amongst themselves. And if the poor accepted the new philosophy and practised it in their own lives and if they did it on a mass scale, the rich would not remain behind. Likewise with the other values and ideals of socialism.

Reconstruction of Indian Polity

The title given to this document is explained by the following paragraph from Jay Prakash Narayan's paper

'Reconstruction of Indian polity (1969) : '1 propose in this paper to describe the main outline of the polity which to my mind is not only most suited for us, but is also most rational and scientific with :a brief statement of the reasons for my views.' The passages from the paper referred to above, which have a direct bearing on political thought, as distinguished from the details of the institutions recommended for India, are reprinted here. I propose in this paper to describe the main outline of the polity which to my mind is not only most suited for us, but is also most rational and scientific, with a brief statement of the reasons for my views.

Common Approach Concerning

It would be fatuous of me to try to give a definition of democracy. Nor is there need to do so. We have chosen democracy as our political ideal and are now concerned with the practical question of how to realise it. The general considerations that follow pertain to this question. Perhaps it would be well, at the outset, to keep in mind that the ideal can never fully be realised in India or anywhere else.

All that is possible is to approach the ideal as nearly as possible. It is for this reason that many political writers narrow down the ideal considerably and advance a realizable definition of democracy. Consider the following from an internationally recognized political authority : 'Government of the people by the people', 'Government of the nation by its representatives' these are fine phrases for arousing enthusiasm and fashioning eloquent perorations. Fine phrases with an empty ring. No people has ever been known to govern itself and none ever will.

All government is oligarchic : it necessarily implies the domination of the many by a few.' Again the same author writes : "The formula "Government of the people by the people" must be replaced by this formula, "Government of the people by an elite sprung from the people".

Furthering Above

The extreme case of political democracy is that in which, people govern themselves directly, making the laws, dispensing justice, and (although this is more difficult) carrying out or overseeing the administrative functions. But no such democracy ever existed, or ever will so long as men live together in large political units. Inevitably, then political democracy must be translated into law and representative government. Democracy does not assume that the 'people' actually govern themselves, and its theory makes plenty of room for leadership Democracy in Western usage stands for the free conflict of ideas and leaders, from among which the electorate makes a choice. These are strong words from wise and learned authorities, but I doubt if they will serve for all times. It might be said that the farthest democracy has advanced in the West is elected oligarchy.

Western democracy may, therefore, be called not democracy but democratic oligarchy. It is questionable, however, if the 'people' will remain permanently satisfied with such a situation. It may also be asked if the world-wide totalitarian assault on democracy does not acquire a point and a relevance on account of the fact that the peoples of the democracies do not experience the glow and satisfaction of self-government. It is further questionable if democrats of all times and climes, social idealists and thinkers, the spirit of man itself will ever remain satisfied with the current Western definition of democracy. Already, I believe; all these elements have combined the thinkers, the idealists, the people, the spirit of man to demand a more satisfying participating democracy. Indeed, it is my firm belief that to the extent to which democracy becomes truly participative, to that extent would the onrush of totalitarianism be stemmed and even rolled backwards. Therefore, while bowing my head to scholarship and learning, and also while remembering that the ideal could never be fully realised. I am for ever pressing forward with the quest for democracy and for discovering the ways and means by which more and more people could govern themselves more and more. Let me now turn, as a part of this quest, to the formulation of some general considerations about democracy. First of all, let it be pointed out that the problem of democracy is basically, and above all, a moral problem. Constitutions, systems of government, parties, elections-all these are relevant to the business of democracy. But unless the moral and spiritual qualities of the people are appropriate, the best of constitutions and political systems will not make democracy work.

The moral qualities and mental attitudes most needed for democracy are : (1) concern for truth; (2) aversion to violence; (3) love of liberty and courage to resist oppression and tyranny; (4) spirit of cooperation; (5) preparedness to adjust self-interest to the larger interest; (6) respect for other's opinions and tolerance; (7) readiness to take responsibility; (8) belief in the fundamental equality of man; (9) faith in the educability of human nature. These qualities and attitudes are not inborn in man. But he can be educated in them and trained to acquire and practise them. This task, let it be emphasised, is beyond the scope of the State.

The quality of the life of society should itself be such that it inculcates these values in its members. The prevailing social ethics, the family, the religious and educational authorities and institutions, the example that the elite set in their own lives, the organs of public opinion-all these have to combine to create the necessary moral climate for democracy to thrive. Thus, it should be clear that the task of preparing the soil in which the plant of democracy may take root and grow is not a political but an educative task.

While the above moral qualities and attitudes have been treated in the abstract, without reference to any particular society in space or time, I should like briefly to deal with one particular moral attitude that seems to be peculiarly relevant to the fate of democracy in modern society. The present is par excellence a materialist age; and whether it is capitalism, socialism or communism, it is the material values that overshadow all other values of life. Man is a mixture of matter and spirit-to use these words in their popular sense-and every man has material needs that have to be satisfied. In that sense every man cannot help but be a materialist. But if the material needs become unlimited and the over-riding activity of mankind becomes an unending endeavour to satisfy the insatiable hunger for more and yet more, there is an imbalance established in human affairs and life becomes wholly materialistic. This is exactly the situation in the West, in spite of its adherence, in large part, to Christianity, one of the noblest spiritual ways of life.

All this may appear to be irrelevant to the question of democracy. I emphatically hold to the contrary, because it seems patent to me that democracy cannot co-exist with the insatiable hunger for more and more material goods that modern industrialism-capitalist, socialist or communist has created. I believe that for man really to enjoy liberty and freedom and to practise self-government, it is necessary voluntarily to limit his wants. Otherwise, the greed for more and yet more will lead to mutual conflict, coercion, spoliation, war; and also to a system of production that will be so complex as to bind democracy band and foot and deliver it to a bureaucratic oligarchy. It is undeniable that there is a conflict today between two values of life, namely, between wanting more goods and wanting more freedom. Those, however, who believe in freedom should have no difficulty in making the choice. In a poor country like India the masses may not yet be faced with this choice, but in the form of an ideal of life, the choice before India is as real as before Europe or America. Which of the two choices India will make depends not upon Parliament or any type of political action, but, among other things, upon the example that the elite of society will set in their personal lives. This issue of voluntary limitation of wants has another fundamental significance for democracy. In the democratic countries the cry is becoming stronger against the growing power of the State and against statism generally. This is a justifiable cry and democrats will have every sympathy with it. Here we have perhaps the most difficult question that democracy faces today, the question as to how to resolve the following dilemma : when there is liberty it leads to abuse and necessitates State interference, and when there is State interference it leads to curtailment of liberty. How then to preserve liberty and prevent its abuse?

There are no political means by which the dilemma can be resolved, there are only moral means. The obverse side of the medal of liberty is responsibility. If the individual is not prepared to take social responsibility, if he uses liberty for self-aggrandizement and neglects or hurts the interests of others, some form of state-ism becomes inevitable. It is here that the pertinence and wisdom of-Gandhiji's concept of trusteeship becomes evident. The only democratic answer to state-ism and totalitarianism is trusteeship.

But trusteeship cannot be practised without voluntary limitation of wants. An individual cannot function as a trustee unless he is prepared to share his possessions with his fellowmen; this he cannot do unless he has learned to curtail his-wants. Thus voluntary limitation of wants, in other words, the rejection of materialism or the unlimited pursuit of material satisfactions, is essential for the achievement and preservation of democracy. Here we are likely to come up against the economists and their 'science' of Economics. For it might be pointed out that the 'laws' of economic growth cannot be by-passed, that economic development must take its natural course, that science and technology cannot be denied. But it is necessary to remember that present-day Economics is a science of a particular type of society which is ruled by a particular philosophy of life the philosophy which we have just considered, namely, the philosophy of unlimited material progress. It is conceivable that there may be other 'sciences' of Economics, pertaining to other types of societies and ruled by other social philosophies. It should be remembered that democracy does not consist merely in its formal institutions. It lives really and truly in the life of the people; it is a way of life. It is not only through the representative assemblies and elected governments that democracy works, but in an equally true sense through the voluntary associations and actions of the citizens which they carry on and establish to deal with their problems, promote their interests and manage their affairs. Professor Harold Laski, when asked how he would judge the worth of a democracy, replied that he would do so by the amount of voluntary activity within it. Democracy has worked best among peoples that have shown initiative and enterprise. Democracy is not merely a question of political rights and people's part in government. Particularly since the First World War, democracy has come to mean more and more social and economic justice, equal opportunity, industrial democracy.

The old distinction between political and economic democracy has been given up and the two concepts have been merged into one to mean full democracy. This is not to suggest that democracy is bound up with 'and such politico-economic ideologies as socialism or communism. It is true that these ideologies had promised full democracy in the sense used above. But experience has shown that in the case of communism there has been not enlargement but a severe curtailment of democracy both political and economic. The old belief that State ownership and management of the means of production, distribution and exchange will lead to economic self-government, elimination of exploitation and equitable distribution of the products of labour, a stateless order of society, has not been confirmed by experience. It is the very opposite that has actually happened. In the case of socialism the position is somewhat better, because socialism preserves the institutions of political democracy. But it is questionable and this has been recognised by, socialists themselves if concentration of economic power in the hands of a central State, even under democratic conditions, works for economic democracy; and, further, if it does not result even in the thwarting and limiting of political democracy itself. It should, however, be pointed out, as it has been indicated above, that the fault is not so much with socialism, as with (a) the centralised State and (b) large-scale industrialisation. In a centralised, unitary State the people are barred from participation in the government, even though they retain and exercise the right of choosing and dismissing it. This latter right too is substantially restricted by the operation of the party system, because it limits the choice of the people. As for large-scale industrialisation, there is a very large measure of agreement among social thinkers that it inevitably leads to shrinkage of democracy. But whatever the experience of the working of socialism or communism the fact remains that the concept of democracy does include social and economic justice, equal opportunity, industrial democracy together with all that is meant by political democracy.

And if communism and socialism have failed so far to lead human society to these goals, the endeavour to reach them must continue to form part of the quest for democracy. It has been indicated above that the answer is moral rather than political or economic. The problem of democracy is intimately connected with such social institutions and attitudes of mind as are represented by the caste system and the practice of untouchability. A society in which men are considered high, low or untouchable according to the families into which they are born, is very far from being democratic. It is quite a different matter that individuals are endowed at birth with different abilities and aptitudes. That is a biological phenomenon, with which caste has nothing to do. It should be appreciated by every Indian democrat that the system of caste hierarchy and untouchability is the greatest and most stubborn enemy of democracy in this country. At the same time it should also be appreciated that vanquishing of this enemy is, again, not a political but an educative task. It is also, but to a much lesser degree, an economic task.

The social stature of the depressed and backward castes will undoubtedly rise with improvement in their economic condition. But it would be a mistake to believe that economic improvement by itself would be sufficient to remove caste distinctions. The economically advanced castes too observe hierarchical distinctions among themselves. In countries like India that have but recently emerged from foreign rule, the problem of democracy is further complicated by the fact of economic backwardness and the absence of recent democratic experience or tradition. The problem of capital formation (which includes the problem of fixing the limits of present consumption and saving), the-direction and utilization of labour and resources and similar problems of economic development are obviously capable of easier and quicker solution under dictatorship-communist or any other-than under democracy. This is one reason for the attraction that communism has for the intelligentsia of the backward countries. Here the people of these countries are faced with a moral choice. Those who have chosen democracy have chosen the higher way of life and have shown that they are more developed as human beings than the others who sacrifice things of the spirit for material things. On closer scrutiny it would appear that under dictatorships-the people are compelled to sacrifice on rather false pretences. Neither in fascist nor communist dictatorships has it been found that the people were given the things for which they were made to sacrifice their freedoms.

The economic development of the countries under dictatorship aims at power rather than peace and prosperity. The standard of living of the common people in Soviet Russia-even after forty-two years of communist dictatorship and despite the phenomena] industrial and economic development-is lower than that of the U.K. or Sweden, considerably lower than that of the U.S.A. The standard in other communist countries is, of course, still lower, except perhaps in Czechoslovakia. Incidentally, we have here the key to the understanding of the question of economic development of the backward countries under democratic regimes. If these countries also wish to build for power, they are doomed. Democratic India cannot compete with China at this game. She will either have to give up her democracy or face defeat in her attempt to build for economico-military power. This is a crucial question for the new democracies to answer : are they going to build for power and war or for peace and happiness? Should the democracies depend upon military power for their defence or upon the forces of peace in the world and the moral strength of their own people? The least that is expected from a nation that calls Gandhi its. Father is that it will refuse to build for power and will build for peace and happiness. As for the second difficulty mentioned above in the building up of democracy in the backward countries namely, the absence of recent democratic experience or tradition, it must be conceded that this difficulty is serious and real enough.

Indeed, some consider it to be so serious as to apprehend the possibility of the rise of dictatorial regimes in these countries. The recent history of several Asian and African countries shows how justified is this fear. The question may be asked, is there time to inculcate the values of democracy in the minds of the people? I personally feel that while the danger in India of a dictatorship, military, or other, cannot be brushed aside lightly, there is no immediate cause for fear. But, even granting that the time is short and democracy is running a race against it for its life, what other guarantee there is for the survival of democracy except the people's intelligent appreciation of the values of democracy and their preparedness to fight for the defence of those values? The only other way to prevent a dictatorship from taking over is to forestall it by setting up another dictatorship-perhaps a 'democratic dictatorship;' that is to say, a dictatorship purposely established by those who believe in democracy in order to save their country from other types of dictatorships that deny the worth and validity of democracy.

The dictatorship of Mustafa Kamal Ataturk which has now developed, outwardly at least, into a Western type of democracy and the two-party system may be cited as a good example of this. The present-day dictators from Cairo to Djakarta all profess to be building up democracy in their own dictatorial ways. While there is no need to distrust their motives, it must be admitted that for the time being at least and no one can tell how long the interregnum will be democracy has been given up. The danger considered above brings to the fore, among other things, the need to strengthen the base of democracy, so that even if something went wrong at the top, the base would-endure and keep the foundations of democracy secure. This was the virtue of the village councils, the town committees, the trade and artisans' guilds of old kingdoms and empires rose and fell, conquerors came and went, but these organs of popular democracy, that drew their sanctions from the people of their own spheres and not from the central State, went on. Apart from the spiritual unity and way of life, it was these grass-root democratic institutions that have been responsible for the continuity of Indian society and culture. I deal below more fully with the question of building these basic structures of democracy. Thus we see that democracy to use an idiom of Mathematics is a 'function' of so many factors, the resultant of so many different activities. There is no single human or social activity by which democracy is created. The house of democracy has many mansions and many types of bricks, and various types of materials and builders are needed to construct it. It is a pity that this is not realised more widely in this country. Otherwise there would not have been such an obsession with politics and other activities could have been consciously undertaken for the building up of democracy.

Picture of Ancient India Polity

It is well-known that the literature on the political and economic institutions of ancient and medieval India is rather scanty. Scholars, however, have gathered and pieced together enough material to give us a fairly reliable picture of ancient Indian polity. I believe a study of this polity and of its relation to the whole ensemble of Indian life and culture should be useful, nay essential for the determination of present political institutions. Political thought has, of course, developed much farther since those days, and new political institutions, such as those of parliamentary democracy, have been fashioned. We must learn from this literature and experience. But the implantation of any idea or institutions that is not adapted to the native soil or grafted upon the roots of our life will not bear fruit or contribute to the organic and healthy growth of the body politic. Indian society has passed through all manner of vicissitudes in the course of its thousands of years of history. But the spirit of India has persisted through them and the main stream of her life has flown uninterruptedly.

At times, the stream disappeared underground, but as in the case of her many subterranean rivers, the limpid waters of India's inner life flowed unbroken under the inert sand of defeat and decline. India is emerging presently from another of such melancholy periods of her history. Therefore, the builders of the future India should take care to explore the hidden founts of her eternal life and go to them for real sustenance. The political institutions that we build today should harmonise with the eternal spirit of India and nurture the founts that have kept her alive.

It may appear irrelevant to some to look to ancient India for sign-posts to guide us on the road to democracy. But India was perhaps the earliest home of democracy and some of her republics had lasted as long as a thousand years. And though kingship or monarchy was the predominant form of Indian polity, kings in the earlier times were elected by and subject to the Kshatriya aristocracy. Even when hereditary kingship became the rule and the Samitis ceased to function, the village and town communities, the merchants' and artisans guilds, the varna order, the dharma, or social ethics, continued to function independently of the central State-with which indeed, the latter did rarely interfere-and to provide a stable' democratic basis for Indian polity. The democracy of the village communities was so stable and efficient that it continued well into the British period.

Therefore, far form being irrelevant to the question of democracy, the ancient polity of India, particularly its underlying principles, should be of the utmost value to us in building up our democracy in the present. 'Community' and self-development and self-regulation of communal life are the distinguishing marks of ancient Indian polity. The State in India evolved through many forms beginning with the small Rigvedic 'kingdom' and developing into vast monarchical empires of the Mauryas and Guptas. In between there were aristocratic republics spreading over the Punjab, Sindh, Eastern U.P. and Northern Bihar. These were the sanghas or ganas. Other forms of State were known variously as rajya, swarajya, bahurajya, dvirajya, valrajya, maharajya, samrajya.

But through them all persisted, and developed according to their own inner laws' the communal bodies. As these bodies were far more stable and enduring than the ever changing States, the latter, whether republican or monarchical, had little authority over them, apart from guaranteeing that they functioned properly within their own jurisdictions and according to their own constitutions and regulations. The State interfered with them only when they transgressed their own proper functions and procedures. There were very rare exceptions to this rule. 'Community' in ancient India had two forms. The first and basic form was the territorial community, the village or township. With the advancement of communal life, these came to be co-ordinated into larger territorial communities, sometimes embracing a whole Kingdom or republic. But their area ever seems to have been very large. The other form of community was the functional or occupational community, the varna. Just as it was natural for man to find communion with neighbours, so it was for him to find it among those who followed the same occupation, even if they were spread over wide, non-contiguous areas. Persons performing the same functions and following the same occupations, shared a common way of life and had common problems, and common rights and common responsibilities towards their larger society. It was thus that the social genius of India developed the functional communities, the four varnas and gave them a theoretical as well as a practical form and basis. Each varna was self-determining and yet integrated with and responsible to the territorial community. The relationship of the two forms of the community and the inter-relationship, between the latter two made up a remarkable, self determining, pattern of a complex ethico-socio-economic life. The varna order of society has been so depraved and distorted that there would be few defenders of it now. Yet, the two fundamental truths of it are undeniable. That human beings have different aptitudes and abilities and every individual should be enabled to pursue and develop his natural gifts and inclinations are scientific truths that not only no one thinks of denying, but that every social scientist desires to make the basis of reorganization of society.

The second truth is voiced in one way or another by the various schools of functional democracy such as guild socialism, pluralistic State, occupational co-operation and others. If our present political institutions are to be soundly based, if they are to draw sustenance from the Indian soil and, in turn, if they are to sustain, revive and strengthen the whole fabric of Indian society, they must be related to the social genius of India described above, and their texture must be woven again with organically self-determining, self-developing communal life, in which occupations, professions and functions are integrated with the community. This is not only a question of constitutional forms or political systems. It is a creative question in the widest sense of the term. It is a question of an ancient country finding its lost soul again. The old village communities have survived in nothing else than their physical existence. They are no longer living communities acting jointly for the solution of individual or communal problems and for the development of their moral and material life. It is not necessary here to go into the story of the destruction of the village communities. It would be enough to note that it was the result of deliberate policy of an alien government that neither understood the character of communal polity nor felt secure in the presence of such strong traditions of self-government and self-help.

Nevertheless, the very fact that the villages do exist physically provides us with a ready-made foundation to build upon, But we do not seem to be going about it in the right manner. Gram Panchayats, no doubt, are being emphasized and established. But this is being done is an alien manner. The principles and methods that are being used will fail to infuse the spirit of community into the empty shells that are our villages today. Nay, they will atomize them yet further. I shall discuss this question more fully in the concluding portion of this paper. A word that figures boldly on the ancient sign-post is dharma. Indian polity held that the State was subject to the dharma, which it was its duty to uphold and protect. The concept of dharma was of great importance in ancient Indian society and it prescribed and regulated individual and group behaviour in all walks of life. This concept of dharma and its role in Indian polity and the wider life of society is another example of that synthetic, organic, communal organization of Indian society which has been discussed above. Communities, territorial or functional, had developed laws and codes of behaviour to regulate the internal life of their communities and groups and their relations with the rest of society. There were in addition codes and laws that were common to and accepted by all of them and that made up the universal social ethics. The ensemble of these social ethics exercised a powerful influence over the State. Communal life having been completely destroyed, the roots of dharma have no soil from which to draw sustenance. Dharma has therefore declined and ceased to exercise any influence, not only upon present polity, which is a wholly foreign implantation and has no roots in the India soil, but upon all social activities, such as commerce, education, labour, administration, priesthood. Unless life in India is again organized on the basis of self-determining and mutually co-ordinating and integrating communities, that organic self-regulation of society which the concept of dharma represented will not be possible. To that extent democracy will remain distantly removed from the life of the people.

Vinobaji is already speaking, for instance, of a gram-dharma (the dharma of the village). But gram-dharma will not arise, as he has stressed, unless the village becomes a community. Only then will it be possible for the village to adopt as its dharma the welfare of all the villagers, so that none goes without food, clothing, a roof over his head, work to do; no child goes without a knowledge of the three R's; none goes without the benefit of a minimum health service.

The ancient concept of dharma has to be revived and the appropriate dharma for a democracy has to be evolved. This, as of old, will not be brought about by a legislative process. It can be none only in an organic manner : dharma must arise from life itself-life that is vital enough, real enough, organic enough to be able to throw up codes and laws for its internal regulation. The experience of recent social engineering may and should be drawn upon, but the main mould of life must be indigenous and consistent with the genius of Indian social organization.

Inherent Nature of Human Being

Man is a social animal and is endowed with social nature. He is born in society, lives and dies in society. His nature makes him crave for 'society', that is to say, for communion with other men Every individual man is unique and has a distinct individuality, but his uniqueness and individuality have meaning and purpose only when be is a member of society. No man can live alone, or if he does, can have any human significance. He is then a freak of nature or an accident of life, he is beyond the pale of human society, he is not man. He is 'wolf-man', or something of that sort, as his rare historical specimens have sometimes been called. Further, the relation of the individual to society is not like that of the grain of sand to the sand dune. The relationship is rather like that of the living cell to the living organism.

Man always lives in organic relationship with other men. It is the totality of these living relationships that constitutes society. Society is not a mere sum of separate individuals. Not even the crowd is an inorganic sum of human grains. Modern Western democracy is based on a negation of the social nature of mad and the true nature of human society. This democracy conceives of society as an inorganic mass of separate grains of individuals; the conception is that of an atomized society. The brick with which the present edifice of democracy polity is constructed is the individual voter and the whole process of democracy rests on the arithmetic of votes. The individual voter casts his vote as an atom of society, not as a living cell in organic relationship with other living cells. It is not the living together that is expressed and represented in the institutions and processes of democracy, but an abstracted individual. It would be a pity if the peoples of Asia, who have such an ancient and rich heritage, should rush to imitate this inorganic polity. Happily, the evidence from Cairo to Djakarta indicates that Asian peoples are having second thoughts, and are seeking to find better forms than parliamentary democracy to express and embody their democratic aspirations.

As far as India is concerned, Gandhiji had long ago pronounced parliamentary democracy to be a failure, and had advanced his own alternative proposals, which were at once so much more consistent with India's tradition and with the true nature of man and human society, and had expressed the hope that India might evolve a 'true science of democracy' and give a 'visible demonstration' of it. The problem of devising the right kind of polity is obviously a part of the larger problem of social reconstruction. While it is true that in the past greed and other false values of life distorted or thwarted the working of man's social nature it is necessary now, when man is beginning consciously to re-order his life, to create economic, political and other institutions that are consistent with that nature. Modern industrialism and the spirit of economism that it has created, a spirit which weighs every human value on the scales of profit-and loss and so-called economic progress, have disintegrated human society and made man an alien among his fellow men. Not only has the community been disintegrated, even the family is languishing in the West, and the mother, the women, who was the centre and soul of the family, is losing her womenhood. The problem of present-day civilization is social integration.

Man is alone and bored, he is 'organization man', he is man ordered about and manipulated by forces beyond his ken and control irrespective of whether it is a 'democracy' or dictatorship. The problem is to put man in touch with man, so that they may live together in meaningful, understandable, controllable relationships. In short, the problem is to re-create the human community. Let me now turn to the community. Territorial contiguity of a number of families, while it is the starting point and a most important condition, does not in itself make a community. The present-day Indian villages, for instance, are not people communities. They were so at one time, but now are mere territorial settlements, life in them being individualistic rather than communal, mineral rather than organic. In the true community there is communion, i.e., sharing, participation, fellowship, as the dictionary puts it; there is identity of interest; a feeling of unity in the midst of diversity; a sense of freedom within the framework of accepted social responsibilities; differentiation of functions converging to the single goal, of the good of the community and its members. Caste, class, race, religion, politics-all these divide men into different, often conflicting groups.

The community brings them together unites them and harmonises their interests. In the community agriculture, industry, capital, labour, skill, intelligence are not at loggerheads with one another, but are synthesized in the service of the community. Production and consumption are not two contra-posed sides of an economic bargain manipulated by distant agencies, but an integrated process serving a single and direct purpose. The community is built up of personal relationships, any choice and free will have their play, within the limits of self-imposed discipline and common culture. In the community there is understanding participation by the members in all communal affairs. The community is a, co-operative society, but the difference between it and the ordinary co-operative society is that co-operation in the community embraces the whole of life, rather than only its economic sector, and all the members of the community rather than only those who purchase shares. Every one in the community has a share in its fortunes and misfortunes. In its internal matters the community is self-regulating and self-determining. Division is poison for the community so the endeavour always is to seek the highest common denominator. It is interesting to recall here that in the Indian village communities there were no elections to executive offices on the present majority-minority pattern, which is a divisive and disruptive process. Instead there was selection by general consensus of opinion, or sometimes, by drawing lots. I do not mean to say by all this that such a community as described above ever existed before, or that it would automatically come about if only people began to dwell in small territorial areas. Had it been so, all the Indian villages would have become ideal communities. What I do, however, wish to say, and say it with all the emphasis at my command, is that such a community must be the ideal of future social reconstruction. Only then will the social nature of man and the great humanist ideals of modern civilization find fulfilment. Only then too will there be true democracy. For the heavily industrialised and urbanised countries of the West, this might be a difficult task-though many thinking Western minds are already giving their serious thought to it. But we in India-and I believe the same is true for other countries of Asia that have not passed under totalitarianism are very favourably situated to launch upon this venture. Before proceeding to consider the community further it may be advisable to deal briefly with the question of science and its impact on social organisation. It may be urged that small local communities might have fitted at one time into the rural pattern of life, but in this age of industrialism they have hardly any place except as odd specimens of a past civilization. Industrialisation and urbanisation, it may be said, necessarily go together. I completely reject this view. The choice is not between urbanisation and rural life. The dichotomy between urban and rural is false and unscientific. Both industry and agriculture are essential for human life and its development.

The question of industry should be looked upon from the point of view of the whole man : it should never be forgotten that industry is for man and not man for industry. Some people talk of science and technology as if they were like forces of nature, like an earthquake, let us say, about which nothing can be done except adjusting ourselves to it. Science and industry are products of the human mind and they should be sent to human purpose. Indeed this is what has already happened; only the human purpose has not been an elevated and worthy one. Science and, its offspring, technology have been chiefly put to the service of private profit and power : the first represented by the capitalist system, the second by the modern centralised State, whether democratic or totalitarian. It is common to call science neutral and amoral and to put the blame on man. The blame, of course, is there, but it is meaningless to call science neutral or amoral. Science, after all, is a product of purposive human endeavour; as such, it cannot be said to be morally neutral. If science does not conduce to human happiness and promote human values of life, it is not science but pseudo-science. The 'science' that has led to the disruption of human society, to the alienation of man from his fellow human beings, to the creation of economic and political Leviathans and to man's increasing subordination to them, to man's automatization, must be rejected as false science and a new science and technology must be discovered to serve a better way of life.

Commercialisation of science has to be replaced by humanisation of science; instead of science being exploited for power and profit, it has to be used for peace and happiness. If man decided that instead of being herded together in large cities it was better to live in small communities, instead of being automatons it was better to be conscious human beings, instead of being a grain in the sand-heap it was better to be a member of a community, it should not be difficult for scientists to evolve the appropriate technology. Thus the society we are visualising here will be neither 'urban' nor 'rural', it will be, if a name has to be given to it, communitarian. In other words, it will truly be society. Development of science has made it possible for the distinction between urban and rural to be abolished. The communities of the future will have a balance of agriculture and industry; they will be agro-industrial; they will make full use of science and technology so as to serve the ends of their life and no more. Owing to geographical and historical conditions agriculture may predominate in one and industry in another, but a balance between them will be the idea of all.

The present monstrosities, the big cities, will have to be decentralised as for as possible to relieve congestion and create healthy conditions of life; and for the rest, they will have to be so reorganized as to be made federations of smaller sized communities, To the extent this is not possible, the big cities will have to be endured, care being taken to see that they do not become bigger, and no new big cities come up. The question may be asked how large should be the local or primary community. There cannot be a cut-and-dried answer; there is no mechanical measure. The primary communities are organic growths and, depending upon many factors, their size varies. Let it be said that they should not be so small that a balanced development of communal life and culture becomes difficult, nor so large that life in them becomes impersonalised. The 'revenue village' in India has a well understood definition, and even though it usually consists of a number of hamlets, all the inhabitants of them do feel a sense of belonging to one another. So in India the revenue village may be taken as the primary community. In States where the revenue village may be too large and an artificial unit, a new demarcation may have to be made. We have so far discussed the local or primary community and shown how it is a creation of man's social nature and the unit with which the structure of society has to be built. Let us now consider how this can be done. Should society be just a sum, a totality, of the primary units? It should be obvious that such a society would be as arithmetic and mineral, or nearly so, as the one, like the present Western society, that is made up of the sum of individuals. Just as in the primary community a number of families come together and cooperate to build a common life, so in order that there may be society, the primary communities must come together and cooperate with other primary communities so as to tackle common problems and promote common aims. Such cooperation and coordination of activities will obviously be impossible between distant and very large numbers of primary communities; mutual intercourse is possible only between neighbouring communities.

Therefore, the next step in the building up of an integrated society is for a number of neighbouring primary communities to come together and cooperate amongst themselves to build, let us say, a regional community. Each single primary community will do all that may be possible with its internal resources. But there will be many things that will be beyond the resources and competence of the primary community. For instance, each primary community might be able to provide for a primary school, primary health services, small irrigation works like wells and village tanks, and village industries. But a number of primary communities must cooperate together in order to provide for a high school, an indoor hospital, a power station and servicing centre, larger industries, larger irrigation works, etc. Thus the regional community comes into existence by an organic process of growth. The circle of community is widened. It will be seen from this that the regional community is not a mere sum of the smaller communities constituting them. It is an integrated community in itself. In other words, at the regional level there is an integration of institutions and activities of their primary communities : the village panchayats are integrated into the regional panchayat; the village cooperatives into the regional cooperative union; the primary schools into the regional high school; the village youth and cultural associations into the regional ones; the village plans into the regional, plan etc.

Just as in its internal administration the primary community is autonomous, so in the spheres in which the primary communities have delegated their powers to the regional community, the latter is autonomous. (The need to, delegate powers arises from the fact that the primary communities are unable by themselves to do everything that needs to be done). The regional community, however, is not a superior or higher body that can control, or interfere with, the internal administration of the primary communities. Each in its sphere is equally sovereign. The regional community in its turn will do all that is within its competence. But, again, there will be many things which will be beyond its competence, such as running a techno-agricultural college, a major irrigation project, production of electricity, manufacture of machines, etc. In order that these tasks be tackled a number of regional communities will have to come together to form a still large community-the district community, let us say. The district community too will be an integrated community and its relationship with the regional communities be of a pattern similar to that of the latter with the primary communities. In this manner the district communities in their turn would, federate together to form the provincial community.

The provincial communities would come together to form the National Community. A day might come when the national communities might federate together to form the World Community. Two conclusions follow from the above. It should be obvious, in the first place, that as we proceed from the inner to the outer circles of communal life and organization, there is less and less to do for the outer communities; so that, when we reach the circle of the National Community it has only a few matters to attend to, such as defence, foreign relations, currency, inter-state coordination and legislation. This being so it should be obvious, in the second place, that such a social organization offers the utmost scope for the people-who are no longer an amorphous mass of human grains but organized in self-governing communities to govern themselves. The communitarian polity that has been described above can alone guarantee the participating democracy which is our ideal and which should be the ideal of all democrats. It will only be in such a society that the individual will be able to, save himself from the fate of robotism to which modern civilization has condemned him and find freedom and self-significance as a member of the community. There is a formidable volume of literature on parliamentary democracy, including in the term systems akin to it, such as the American presidential democracy.

There is also a vast literature on the party system which appears in the wake of this type of democracy. I believe it would be fair to say that even the most ardent defenders of parliamentary democracy agree that it has serious defects. But they console themselves with the thought (a) that there is no better alternative; and (b) that, within limits, it is possible to amend and improve it. No one will deny that the system is capable of much improvement and it is undergoing change all the time, though not always for the better. But no matter how much improved, its fundamental defects will yet remain, because they are the very premises on which its entire structure has been raised. The fundamental defect, from which other serious defects issue, is that this form of democracy is based on the vote of the individual. We have already examined this situation and found that it is the atomization of society that is responsible for this kind of political system. But that does not alter the fact that the system is based on a false premise-the State cannot be an arithmetical sum of individuals. The people, the nation, the community can ever be equated with the sum of individual voters. The partisans of parliamentary democracy claim that under it the government is at least representative of the majority of the voters, if not of the people, First of all, this is not true. More often than it is commonly believed governments elected under universal adult suffrage are minority governments, in the sense that they represent a minority of the voters. Wherever there are more than two parties, this happens quite often, but even under two party systems, it is not a rare phenomenon. At the last General Election in this country [19571, for instance, minority governments were established in a majority of the States, i.e., seven out of the thirteen States, excluding Union Territories. In this way the 'minority' States were : Bihar (Congress : 44.47%); Bombay (Congress : 48.66%); Kerala (Communist : 37.48%); Madras (Congress; 46.52%); Orissa (Congress : 40.01%); Uttar Pradesh (Congress : 46.29%) West Bengal (Congress : 49.20%). Perhaps the most serious fault of parliamentary democracy, from the point of view of democracy itself, is its inherent tendency toward centralism. At one extreme of its political spectrum is the national State and at the other the individual voter, with a blank in between. The local bodies that may exist have (a) little self-government powers, and (b) no direct or indirect influence on the national State. Add to this the complexities of a highly industrialised civilization that are beyond even the understanding of the ordinary citizen, and you have a central State of overwhelming power and resources and the individual voter reduced to abject helplessness. The 'sovereign people' being dispersed over the length and breadth of the country like particles of sand over the desert and having no other organized political force than the national State itself to interpose between themselves and that State, the latter naturally becomes all powerful. The issue of power in such a State is decided not by the fictitious 'people' but by a balance between political parties and such organized interests as industrialists and bankers and powerful labour unions.

The people represent a wholeness, while the organized interests the sectional. Even a sum of the sections cannot make up the whole. Only their organic integration can do so. Such integration takes place only in the community-at its various levels. In the communal or communitarian democracy that we are advocating there are a natural decentralization and a multi central pluralistic State. A natural outcome of centralization of power and administration is bureaucracy. The central executive or cabinet is so over-burdened with work that it is compelled to leave more and more to, and depend more and more upon, the permanent officials, who in course of time gather more and more power for themselves. This soon leads to a dangerous autocracy, the autocracy of the bureaucrat, which is difficult to fight because it 'works in the shadows' and is hard to get at. They only answer to the problem of bureaucracy is more and more decentralization so that the people directly participate in the administration of their affairs and control the civil servants who owe their jobs and are directly responsible to them. This is exactly what will happen in the communitarian democracy outlined here. The communal administrations might make mistakes and there might be inefficiency. But as they themselves will be the sufferers, they will learn and improve things. Moreover, during the British rule did we not say to ourselves repeatedly that good government was no substitute for self-government? Is that less true now? An inevitable concomitant of parliamentary democracy is the party system. So much has been written in criticism of this system that it seems unnecessary to dwell upon it here at any length. Some criticism of it has been implicit in what has been-aid above. It is clear that parliamentary democracy cannot work without parties.

Parties of a sort will perhaps exist everywhere and at all times. Even in the family there may be parties. In the ancient Indian republics, which were aristocratic democracies, parties and factions were a common feature. But the highly organized, centralised mass parties of modern times are a far cry from the factions of old, whether of the ancient Indian republics or the Greek city states. The old democracies were small and the factions and the people were not so far removed from one another. The people therefore could judge them and the issues that were raised with intimate understanding. The issues in those days were also simple enough. All this has changed now and parties have become a sort of state within the state. They are now the real arbiters of the people's fate, whose control over them is fictional. The citizens who cast their votes for the parties have nothing to do with the running of the parties, they are complete outsiders. Even the enrolled members of the parties have no say either in the policy-making or the inner administration of the parties. The parties are run by caucuses that are beyond democratic control. Party rivalries, we have seen above, give birth to democracy, depress political ethics, put a premium on unscrupulousness and aptitude for manipulation and intrigue. Parties create dissensions where unity is called for, exaggerate differences where they should be minimised. Parties often put parties interest over the national interests. Because centralisation of power prevents the citizen from participating in government, the parties, that is to say, small caucuses of politicians, rule in the name of the people and create the illusion of democracy and self-government. No doubt the party system has its good points and because parliamentary democracy cannot work without it, those who, swear by that type of democracy and see no alternative to it are prepared to accept the evils of the party system as inevitable and satisfy themselves by pointing out its virtues.

For my part, it is not the party system that is the main culprit, but parliamentary democracy itself, which gives it rise. In the communitarian democracy that I have proposed here, there may conceivably be parties, but they are likely to be local factions, and, in any case, their role in the State will not be as commanding as that of the parties in the parliamentary system. Another serious fault of parliamentary democracy is the system of election that it fosters and requires for its proper functioning. First of all, the system is very expensive and appallingly wasteful. The fabulous expenses involved have the effect of mortgaging democracy to moneyed interests or large sectional organizations such as trade unions. As compared with this the election expenses in the communitarian system would cost practically nothing. It would have been a matter of some consolation if the huge expenditure had resulted in any public good. In fact, the result is just to the contrary. A general election, as noted above, creates unnecessary passion and excitement; instead of educating and enlightening the people it befogs their mind; instead of resulting in the election of able and good men, it tends to favour demagoguery. Serious political and economic issues and other questions of policy, it is obvious, should be considered calmly and dispassionately and not in the heat of partisan warfare. That is why I hold that the practice of general elections should be abolished. The elected houses should be continuous in nature, with a part of them being renewed periodically.

Objective of Community's Economy

This is not the place to deal at any length with the Economy of the Community. For that a separate paper would be necessary. However, a treatment of the policy would be incomplete without a brief description of the economy that would underlie it. Society is a complex whole, as man himself is; and, therefore, social and human reconstruction requires an all-sided approach. The aim of the community's economy is the welfare of the community and each of its members. Its aim cannot be individual profit, exclusive of the welfare of other individuals in the community. The community's economy is neither exploitative nor competitive : it is co-operative and co-sharing. The community comprehends the whole of man and is interested in his all-sided development.

The life of the community is balanced and not one-sided. The economy of the community must, therefore, be subordinate to, and subserve, the aim of a balanced development of human life. Therefore, it cannot be an economy of unlimited wants, as it is in the existing society. The present 'science' of economics would be inapplicable to a balanced society. For it, a new science of economics will have to be worked out. In this country Gandhiji and Shri J.C. Kumarappa have laid the foundations, of such a new economics. The community is an enlarged family, and like the family it represents the eternal flow of life. Just as the family is interested not only in its present members but even in those who are unborn, so the community thinks of future generations. Its economy, therefore, is not wasteful. It is particularly careful about the non-renewable resources of nature which are being wasted at such a criminal rate by the so-called advanced nations of the world. A balanced economy concerned with future generations of men, that is, with life rather than death, would try to do its best to return to nature what it takes from it. It will, therefore, try to restrict consumption as far as possible to renewable resources and use as little as possible of the resources it cannot put back. The economy of the community is in cooperative harmony with nature, while present-day economy both of the West and East is at perpetual and destructive war with nature. The economy of the community, further, should be as self-sufficient as possible.

The idea of self-sufficiency, in this age of international trade, strikes many as parochial, isolationist, reactionary. But for the community it is most natural. The primary concern of the community is to provide for satisfaction of the primary needs of its members. It is, therefore, natural for it to produce all it can to provide for them food, clothing, shelter and other necessaries of life. It is also the community's responsibility see to that every able-bodied individual in the community finds useful employment. But if the economic activities of the community are not primarily related to its needs, the community would be at the mercy of the market-not only national, but also the international market-which may spell unemployment and economic ruin for it. We have already discussed the effects of the atomization of society and seen how modern industrial organization has made the individual a helpless human particle ruled by forces which he neither understands nor can control. Therefore, it was pointed out that the institutions and processes of society must be adapted to the human scale and man must be made the master of his fate. Following that line of thought we arrived at the commonitarian way of life.

But, if having reached the community, we again reverse the process and make it subject to the domination of macro-economics, we would mind ourselves exactly where we started from. There would then be no other fate left for man but robotism. Therefore, it is inescapable that in the economic sphere the community should, in the first instance, engage in activities that would be completely under its control. That is the sphere of production for self-consumption or consumption within the community. It is obvious that such production must in the first place, be in the field of primary needs of life. The community would obviously have other than primary needs. No community would be able to produce all that it needs. Even in the sphere of necessaries of life, every community may not be able to produce all that may be required. No community can be self-sufficient in every thing. The question is how are those other needs to be satisfied? The economic life of the communitarian society would be so organized that human needs are satisfied as near at home as possible first, in the primary community, then in the regional, district, provincial, national and international community in that ascending order. This means that each expanding area of community would be as self sufficient as possible.

Incidentally, this would save much of the unnecessary energy and time devoted today to the business of commerce, advertisement, etc. This would naturally set the pattern for planning. Planning would begin from the primary community and therefrom fan outwards. In our scheme of things the regional plan, i.e., the plan of the regional community, would be the pivotal plan. This would mean that the regional plan and not the village plan, which would be too small for the purpose would be the unit out of which the whole national plan would have to be constructed. The existence of large, unbalanced cities would complicate communitarian planning, and necessary adjustments would have to be made. The towns would of course, be integrated with the regional, and district communities. But the integration of the cities would be difficult. It will be recalled that I have already suggested that as far as possible the cities should be re-constituted as federations of communities. All natural resources would belong to the community. How they would be divided between the communities would be decided upon by common agreement. Generally, speaking each community would have possession of the natural resources that falls within its boundaries. But there are resources that are unevenly distributed such as forests, mines, etc. These would have to be shared by all by common agreement. It follows that land would belong to the community; and in the nature of things, each primary community would own the land that falls within its area. Great economic inequality is inconsistent with community-, spirit. Up to a point difference in income or wealth may be tolerable. Vinobaji gives a homely illustration to drive this home. He gives the example of the five figures of the human hand. They are unequal, but the inequality is reasonable; so that, in spite of it, the fingers can cooperate and work together. But if the difference had been too great, so that one finger was only a few inches long while the next was measured, in feet the hand would have been utterly useless. In the community, the position of the worker would be central, because it would be realized that work is the most essential thing required for the community. Without work the community could not exist.

Therefore, every adult in the community would be a worker. At the same time, work would be a meaningful expression of human powers, rather than meaningless drudgery, because the worker would be a responsible participant in the work process. There would be no over-specialization tending to reduce the worker to an automation. Rather, the agro-industrial nature of the communal life would make it possible for him to follow a diversified occupation. A few words about the organization of industry, commerce, etc. I have already stressed the agro-industrial character of the communities-as opposed to purely agricultural or purely industrial. I have also stressed the need for a new kind of technology, adapted to the scale of man. A social organization and technology of the kind proposed, here would assure that the bulk of industrial and other economic institutions would remain confined within the region and district. There would be some institutions of provincial, and a few of national dimensions. These institutions might be of the private, cooperative or communal type. In the primary, regional and district communities a large part, may be the greater part, of industry and commerce would naturally be of the owner-worker type. The rest would be cooperative or communal. A few units might be of the private employer-employee type. The provincial and national undertakings would be of the cooperative, communal-or even private type. Perhaps a word of explanation is necessary about the communal undertakings. They would be undertakings established by the communities and run either (a) by bodies set up for that purpose by the communities concerned, and working with full participation of the employees; or (b) by bodies directly set up by the employees themselves. Self-government in industry, as in every other economic undertaking, would be a cardinal principle of the communitarian economy. In owner-worker units, the problem does not arise.

Cooperatives formed only of producers also do not raise any problem in this regard. But in such undertakings, large or small, where there are employers, managers, technicians and workers-no matter who the employer may be a joint body representing all the elements would be set up for internal self-government. The idea of classes at war with each other is foreign to the communitarian order of society and opposed to the spirit or community. That spirit requires harmonization of interests, which is possible only on the basis or aim, snaring and acceptance of responsibility the cardinal principles of community life. It follows that such things as strikes and lockouts would be foreign to the communitarian way of life. Non-cooperation might be a possible course of action in extreme : cases involving moral issues.

4

JAY PRAKASH NARAYAN AND CSP

Rise of the Party

The Congress Socialist Party grew out of the experiences of the last two national struggles. It was formed at the end of the last civil disobedience movement by such Congressman as came to believe that a new orientation of the national movement had become necessary a redefinition of its objectives and revision of its methods. The initiative in this direction could be taken only by those who had a theoretical grasp of the forces of our present society. These naturally were those Congressmen who had come under the influence of and accept the Marxian Socialism. It was natural, therefore, that the Organisation that sprang up to meet the needs of the situation took the description "Socialist." The word "Congress" prefixed to "Socialist" only signified the organic relationship past, present and future of the organization with the national, movement. The socialist forces that were already in existence in the country were completely out of touch with the Congress and had no influence on the national movement. Therefore, there did not take place, as otherwise there would have, a fusion of the Congress Socialist Party with the groups previously existing. Given the adoption of correct and sensible tactics by all the parties concerned, there is every likelihood of such a fusion taking place at a later stage.

Party's Functions

The immediate task before us is to develop the national movement into areal anti-imperialist movement-a movement aiming at freedom from the foreign power and the native system of exploitation. For this it is necessary to wean the anti-imperialist elements in the Congress away from its present bourgeois leadership and to bring them under the leadership of revolutionary socialism. This task can be accomplished only if there is within the Congress an organized body of Marxian Socialists. In other words, our Party alone can, in the present conditions, perform this task.

The strengthening and classification of anti-imperialist forces in the Congress. Congress Socialist Party depends largely on the strength and activity of our Party. For fulfilling the Party's task it will also be necessary to co-ordinate all the other anti-imperialist forces in the country.

Work within the Congress consistent with its task, the Party should take only an anti-imperialist stand on Congress platforms. We should not, in this connection make the mistake of placing a full socialist programme before the Congress. An anti-imperialist programme should be evolved for this purpose suiting the needs of workers, peasants and the lower middle classes. It being the task of the Party to bring the anti-imperialist elements under its ideological influence, it is necessary for us to be as tactful as possible. We should on no account alienate these elements by intolerance and impatience.

The Congress constructive programme should not be obstructed or interfered with. It should, however, be scientifically criticized and exposed. In Congress elections, we should not show keenness to "capture" committees and offices nor should we form alliance with politically undesirable groups for the purpose.

Party's Objectives

This does not mean that the Party should not carry on socialist propaganda from its own platform. It must continue to do so and do it more systematically and rigorously. It follows that the Party's own programme must be a Marxist one, otherwise Party will fail to fulfill its task and leadership. Marxism alone can guide the anti-imperialist forces to their ultimate destiny.

Party members must, therefore, fully understand the technique of revolution, the theory and practice of the class struggle, the nature of the state and the processes leading to the socialist society. At the annual conference help at Faizpur on 23-24 December 1936, the following resolutions were passed. The chief task facing us and all other anti-imperialists is the creation of a powerful national front against imperialism.

This is not a task that has to be begun anew. The struggle against imperialism is on and has been on for many years past. It has now to be widened, integrated and raised to a higher stage of intensity. While the working class and the peasantry has led in the past and is leading today important militant struggles against imperialism, the main organized expression of the anti-imperialist movement have been the Indian National Congress. But as is evident it has not yet become an adequately consistent and effective anti-imperialist force. It does not yet embrace the broadest possible sector of the masses whether organized or unorganized and still stands aloof from their day to day struggle for the satisfaction of their pressing immediate needs. It is the task of all anti-imperialists in the country to bring together and unite all anti-imperialist sectors and to build up a mighty front against imperialism made up of the broadest possible sector of the masses. It is clear that in our attempt to do so, it is the Congress that we must take as the basis and starting point, and we must attempt to make it an all embracing united front against imperialism.

The Congress has already succeeded to a large extent in uniting wide forces of the Indian people for the national struggle and remains to day the principal existing mass organization of diverse elements seeking national liberation. It is for us now to find means to assist and extend to that unity to a still wider front. This task though being a single whole, can be divided, for the purpose of elucidation into three main parts : our work within the Congress; our work among the masses outside the Congress; the task of integrating the anti-imperialist struggle outside and inside the Congress and consolidating the leadership of the anti-imperialist and left forces. The Thesis is mainly concerned with the elaboration of the triple task. The Congress is organized at present on the basis of individual membership.

Its members come mainly from the peasantry and middle class. Most of these members do not take any active part in the anti-imperialist movement and simply meet once a year to elect their delegates and representatives. The Congress Committees do not have any day to day programme of work. They have usually no contacts with the organization of peasants and workers and do not take any appreciable part in their day to day struggle. The only contact they could have had with the masses, apart from the fact that it was not calculated to develop mass struggle, was through the "constructive programme". But this programme too is in the hands not of the Congress Committees but autonomous associations like-the A.I.S.A., A.I.V.I.A. etc. The form of open struggle-disobedience of specific laws-that the Congress has so far used does not give the masses wide scope for participation. It is not in fact a form of mass struggle which can develop only out of the day to day struggle against exploitation and oppression. The reason for this is that while the Congress is a mass organization, its leadership is predominantly bourgeois. This leadership is unable within the framework of its conceptions and interests to develop the struggle of the masses to a higher level. But it should be kept in view that the Congress leadership is no longer undivided.

Recently a conscious Left has been forming within the Congress and this development is reflecting itself in the leadership also, in which a sharp division is taking place. But as yet Left is largely ineffective leadership is in the hands of the Right. This should not be understood to mean that the class composition of the Right is itself bourgeois. A part of it is undoubtedly so. On the whole it is petty bourgeois but it is under the dominance of bourgeois interests and bound by the limitations of the Indian bourgeoisie. This analysis of the character of the Congress defines our task within it. In the words of Meerut Thesis it is to "went the anti-imperialist elements in the Congress away from its, present bourgeois leadership and to bring them under the influence of Revolutionary Socialism." The present thesis must further elucidate this. The Meerut Thesis conceives of the task in too narrow a manner. Our task within the Congress is not only to wean away the anti-imperialist elements from bourgeois leadership but also to develop and broaden the Congress itself as to transform it, into a powerful anti-imperialist front. The problem is not only the one of the change of leadership. It requires a complete reorganization of the Congress from the bottom upwards. As it has already been pointed out this cannot be done by confining our activities to Congress alone.. Here, however, let us see what we have to do within the Congress.

Taking the organizational aspect first, we must work for the democratization of its constitution so as to give more initiative to the primary members and committees and should endeavour to enlarge the membership and extend the organizations of the Congress further and make them active and alive. We should further try to bring the masses into the Congress by securing their representation in the committees of the latter. Till this is done we should build up a close link between such organizations and committees for the purpose of work.

Its Programme

As for the programme of the Congress, we should so shape it that it comes actively to develop the struggle of the masses taking their immediate demands as a basis. The formation of peasants' and workers unions and active support to the struggle conducted by them should be kept in the fore-front of this, programme. In all other possible ways also, working on the principles laid down above, we should endeavour to provide Congress Committee with a programme of day to day work among the masses. We should try to rally the rank and file of the Congress workers around this alternative programme. The political back-wardness of the rank and file is due to their lack of contact with the economic struggle of the masses. Propaganda alone will not radicalize them. They must be drawn into the peasant and labour movements so that they may realize that-our programme is a more dynamic one and will raise the anti-imperialist struggle to a higher pitch. The Meerut Thesis declared that we have to bring the anti-imperialist movement under the leadership of Revolutionary Socialism. It is necessary to further elucidate this. The anti-imperialist struggle in India is multi-class struggle of the peasantry and the working and middle classes. The working class in India though organizationally weak and politically not sufficiently conscious of its role, is none-the-less potentially the most revolutionary class.

The struggle of the Indian-masses for freedom will not reach its objective unless the working class is the vanguard of that struggle. Therefore, it is our task as Socialists to see that it assumes its historic role in the national movement. The leadership of Revolutionary Socialism can mean nothing else.

Development of Independent Organisation

The anti-imperialist struggle cannot be separated from the day to day struggle of the masses. The development of the latter is the basis for a successful fight against imperialism. Therefore, our foremost task outside the Congress is to develop independent organizations of the peasants and workers and of other exploited sections of the people. Besides these class organizations we should also attempt to organize the youth of the country so as to mobilise the most active elements of the lower middle class. We should not be content with the formation of these separate organizations.

We should try to harness them in the anti-imperialist front. This should ultimately lead us, as already pointed out, to the masses mobilized in these organizations entering the Congress through collective representation. Thus will the Congress become a wide national front against imperialism. This transformation is bound to change the entire structure and leadership of the Congress which will be composed of the strongly welded alliance of the various anti-imperialist classes, organized and unorganized consolidation of Socialist forces.

In the conditions of India, the conscious leadership of the anti-imperialist movement falls on the Socialist forces. These forces are unfortunately still divided. The Party from the beginning has stood for unity in the socialist ranks. It is of the utmost importance that in the Congress, in the mass movement outside, in all spheres of anti-imperialist activity a united lead is given. If Socialists speak with a divided voice there will be utter confusion and it will only retard the national struggle. Till such unity is arrived at the minimum that is necessary is agreement on the immediate tasks and lines of action. On the basis of this agreement the various Socialist groups should work together till the time we are in a position to form a united party. Apart from unity of agreement among Socialist ranks, it is necessary that the forces of the Left are also consolidates and an understanding developed within its leadership. The Party should continue its efforts in this direction.

Party's Structure

Our Party has generally grown in the last year. In certain, provinces there has been a setback and the growth has not been uniform everywhere. While there are parties with a, membership of hundreds, certain other parties, also quite, active, have not enlarged their organization beyond a few score of members. It is obvious that the line of development and the scope of organization have not clearly been laid down. Without prejudice to the Marxist basis of our Party, it is necessary to enlarge the membership of the Party so as to include a wider section of Congress workers and conscious elements active in the labour, peasant and other movements.

Purposes of the Party

The objects of the Congress Socialist Party, as laid down in its Constitutions, are "the achievement of complete independence, in the sense of separation from the British Empire and the establishment of a socialist society." This is direct and simple enough. The Party has two objects : The first is the same as that of the Indian National Congress, except that the Party wishés to make it clear that the complete independence of India must include separation from the British Empire. The second object of the Party means that Independent India must reorganise its economic life on a socialist basis. If the ultimate objective is to make the masses politically, and economically free, to make them prosperous and happy, to free them from all manner of exploitation, to give them unfettered opportunity for development, then, Socialism becomes a goal to which one must irresistibly be drawn.

If again, the objective is to take bold of the chaotic and conflicting forces of society and to fashion the latter according to the ideal of utmost social good and to harness of all conscious, directives of human intelligence in the service of the commonwealth, then, again, Socialism becomes an resectable destination. If then, these be our objectives, it should take little argument, to show that Socialism is as definitely "indicated" in India as elsewhere. In India too there is poverty, nay, starvation, on the one hand and wealth and luxury on the other; in India too there is exploitation; the means of production here also are in private hands. That is, the root evil of modern society, namely, economic and social inequality, exists in India too as does its cause; the exploitation of the great many by the very few. And this is not the result of British rule. It is independent of it and will continue even after it. The ending of the foreign domination would not automatically solve Indian's problem of poverty; would not put a stop to the exploitation of the vast many; would not in fact, mean the accomplishment of any of the objectives which we have started with. Economic freedom is also indispensable.

As far as we socialists are concerned economic freedom means only one thing to us-Socialism. Without Socialism, economic freedom would be a sham, and moonshine. The present programme of the Congress falls far short of these ideals. It might ameliorate the conditions of the masses to a certain extent, but it will neither rid them of exploitation nor put them in power.

Far from effecting revolutionary changes in it, it leaves the economic structure of society intact. It leaves capitalists, landlords and princes on the one side and workers, tenants and subjects on the other. It leaves the means of production in the hands of private individuals, except in the sphere of key industries. The entire economic organisation, based as it is on the exploitation of the poor and middle classes, is preserved. This is not economic freedom. The preamble and substance of the Karachi Resolution are at wide variance with each other. What we endeavour to do is to remove this variance and bring them close together. When the Congress professes the economic freedom of the masses, let it distinctly state what that freedom means. The Congress may be unprepared for the acceptance of such a minimum, programme as we advocate. But it is one thing to say that we are not ready for any further definition of our goal-which of course may be disputed-and quite another, as latterly repeated ad nauseam, that Socialism is moonshine; that it is unsuited to the Indian climate; that Indian socialists are merely adventuring in the realm of theory; that they are only quoting a rusty old German Jew who called himself Karl Heinrich Marx; and the rest of the drivel. I do not desire to suggest that at Karachi, the Congress should have outlined a full-grown programme of Socialism.

What it must do, however, is to accept such a minimum economic programme as will, when put to practice, free the masses from economic exploitation and transfer full political-

and economic power into their hands. It is such a programme that the Congress Socialist Party is advocating. What, there does the Congress Socialist Party propose? 'What must the Swaraj Government do in addition to nationalising key industries in order to realise the economic freedom of the masses; in order to rid them of exploitation, injustice, suffering, poverty, ignorance? The measures that are necessary, in the opinion of the Party to achieve this are clearly set forth in the Objectives section of the Programme of the All-India Congress, Socialist Party.

Its programmes are as follows :

1. Development of the economic life of the country to be planned and controlled by the state.
2. Transfer of all power to the producing masses.
3. Socialisation of key and principal industries (e g. Steel, Cotton, Jute, Railways, Shipping, Planations, Mines), Banks, Insurance and Public Outlines, with a view to the progressive socialization of all the instruments of production, distribution an exchange.
4. State monopoly of foreign trade.
5. Organisation of co-operatives for production, distribution and credit in the unsocialized sector of economic life.
6. Elimination of princes and landlords and all other classes of exploiters without compensation.
7. Redistribution of land to peasants.
8. Encouragement and promotion of co-operative and collective farming by the State.

9. "To every one according to his needs and from everyone according to his capacity" to be the basis ultimately of distribution and production of economic goods.

10. Recognition of the right to work or maintenance by the State.

11. Liquidation of debts owing by peasants and workers.

12. Adult franchise on a functional basis.

13. Repudiation of the so-called Public Debt of India.

14. No discrimination between the sexes by the State.

15. No support to or discrimination between religions by the State and no recognition of any distinction based on caste or community.

There are fifteen measures as we see. They look forbidding appear to be too drastic; too extreme; too foreign sounding. They are, in fact, simple enough, reasonable enough, just and practicable enough.

And as for their foreign sound well, they sound no more foreign than the Constituent Assembly, the Legislative Council, the Tariff Board, the siren of the cotton mills or the hooting of the latest Cadillac (shall we say?) They are all intended to establish the rather simple principle that the abolition of private ownership, of functional property, which, as we saw, was the real villain of the piece-the source of all our evils or most of them. They are further intended to establish the most eminently reasonable of principles of social life-social planning.

Criticism of C.S.P.'s Policy Against Congress

The policy that the Congress Socialist Party has followed in recent months with regard to the Congress has come in for a good deal of criticism and abuse. I believe, however, that a little dispassionate thinking would show the correctness of this policy. Unfortunately, the prevailing atmosphere is not too conductive to dispassionate thought.

There is mutual distrust and ill-will, deliberate confusion of issues, empty heroics. In, certain quarters it is the fashion to attribute motives to whoever disagrees with you. Thus, it has been suggested by some of my leftist friends that my recent policies have been dictated by my desire to be elevated to the Congress Working Committee. This way of political understanding throws some light on, the depths to which a section of the left movement has descended. If my friends find such a motive behind may policies, it is little wonder that in every move of the Congress Working Committee they sense a deal with imperialism. It is in public interest to refer-even at the risk of indecorum-to a personal matter. Since my membership of the Congress Working Committee is on the brain of some of my, friends, I should like to tell them that the doors of the Working Committee have, since the time we were first appointed on it, been always open to me and to some other leading members of the C.S.P. I resigned my membership in 1936 of my own accord, and since have refused my seat every time it has been offered to me. At the Haripura Congress Acharya Narendradeva, and Achyut Patwardhan refused their seats that were offered again by the President, Babu Subhas Chandra Bose. At Calcutta, Dr. Rajendra Prasad again invited us to, serve on the Committee, which offer he repeated at Bombay; but Narendradevji again declined the offer on behalf of the today. I should add that our refusal of membership never implied, any disrespect to the Congress Working Committee, to be a, member of which is a great national honour. Nor did it imply and deviation from the principle of composite leadership which we have always held as we hold it even today. To turn now to the subject-matters. Our present policy has been attacked on the ground that it is a surrender to-Gandhism. Socialism vs. Gandhism is not the present issue, however. We are faced with the task of preparing for and launching a national struggle against imperialism. This is not a socialist but a nationalist task to be carried out by socialists, Gandhians and others. Our only crime, therefore, is that we continue to insist on the unity of the Congress as the only guarantee of national unity and a national struggles. Our further crime is that we insists that unity of the Congress involves the unity of its leadership, because we cannot, particularly in such a crisis as the present, split the leadership and keep the Congress together.

Our still further crime is that we are being guided not by what is good for the Congress Socialist Party or for that heterogeneous and vague thing called the left, but by what is good for the whole the left and right together. We believe that we have reached a dangerous point when the certain sections of the Left have begun to look upon themselves not as a wing of a body, but as a whole body itself, with interests distinct and separate from the body of which it is a part. The Congress Socialist Party was formed not to develop into a rival to the Congress, but to work within the Congress, to strengthen it, to mould and shape its policies. In the five years that the Party has functioned, it has succeeded appreciably in influencing Congress policy, number of Congress decision bear clearly the impress of our propaganda.

Due to the pioneering work of the Party, since the depressing days of 1934, when Civil Disobedience had to be called off and all through the upsurge of parliamentarianism, a vigorous left wing developed in the Congress which even penetrated the ranks of the leadership. The Programme of peasant organization which we placed before the Congress, though unaccepted officially by it, yet won the approval of quite a number of provincial and other Committees and a large number of Congressmen. But in spite of all our efforts the Official programme of-the Congress is still Gandhiji's programme of 1920. Also, while a new leadership has arisen, the predominant leadership is still in the hands of the Old Guard. The old leaders have been at the helm for thirty years. During this period they have brought new life, new strength, new consciousness to the masses. They represent a vital national force-still the most influential in their country. In these circumstances, what are we to do, particularly when a world crisis demands immediate action? Conceivably, given another five years, the balance of influence within the Congress and the country could have been changed and old, as always, would have given place to the new. I should interpolate a remark here that even today the influence of the left leadership would have been much greater had Sjt. Subhas Chandra Bose followed the advice of our Party and had the communists and other leftists the guts to tender the same advice to him. We advised Subhas Babu, in spite of all that had happened, not to resign from the Presidentship of the Congress. Had he followed our advice we would not only have escaped all the sorry developments of the past months, but we would have also had a Working Committee with a large leftists' voice. Subhas Babu himself would have been their President, Pandit Jawaharlal Nehru would have been the General Secretary, Sjt. Sarat Chandra Bose and two leftists would have been among the members. It will be remembered that this was the minimum arrangement to which the old Guard was agreeable. Let me revert to the question, in the present circumstances what is our duty? To answer it, first let me ask whether we have any other instrument than the Congress for waging a national struggle and maintaining national unity. Throughout history we have had to contend with disintegrating factors and sometimes have even over-whelmed the forces of national., unity. Even today excepting the Congress there is no other consolidating factor in our social or political life. The Congress represented and still represents, and from all appearances, will continue to represent (much as the communists may dislike the prospect) the widest, the strongest front against imperialism in India. If India goes to war with imperialism with any chance of success, that war has to be waged under the tricolour flag. People talk loosely of Kisans, mazdoors, youths, and students as if they stand outside of the Congress. What are meant by these generic terms, however, are the Kisan Sabha, the Trade Union Congress, and the Students' Federation. These bodies have potentiality for the future, but at present except in a few provinces, their organisation is elementary.

Their role in our national struggle will be important and it must be the task of Socialists as well as of other progressive elements to make that role even more important by strenuous organisational work. Their role is, however, clearly of an auxiliary character. The Congress must lead the struggle and the active cooperation and participation of these bodies will be an added factor of strength. But it is crystal clear that today, neither the Kisan Sabha nor the Trade Union Congress in their present state of development can hope to fight imperialism with any degree of success. That task unquestionably be-, longs to the Congress. This is the situation facing us when looked at through uncoloured glasses. The Congress alone is the country's salvation. And let us remember the Congress means the whole and not part of it. A limb torn from a body does not have its proportionate strength and ability. It merely dies. I have said above that we are faced today with preparing for and launching a national struggle. I have shown that this struggle can be launched by the Congress alone. Now, let us examine another set of facts. The effective leadership of the Congress is in the hands of Gandhiji. It is obvious that if the Congress starts a struggle today it would be in accordance with the programme that Gandhiji lays down. We can influence that programme but we cannot determine it. The technique of the struggle would therefore naturally be the old Gandhian technique, whether any one likes it or not. An acceptance of these facts does not mean surrender to Gandhism.

We have not ceased to propagate socialism. We have not stopped working in the Kisan Sabhas and Trade Unions and developing the peasant and labour movements. The first strike for a War-bonus was led by the C.S.P. in the Gaya Cotton Textile Mill and the first War-bonus victory was won by the Dalmianagar workers under the C.S.P.'s leadership. In Bihar, the U.P., Bombay, Bengal and elsewhere members of the Party have been as active as before in the struggles of the workers. The same is true of the peasant movement. Where worker has suffered in these spheres it has been due to the withdrawal of Party cadres into the new activities of preparation for the national struggle-such as intensive organisation of the Congress Committees and intensive propaganda, volunteer organisation, etc. However, the situation in which we find ourselves is not such that can expect to develop the national struggle out of our-own plan of action. We carry on our own work and propagate our plea, but we at the same time desire an immediate struggle. When we know that there is no prospect of a struggle being started under any other leadership, but the present, is it not the madness to attack the leadership, to seek to discredit it, to weaken it? Shall we thereby bring the struggle nearer or push it away? All these years we have heard the theories of united leadership and united front propounded. Now, when the hour has arrived to put these theories into practice, to act up to them, gutless revolutionaries are scurrying away from their implications. United leadership was held to be necessary in the interest of a united national struggle. This theory was mouthed incessantly by our Communist friends at a time when the Congress was engaged in parliamentary work and struggle seemed distant. Now when the parliamentary work has been given up and the Congress is on the eve of struggle our Communist theorists have thought it wise to fling their theory to the wind and concentrate on attacking the present leadership. In this manner they shall only contribute to the sabotaging of the struggle. I think it is necessary for us to realise the limitations in which we have to work. By disregarding them we only strengthen them.

A fight against the present leadership now is not only inadvisable, it is positively harmful. If a national struggle as opposed to sectional, factional or partial can be launched by Mahatma Gandhi alone, it is suicidal to fight him. It is necessary to lend him our fullest cooperation and loyalty in everything that is preparatory for struggle. We must submit to his condition. If, then, there is no struggle we may part company with him and then take the responsibility of the struggle ourselves if we have the strength. Many people believe that in these circumstances, the Congress Socialist Party becomes superfluous. I should like to remind friends that we are to be guided by what is good for the whole movement and not by the necessity of blowing our own trumpet at all times. If our policy is correct the C.S.P. will draw strength from it and as in 1934 again show that of all the groups mouthing Marxism, it is the only on which understands how to apply Marxism to India. This is not the place to go into the matter here, but it would be interesting to show how at every critical stage in the last five years the Congress Socialist Party showed the way and others followed or proved their folly. In 1934 the wise communists went out of the Congress and were out to destroy it. We were in it and in to build and strengthen it. In 1936 they too filed in, to build of ti destroy, history alone will show.

In 1936 the C.S.P opposed the acceptance of ministerial offices by the Congress. The Communists were first for accepting them with a radical programme. Later when they found that the Anti-Ministry cry was becoming popular in the Congress Left, they veered round to it as they may not be isolated. During the General Elections, the C.S.P. supported the Congress wholeheartedly. The Communists opposed the Congress in one constituency only to show their own importance and to blow their own little trumpet. At Tripuri, they spoke passionately of unity and united leadership but again their fear Of isolation drove them to, action which could lead only to contrary results. At Calcutta, the C.S.P. boldly advised Sjt. Subhas Chandra Bose to withdraw his resignation from the Presidentship; the Communists—lost their guts and kept mum. Coming to recent events, the C.S.P. did not subscribe to the addendum to the Independence Pledge; the Communists swallowed it. One hopes that they are faithfully carrying out their vow, otherwise there is danger that fraud may be discovered and Mahatma Gandhi may refuse to launch the struggle after all. The C.S.P. supported Maulana Abul Kalam Azad in the Congress Presidential election, the Communists were neutral. Comrade P.C. Joshi declared in a public statement that voting for Maulana Azad would mean supporting the policy of the Working Committee. Strange argument!

When the Communists voted for Roosevelt in America, did it mean that they supported the whole of Roosevelt's policy? In such a thing as a presidential contest one votes for the candidate whose election would advance the nation's cause generally. If one must have a President with whose policies one must always be in agreement, one has only one course open, i.e., to set up a candidate every time from one's own Party or Group. There are thousand and one ways of expressing one's difference from the Working Committee and this both the C.S.P. and the Communists have been : doing. Voting for Maulana Azad could never have prevented. Comrade Joshi from pointing out his difference from the Working Committee. I agree that it would have prevented him from calling Maulana Azad an agent of imperialism! Then a last instance. The C.S.P. clearly dissociated itself from the anti-compromise conference, the Communists were neutral to it. Their growing neutrality is an index of their growing political, impotency. I had not intended to devote so much space to this matter. The list can be enlarged, more so when we leave the realm of policies and enter into that of tactics. To return to my point. Far from becoming superfluous, the Congress Socialist Party has to be in the forefront of the struggle and the preparations for it. It must remain, as it has been so far, the active element in the Congress Committee, guiding them in organisational and agitational work. It must by carrying on its mass work continue to prepare that basis for struggle that is important than anything else. It must influence Congress policy by criticism and propaganda as it has done so far. The time has come for the Congress, Socialist Party to workout what it has preached so far. I am grateful to you for the honour you have done mo. by inviting me to preside over this conference. Being the first Provincial Conference of your Party, it possesses a unique importance. Much of the future of our movement in this, province will depend upon the lead that this conference gives. I, therefore, wish that you have entrusted the responsibility of conducting its proceedings to abler and more experienced hands. However, I hope that with your cooperation I shall be able to discharge my duties to your satisfaction. Bengal, of all the provinces in India, has occupied a premier political position. It has been in the vanguard of the country's freedom movement since the beginning.

In suffering and sacrifice it is easily the first province in the country. Even at the present moment, whole districts of the province are subject to virtual martial law. Thousands of Bengal's youngmen some of them with the promise of the most brilliant careers lie wasting in jails, without as much as charge having been framed against them in a court of law. The Bengal Government enjoys the unique but doubtful reputation of depriving its citizens of their liberty without having proved their guilt. And yet the Governor of the province, Sir John Anderson, remarked the other day that it was ignorance that prompted people to demand the release or trial of the detenus. It is true that the public does not possess the facts that the Secret Service has made available to Sir John. But that is no reason why the public should condone acts which offend against all canons of civilized law. If Sir John Anderson is so sure of his facts, why does he not produce them in a court of law and have them established? As long as his Government refuses to do this, the public will continue to condemn its-action and to demand the release of those who have been-deprived of their liberty without any known cause. In the words of Babu Rajendra Prasad, the President of the Congress the Government "have no reason to complain if the public-are not prepared to accept their view, subversive as it is of all recognised principles of civilized jurisprudence." The demand for justice being done to the detenus has been brushed aside by the Governor of Bengal as ignorance or pro-terrorism. Under the latter pretest, all efforts in behalf of the detenus have been suppressed in this province, thanks to the black laws with which the executive has provided itself here. Outside Bengal where the black laws have no jurisdiction, the detenu agitation is disposed of on the plea of ignorance.

Official effrontery never before presented itself in a more branen form. It is well that the Government should realise clearly and once for all that the demand for the release of the detenus has nothing to do with terrorism nor is it based on ignorance. It is based, as a matter of fact, on one of the most elementary principles of civilized society, viz., that no person should be deprived of his liberty without due processes of law. The country's case in this connection cannot be put better than in these words of the President of the Congress : "The Governor of Bengal in his address to the Bengal Legislative Council divided those who pressed for the release or in the alternative for the trial of Bengal detenus into two classes, viz., those who were in secret sympathy with terrorism and therefore should be regarded as out of court and those who though well-meaning were ignorant of the real state of affairs and therefore deserved no consideration. He ignored the third class which I believe, is the largest in the country and which has among it persons holding diverse political views and belonging to diverse parties.

That third class comprises persons who hold the liberty of person as sacred and who strongly believe that none should be deprived of his or her liberty except as a result of a trial openly held in accordance with canons of civilized law."

Realisation of Gravity of Detenu

The country has only recently begun to realise the gravity of the detenu question. Till practically the middle of last year we were in the midst of a great national struggle. Every province at that time had its own troubles, its own share of repression. Bengal, though being incomparably the worst sufferer of all remained, therefore, a provincial issue. But not entirely so. Even during that period such eminent leaders as Pandit Jawaharlal Nehru showed considerable concern for the province and you are all aware that it was for pleading : your case that he was imprisoned. When the Satyagraha movement was withdrawn, the strain of the struggle left us unprepared to take up immediately any such issue as that of Bengal. Gradually, however, the Bengal question, particularly the question of the detenus rose to prominence. It has now become a countrywide issue, though much remains to be done. It should be a matter of satisfaction to us that our Party has played a considerable part in bringing this issue to the fore.

The Detenu Day which we observed last March in a way marked the beginning of this agitation on an all-India basis. It should also be a matter of satisfaction for all of us that the President of the Congress, Babu Rajendra Prasad, has been giving his particular attention to this question since he assumed office. But, as I said above, there remains a great deal to be done yet. The demand for the release of the detenus is still very feeble. Much more publicity is required to be given to this question than it has received so far. And the publicity should be extended to foreign countries also, particularly to England. Mr. C.F. Andrews has already led the way in this direction. He must be followed up by others. On behalf of my Party I assure the people of Bengal, and the detenus particularly, that we shall always stand by them and do all we can to help them. The question of the detenus is not the only outstanding problem in Bengal. Under the pretext of putting down terrorism, the Bengal Government has made all national and mass activities impossible. Many Congress bodies, Khadi organisations, trade unions peasant organizations, student associations, presses and publications have been placed under a ban. Those which are not actually banned have to live under the perpetual surveillance of the Secret Service. To strengthen my assertion I shall quote again from the-statement of the Congress President. "But today they are bent on perpetuating the lawless laws", runs the statement, "depriving people of personal liberty, liberty of association and liberty of expression of views on the platform and through the press at the will of the executive, and they have been, enforcing such laws with all their rigour and not unoften misapplying them to conditions for which they were never intended. Consider the number of presses and newspapers which have been penalized, the number of Associations, including Labour organizations and Congress organizations which are banned, the number of individuals who have been deprived of their liberty without any of those being tried and condemned by a court of law, and it becomes clear to what extent the Government can go even when things are more or less quiet." There is no need of my going into the details of this question. You who belong to this province know them much better than I do. The real question before us is what can we do in the matter? It is clear that Bengal alone is helpless. The other provinces must come to its aid. As in the case of the detenus publicity is the chief remedy here also. The public does not know all the facts. I believe that if all that was happening in Bengal was made known to the country and to the civilized world outside, such a storm of protest and condemnation would be let loose that even the Bengal Government would be compelled to bend down before it. This cannot be done, however, unless there is an organization which takes it up as its sole activity. I wish to place before you a suggestion in this regard, though I must tell you that I am not its author. Bengal, though suffering the most from the evils of an arbitrary rule is not alone in its suffering.

The whole country is in a manner subject to it and acts of high-handedness and unlawful victimization are not uncommon elsewhere even in normal times. Most of these acts would not be committed if the public were a little vigilant and if there were some organization, the task of which was to bring such, acts to light and put up a fight against them, through the lawcourts, the legislatures, the press and the platform. It is, therefore, suggested that a non-political association should be formed, the business of which should be to defend the ordinary right of citizenship rights that are enjoyed by every member of any civilized society. You have heard of the Civil Liberties Union of the U.S.A., which under the able leadership of Mr. Roger Baldwin has done extremely valuable work. There are also many international organizations for the protection of the working man's rights and interests. This association which is suggested here should also be on similar lines. It should be formed not of political workers but of leading jurists of the country, eminent publicists and journalists; women workers (for women are the worst sufferers) social workers, like some of those of the Servants of India Society, and.... It should be an all-India body and should have intimate contacts with kindred foreign organizations. It should collect facts, publish literature, organize legal defence, raise funds for sufferers; do foreign propaganda; cause questions, resolutions etc. to be asked or moved in the legislatures and so on. It is not a pity that in spite of all that has happened in Bengal, there is not even one pamphlet published which gives even the bare facts? Such a pamphlet should have been placed in the bands of every public man in India, every member of Parliament, every organization in Europe and America, that is interested in the civil liberties of the people. If we turn the merciless lights of publicity on every act of official excess, we shall be able if not to totally stop them, at least, to reduce them greatly. There has been recently some talk of foreign propaganda. It may be true that general nationalist propaganda in the West is not very fruitfuls but I have no doubt that a propaganda which exposes specific acts and measures of official terrorism will prove effective. I may add that its efficacy will be in proportion to the accuracy and regard for truth that the Association shows in its work. I think that there is ample material in the country to form such an association.

The first step is to find a competent individual with a status in public life, who has travelled in the country and abroad to take the initiative. Such an individual must give his whole time to the association and should be paid by it. I do not think that the cost of running such an association would be more than Rs. 50001/- per year-a sum which can be easily raised for a cause such as this. I do hope that some one from Bengal would come forward and take up the work. I hope you will not misunderstand me and take me as saying that this Association alone will be sufficient to deal with the problem. The Association will do very valuable work, but not the whole of it. I have already suggested other necessary measures. I shall take up next certain other issues which loom large on the political horizon of Bengal.

Calculation of Communal Award

The first of these is the communal problem. Bengal is out of those provinces, the minority community of which is said to have been wronged most by the so-called Communal Award While non-Hindu minorities have been given special treatment elsewhere, the Hindu minority of this province has been particularly discriminated against. The Hindu politicians of the province are naturally in a flurry over this and have formed a party which is called paradoxically enough, the "Nationalist Party". Let us look at this question little more closely. The question whether the Communal Award is good or bad is one which admits of no controversy. There cannot be two opinions about it. For me it is sufficient reason to condemn it that it is an award of the British Premier. That high executive of imperialism could not have been allowed to commit-such a grave public lapse as to do India a good turn.

The Communal Award was deliberately calculated to exploit the communal tension in the interests of imperialism. Subsequent events have borne this out. We shall have further proofs when the New Constitution begins to work. That a few individuals of this or that community have benefited or will benefit by it does not alter the basic reality. The Communal Award is the greatest single anti-national factor in our political life today. And that brings us to the real problem. Granted that the Communal Award is bad, what should be our attitude towards it? Shall we be foolish and play into the hands of the imperialists or shall we be wise and foil their attempts? I, When we say that the Communal Award is bad, what do we mean? Where does its badness lie? Does it lie in the fact that so many seats have been given to the Muslims and so many to the Hindus or in the fact that it has become an instrument of communal discord? From the nationalist point of view, it matters not a whit how many seats Muslims or Hindus have got. They are both Indians, and, granting that seats do any good, whichever community benefits, the nation benefits. The real mischief of the Communal Award is in its potency to take advantage of our... in sowing seeds of discord. If that be so, are we acting in the national interest if we deliberately aggravate that mischief? If the Muslims or Sikhs get a few more seats than the Hindus, India is not the loser; but if we fall out and quarrel among ourselves, we not only lose heavily but we do so to the tremendous profit of the outsider. To fight over the Communal Award is like the serpent swallowing his own tail. The exasperated "nationalist" may cry "what is the solution, then?" The solution or what? I shall ask him. If he is looking for a solution which will set right the disproportion between Hindu and Muslim representation in the Bengal Legislative Council, I am afraid, I have no such solution for him. I am not even interested in the question of few seats more or less for this or that community.... of the least consequence to our struggles for freedom. If, however, he is looking for a solution which will bring both Muslims and Hindus in their full strength into the freedom movement, I do have an answer for him and I believe, the only answer. The communal question in Bengal as in other parts of the country is largely an economic question and has resulted from the fact that the Muslims are nearly all tenants, and the landlords are nearly all Hindus.

There has always been a serious conflict between the Bengal tenant and landlord; and peasant uprisings have been quite frequent here. But since the class division nearly-coincides with the communal division this conflict and these clashes have often been given a communal colour. It is well-known that religious fanaticism and economic radicalism often go hand-in-hand among the Muslim masses of the province. Just as the Irish under Protestant. Britain clung fanatically to their Catholicism and the Czechs under Catholic Austria turned free thinkers, so the Muslim peasants of Bengal under Hindu landlords are as easily susceptible to communal passion as to the idea of the abolition of zamindaris. In a modified form this is true even outside Bengal. Where the class and communal divisions cross each other, instead of coinciding, the communal question is confined to the upper layer of the social stratum to men who are desirous of posts and positions, seats and titles. This being the background of the communal problem, how is it to be solved? It is clear that if we continued to wrangle for seats in the legislatures, we shall only aggravate the malady. The masses whether Muslim, Hindu or of any other community, have no interest in the communal distribution of these seats. It may be that today they are persuaded by demagogues into supporting this or the other proportion of communal representation, but their basic interest lies in an entirely different manner of representation. The Hindu labourer and the Muslim labourer have identical interests and if they are made conscious of them, they would forthwith denounce and repudiate communal representation and demand the representation of their common economic and political interests. The communal question, as it exists today, affects only a small class, the class which is directly interested, purely for the gratification of personal ambitions and desires, in legislative elections and jobs and employments in the departments of the Government. This advantage of broader causes of communal conflict such as exist in Bengal due to the economic circumstances, I have already mentioned, seek, and, unfortunately succeed to give to their claims and wranglings, a much wider sanction than they would have otherwise possessed. What is the duty of the "nationalist" in these circumstances? In my humble opinion there are only two courses he must follow, if he genuinely desires to solve the communal problem. Let me remind him again that problem consists not in amending the percentages of communal seats so as to suit better the claim of this or the other community which invariably means the self-seeking upper fringe of that community but to endeavour to bring all the various communities wholeheartedly into the freedom movement. The courses that suggest themselves to me are : firstly, a total withdrawal from the wrangling for legislative seats; secondly, the linking up of the freedom movement with the economic struggle of the masses. My first suggestion would seem to cut the ground from-under the feet of the Bengal Nationalist Party, which, I do not wish to deny, enjoys a great popularity among the Hindu population of the Province.

The popularity rests, howevers nor so much on the issue being a popular one, as in the fact that the educated upper class in this province has taken advantage of its prestige and of the estranged relations between the two communities to arouse popular sentiment on this entirely false issue. For the issue is a false one. The millions of the Hindus of this province cannot in any manner gain by a few more Hindu seats in the Bengal Legislative Council. Nor do, those millions have interests which are different from the interests of the Muslim millions. The Bengal Nationalist Party, unlike such parties in some other provinces, is formed of genuine, even militant, Congressmen I ask these friends if they are in any way helping the freedom movement the cause of the people of the country by generating the hostilities, the suspicions, the bickerings, which must be the natural issue of their policy. I ask them if they are not weakening the movement for independence, if not diverting it into fruitless, nay, dangerous channels? The Congress exists and Congressmen exist not to fight the Communal Award but the system whose instrument it is. I now come to the second course. I have said that we must link the freedom movement with the economic struggle of the masses. This, of course, is a basic tactics with us. But just now I have to discuss it only as a solvent of the communal, problem. Later I shall return to it to consider it as a technique of mass action. The communal problem exists, i.e., we fail to draw, let us say, the Muslim masses, into the national struggle, because we fail to inspire confidence in them. Our movement is not a mass movement. It is not the problem of the masses that we discuss, that guide our action, that determine our social philosophy.

Our outlook is yet limited by middle class ambitions and desires. That is why the distribution of seats looms so large, on our horizon. If we were leading a genuine mass movement, the masses of all communities would gather round our banner, in other words, the communal problem would have ceased to exist. As an instance of how we fail to inspire confidence among the masses let me remind you of how the Bengal Swaraj Party-years ago caused a Tenancy Bill to be passed through the Legislative Council in the teeth of the opposition of the ryots. You will recall that Muslim opinion was bitterly hostile to that Bill. Consider for a moment what would have been the-effect had the Swaraj Party brought in, as it would have if it verily mass party, a Bill which was in the interest of the ryots. It would have secured the unstinted support of the Muslim-Community at least, of the 98 per cent of it. But, as it happened, the Swarajists only succeeded in creating the impression that the Congress was a Hindu and Zamindar organization. This, as every one can see, was a fatal impression as far as-creating confidence was concerned. It is clear from this incident that if we adopt a programme which is in the interest of the masses if we participate in their struggle for economic emancipation, we shall have no difficulty in getting their support and following. And when we do that, the communal problem disappears, because the masses include all communities. I, therefore, suggest that if Bengal Congressmen want to solve the communal problem, they must, first, unequivocally declare for the abolition of the Zamindari system, and, second they must seriously set out to acquire into the present difficulties of the terants and organize them for their removal. A tenants' movement, with the slogan of abolition of zamindaris in the foreground, is the best and only solution of the communal problem in Bengal. Besides liquirating this problem, such a movement will also prepare the masses for the achievement of independence political and economic.

Problem of Unemployment in Bengal

Now I shall touch a little upon the subject of unemployment in Bengal. Unemployment among the poor is a chronic ailment all over India. But middle class unemployment is perhaps the most acute in Bengal. If there is any social phenomenon more responsible than, another, for turning men's minds to the examination of existing society and to proposals for the creation of a better one, it is unemployment. There is no more forceful argument against it than the status quo. What is the solution of the unemployment problem? Is it provincialism, nationalism? It is strange that in such an intellectually progressive province as Bengal, provincialism should be considered in certain, sections, as a solution of problem, the roots of which are very, much deeper. It is not a problem which admits of such an, easy solution. Unemployment results from the maladjustment between production and consumption which is an irremovable feature of capitalist society. It can be cured only when this maladjustment is cured, i.e., when society is reorganized on a socialist basis. We see this being demonstrated in the present world. While every capitalist country is suffering from unemployment, Soviet Russia, which is yet only on the road to Socialism, is entirely free from it. It follows from what I have said that not even national independence will be able to remove unemployment. We have only to look at the independent countries of the world to be convinced of this. Socialism is its only cure.

5

C.S.P. AND NEW CONSTITUTION

Now I wish to consider with you the attitude that we should adopt towards the New Constitution that has been forget for us by the imperial power. You recall that the Working Committee of the Congress decided at Wardha that this question should be settled only at the Lucknow Congress. The final decision always lies with the annual session of the Congress. What the Working Committee really meant to say was that it was not prepared to express its opinion yet.

The Working Committee not only refused to, express its opinion as a committee, it also placed a ban, through its President, on its members from expressing their individual opinions. The result is that the country is deprived of the guidance of these leaders in discussing, analysing, examining this complicated question. It is not clear to me how this state of things has been considered desirable by our leaders. Unless the question is previously discussed threadbare and unless the opinion of the Congress leaders is known beforehand, it would not be possible to reach an intelligent and democratic decision at Lucknow. A few speeches cannot be expected to consolidate opinion in a few hours at the Congress Session. Perhaps the President was anxious to maintain the unity of his cabinet. But, the reported resignation of Sardar Sardul Singh shows that policy too has its dangers. You are a aware, I expect, of the move made to convene a conference of those Congressmen who are opposed to the policy of acceptance of ministerial offices under the new constitution which has been advocated by certain Congress leaders. We expect that this move will help to mobilize opinion on this issue and give the much desired lead. In this connection, I am happy to note, that the Bengal Nationalist Party has already decided against acceptance of offices and, if I mistake not, Your Dinajpur Political Conference also reached the same decision. I take this opportunity to place my views and the views of my Party before you in this regard. What is the situation before us ? Briefly, that the imperialist power is attempting to force upon us advice for, the further Perpetuation of its domination. I need not describe that device to you with all its traps and dangers.

It has been fully analysed in the Indian Press and it has declared that it would rather struggle under the existing order of things than have the new dispensation. The new dispensation will however be upon us in a few months, inspite of our rejection. The question is what should we do with it ? Before going into details, let us consider some broad principles of policy. Remember, I am discussing the issue from the point of view of the Congress, i.e., trying to discover what should be the policy of the Congress in this regard. The first course that suggests itself is to work the constitution for what it is worth. This is the policy that the Liberal Party would adopt, notwithstanding its severe condemnation of the constitution. In doing that the Liberal Party would be acting logically, mind you, I do not say correctly. Logically, because the Liberal Party knows only one method of political work constitutionalism. Now, the Congress long ago gave up its belief in constitutionalism respective strengths of the Liberal and Congress parties show which has been the more fruitful and correct of the two and embraced direct action as its basic policy. Direct action and constitutionalism are incompatible. The Congress cannot truthfully profess its faith in the former if it agrees to work the constitution. I need not dilate on this point because I think no Congressman will be found to disagree with, it. I doubt if even the great ministry enthusiast, Mr. Satyamurti will disagree. But there is a catch in this agreement. While the ministerialists, by which term I mean those Congressman who favour holding of ministerial offices hastily agree that the Congress cannot even contemplate holding of offices the proposals they put forth virtually amount to the same thing. But we shall examine this question later. So, if it is agreed that we cannot work the constitution, what must we do? What policy should the Congress accept. Our answer is that where possible, i.e., where the Congress has a majority, we should make its working impossible. The Working Committee in its resolution on the J. P. C. Report said that "the Joint Parliamentary Committee scheme designed as it is to facilitate and perpetuate the domination and exploitation of this country by an alien people under a costly mask is fraught with greater mischief and danger than even the present constitution." And, further on, that "This Committee is of opinion that the said scheme should be rejected well knowing that the rejection must involve the necessity of struggling under the present constitution humiliating and intolerable as it is." Such being the opinion of the Congress does it not follow as a natural corollary that the Congress policy should be to carry out the decision of rejection by forcing the Governor to continue the administration by the exercise of his special powers? Last is policy should be considered futile and barren, I quote some very interesting remarks of a British statesman. Captain

Wedgewood Benn, writing on the 'Outlook on the Indian Reforms' in the "Political Quarterly" for July-September 1935 hazards some guesses about the policy that the' Congress would be likely to follow with regard to what he has termed the Indian Reforms. He begins by asking : "The most powerful, the best organised and the most important of all Indian National parties is the Congress. What will they do? He thinks that "in all, but a few of the Provincial Assemblies, they (Congress candidates) will secure a victory". Then he goes on to say that and this is interesting, "the Congress candidates, it elected, will undoubtedly attempt to wreck the constitution". Discussing the underlying principle of Congress policy he says "The issues they (Congress members of Legislatures) will present will not be offered as local at all. Everything will be put into the guise of opposition to the hated British Domination. The issue which they wish to keep before the public, that of British versus India will be most clearly presented of course." I want you to take special note of this, "if they can force the Governor into the use of autocratic powers which he now possesses in an unprecedented degree."

This is a most significant statement coming asset does from such high quarters. Capt. Benn adds : "The technique of the Irish, which has been closely studied in India will be copied, possibly with success." Looking at the present drift of Congress policy, one doubts, if it will be. However, Capt. Benn has gone to the root of the problem. If there is any issue which it is the duty of the Congress to keep perpetually before the public, it is that of Britain versus India, as he puts it. And by forcing the Governor to continue his administration without the aid of ministers this issue is kept alive. To elucidate this point further, as it does not seem to be clear to many of us, it is better to look for a while at a very important aspect of the new constitution which I am afraid has not been kept before the public eye as prominently as it ought to have been. The new constitution without transferring any real power to the ministers creates the fiction of responsible government in the provinces. The British Power withdraws itself into the background keeping all the leading strings in its hands. This means that the issue Britain versus India, is covered up by this subterfuge. The issue, in fact, is turned into "the people versus the party in office," in other words, one part of the people versus the other part. This from the British point of view is a master stroke of political craft. By thus blurring the issue, the British politicians wish to destroy the directness and keenness of the Indian struggle. They further seek to shift the responsibility of carrying on an unpopular administration to the shoulders of Indian ministers, thus hoping to dull the edge of popular resentment against them. There is a difference between Indian ministers and "members of Government" of the present, and the ministers of the new constitution. At present the position is that the foreign power is able to secure the services of individual Indians, who in return for a title and a consideration carry on the administration for the British.

Under the new arrangements, ministers will represent parties which in turn will represent a section of the electorate. For the actions of the ministry, a party, and ultimately a section of the people itself, will be responsible, at least in theory and not the British Government. What use a clever governor will make of this situation can well be imagined. Of course it is obvious what will happen. It has often been said that imperialism has attempted through this constitution to strengthen itself in the face of gathering mass of discontent by rallying around it the vested interests in the country. These "responsible" ministries would be the constitutional mechanism through which this plan would be put into practice. The vested interests will become a facade behind which imperialism will continue its rule. But I am digressing. To return to the original point, I was saying that the issue of India versus.

Britain can most clearly be brought out only by forcing the suspension of the constitution, where this is possible. This is a course desirable for another reason also. We rejected the J.P.C. Report. After the Report has been made a fact in the new constitution, shall we drop our policy of rejection. Remember that the British have always been counting on the constitution being worked. It is with that belief. Bat they went on, most cynically disregarding the council even of their Indian friends, with their reactionary I measure. The Government members in the Legislative Assembly have often mockingly replied to the Opposition that however much it may howl against the "reforms" every one would come back and work them. Under these circumstances it is the duty of the Congress party wherever in a majority to defeat the objects of the foreign power and to foil their well laid plans by showing that the constitution they have laboured so long to perfect is a broken reed and that Governor must carry in the administration himself. The impression that this will create in India and abroad would be infinitely superior to any thing that can be achieved by any other tactics. From the point of view of keeping up the spirit of the Congress which after all is the thing that matters there can be no better course to follow. It is said that there will be no popular enthusiasm for this policy, because it will not enable the Congress party to throw any crumbs to the people.

This is a pathetic plea. The manner in which the electorate responds depends entirely on the manner in which the issue is presented to it. If we go to it in a defeatist, apologist frame of mind, it is clear we shall fail to inspire confidence. If, on the other hand, our campaign is marked with vigour,

our case presented aggressively, the electorate is bound to respond. Suppose that on this constitutional issue a whirlwind propaganda is carried on, raising the one issue of wrecking the constitution on the ground that it has been thrust on us forcibly and is a mischievous device for our further enslavement. I feel sure that in that case we shall be able to arouse sufficient enthusiasm to be returned every time in a majority. Even if we don't we shall have done excellent political propaganda during the election campaign which will prove its utility when we resort to direct action again. For all our efforts must lead to that. There is another important aspect of this policy which makes its acceptance well nigh imperative by the Congress. In its resolution on the J.P.C. Report the Working Committee declared that "the only satisfactory alternative (to the constitution adumbrated in the Report) is a constitution drawn up by a Constituent Assembly." I might remark parenthetically that it is curious to note that since the half-hearted reference to the Constituent Assembly made at the last Assembly elections, there has been no talk about it again. Indeed, a member of the Working Committee, Dr. Pattabbi Sitaramayya, has in a recent interview poobpoohed the whole idea as applied to current politics. "To talk of the latter (the Constituent Assembly)," he concludes his interview, "in our retreat is to cover it up with undue hope if not bluff." One wonders if the Working Committee was bluffing when it made the solemn declaration I have just quoted. At any rate, I wonder if the President's ban on his colleagues is only in regard to the ministry question or also on making light in the manner of the Andhra Doctor, of the considered decisions of the cabinet. However, if the only satisfactory alternative to a constitution devised in Westminister is a constitution drawn up by & Constituent Assembly, is it not our duty to raise the slogan of the Constituent Assembly during the coming election and place it before the electorate as the only alternative, as we have in our resolution ? It may be urged that the Constituent Assembly is a distant prospect and therefore it is mere bluff, as Dr. Pattabhi says, to talk of it as an alternative to any current political measure. Is the Constituent Assembly more distant than independence, and yet have we not "declared" independence from a thousand platforms ? Moreover, why, if it is a distant prospect, was it made a slogan at the last, Assembly elections ? In its resolution from which I have quoted before, the Working Committee expressed pleasure that the "demand for a Constituent Assembly has been endorsed in a clear and unambiguous manner by the country at the recent general election to the Legislative Assembly." That demand was put forward as an alternative to the J P.C. scheme which we were asked to reject. Now when that scheme is actually being foisted on us, should it not be our policy to raise the issue of the Constituent Assembly still more vigorously ? But if we do that on the one hand, we must say on the other that, where we can, we shall wresk that constitution by making its working impossible. Just as when the constitution was in the making and we were asked to consider it, rejection and the Constituent Assembly were complementary part of a whole policy, so now when the constitution is an accomplished fact and we are asked to work it, wrecking and the Constituent Assembly are again the inseparable complements of any self-respecting policy that we may adopt. The slogan of the Constituent Assembly cannot be part of any election programme which contemplates acceptance of offices under the new constitution. Its counterpart can only be the slogan of wrecking. Let us now consider the alternative proposal. I have said before that an objection is raised to this policy on the ground that the electorate would lose interest in it because it would not get any concrete and immediate benefits from it.

Suppose that we adopt such a programme of benefits. If we really wanted to give benefits, we would have to remain in office as long as possible, because going out in that case would be a barren policy. At the same time it is well-known to much scope for ameliorative measures the constitution provides. In other words, we will have to work the reforms, and will have the satisfaction of finding at the end of the terms of our ministries that very little has been done for the people so little, indeed, that they have become as much dissatisfied with us a, with the British. We shall also find that we have succeeded in killing that mentality of fight against government which is the soul of the Congress movement and in its place have taught the people to look for loaves and fishes to it. The argument of not being able to do any thing for the people if we follow a wrecking policy, leads inevitably to constitutionalism. There is no half-way house. I have considered so far only our tactics in case the Congress has a majority. What should be its policy where it failed to be so successful ? Before taking up that question, let me examine briefly the case of those who are advocating acceptance of offices.

First of all, we note that they absolutely overlook all the considerations I have urged. All the underlying principles of our movement, its psychological foundations, our past commitments all these are given the go by. It is interesting to recall in this regard the old policy of the Congress when it decided in 1926 to contest elections. The A.I.C.C. laid it down that "Congressmen in the legislature shall refuse to accept offices in the gift of government until, in the opinion of the Congress, a satisfactory response is made by the Government". I wish to draw your attention particularly to the condition for accepting offices. The Government must make a satisfactory response. Considering the objectives of the Congress of those days, it was an honourable and self-respecting decision, consistent with the spirit of the times.

The present Congress has travelled far away from its old objectives and it no longer looks for a "response" from the British Government. Is it not regretful therefore that Congressmen should advocate acceptance of offices under the present circumstances, and with no qualifications. It might be said : that the offices are no longer in the gift of the Government.. That would be a very superficial view of the matter. There is no popular sanction behind the constitution. The whole thing is a gift of the Government withal a most unwelcome gift. Thus the first thing the ministerialist seeks to do is to destroy a valuable psychological aspect of Congress policy. What does it offer in return? It is difficult to say, because this point has not been made clear yet. Mr. Satyamurti an& certain others have spoken of benefits and ameliorative measures, of clothing the service in khadi, of flying the national, Rag government buildings and so on. A rather doubtful fare. The Congress which has stood for large measures cannot forsake them and seek to appeal to the electorate with a programme of petty reforms. If the Congress did so it will divert the public mind from the basic and fundamental issues and teach the electorate and the people to look to the government for petty favours. This would means the diverting of mass energy into fruitless channels and therefore the weakening of the national movement. At the same time, it is obvious that if the Congress adopts a programme consistent with Congress policy and objective, it will be of such a far-reaching character that no Congress ministry would be allowed to carry it out.

A Congress ministry can only be a very short-lived experiment under these conditions, leading us nowhere and greatly damaging some of our basic ideas and Principles. Here, I wish to pause a little to consider the suggestion that Mr. C.R. Reddy has made in a recent speech in the south. He suggested that there was a midway house between wrecking and working the constitution. The Congress Party should seek election on a Proper Congress ticket and, if returned in a majority, it should take office, and try to work out its programme. If obstructed by the Governor, it should resign and seek re-election on the issue which created the deadlock. This kind of political strategy can be suggested only by one who is used to thinking on constitutional lines alone. Consider, what this strategy does, it drops the slogan of basic opposition to the new constitution, of rejecting and wrecking it, of the Constituent Assembly, it destroys the valuable mentality that has been generated in the course of our struggle of always looking at the government as an opponent, it creates illusions in the people's and regarding the capacity of ministries to solve their difficulties, and so on. Let us look at the other side of the shield. What does it achieve ? Nothing except that a few Congressmen occupy the seats of government for some time the time will depend on how soon Mr. Reddy considers the ground to have been prepared for a spectacular walk-out. The constituents would not have "benefited", at all, because the deadlock would prevent the ministers from benefiting them. In other words, this strategy does not even have the merit of the pucca constitutionalist who gives the people what tiny benefits he finds possible to give. On the other hand the fight against the governor takes place not on the fundamental issue of India versus Britain but on something of much lesser importance. Mr. Reddy's suggestion is as dangerous as any other. I do not wish to devote much more time to this question. However, let me mention a few more dangers and risks that lie hidden in the programme of the ministerialists. Take the election campaign itself. If it is decided that Congress should accept offices, then every attempt would be made by the Congress party to secure a majority.

This would inevitably lead to compromise with non-Congress groups and the modification of the Congress programme in such a manner as to allow nor-Congress and vested interests to join the Congress campaign. It was a genuine surprise to me when I came across a Hindi manifesto of the U.P. Congress Parliamentary Committee, issued over the signature of its assistant secretary during the last Assembly election, setting forth reasons why the landlords of the province must support the Congress candidates. The manifesto, in short, tried to make out that the Congress has always stood for and defended the right of the landlords. It is interesting to note that the spirit of this manifesto runs wholly counter to another of the same committee, issued in English for the general voter. It is also interesting to recall that in this same province, a few years ago, a resolution was passed by the Provincial Political Conference advocating the elimination of all middlemen between the tiller of the soil and the State. I have brought up this matter merely to show how the exigencies of winning a majority leads to watering down, vulgarising and distorting of even the present Congress ideals, moderate as they are. I do not for a moment believe that U.P. was an exception in this regard. This sort of thing must have happened everywhere. So we see that at the very outset of this policy in the election campaign itself, there is compromise and a drift to the right. Whereas the election campaign should be utilised for raising fundamental issues, for educating the masses, for organising them, we will be led to make compromises and to give up the more revolutionary slogans and programmes. Then the dangers after the ministries have been actually formed are not negligible the dangers, I mean, of demoralization, leading in the end to constitutionalism on the one hand and serious disruption of the Congress ranks on the other. So far I have discussed with you only the policy which should be followed in the case of the Congress securing majorities. I have taken so much of your time in discussing this question because I felt that of all present issues it is of the greatest significance to the growth of the freedom movement. Now, I shall briefly touch upon the policy the Congress Party should follow where in a minority.

The policy of the old Swaraj Party was "one of determined resistance and obstruction to every activity, Governmental or other, that may impede the nation's progress towards Swaraj" coupled with enactment of ameliorative measures. We suggest an improvement upon this. Mere obstruction will not be sufficient. We must also use the legislatures as tribunes for voicing the people's grievances, their rights and demands. The most effective form of legislative activity is one which brings the struggle that is waged outside into the legislative chamber. This means that the Congress must attempt to develop mass activity in the shape of an economic agitation of peasants, workers and other exploited groups, and use the legislature to further that activity. Without linking up in some such manner legislative work with an agitation outside, the former becomes utterly sterile and ineffective. I need not dilate on this point any further. The policy in cases where the Congress is in a minority is not difficult to determine. There are also a number of instances in history to guide us in this regard. In concluding my remarks on the constitutional issue, I should like to state, as a resume of what I have said already, the underlying principle of our entire policy in the matter of legislative work.

We believe that legislatures have to be used only in order to strengthen and support the revolutionary work outside. For us there is no parliamentary work, as such. I remember Mr. Rajagopalachari saying at Jubbulpore, in his speech on our resolution concerning the work of the Congress Party in the Assembly, that when we go to the legislative chamber we must do what is customarily done there. What he meant to say was that we must work there on approved constitutional lines. According to him our insistence, for example, on the slogan of the Constituent Assembly having been raised in the Assembly chamber, was misplaced tactics. That was a slogan which had to be raised outside at the proper time. Our whole conception of legislative activity is opposed to, this. We hole that when we go to the legislatures our purpose should be not only to inflict constitutional defeats on the Government but also to raise fundamental slogans for the purposed of propaganda, to relate the work within to the day-today struggles of the masses outside, to expose Imperialism to, obstruct its working. This, of course, means that the Congress while sending its members into the legislature must simultaneously engage itself in organizing the grievances of the masses outside. A strong labour and peasant movement outside coupled with revolutionary use of legislatures that is the principle which ought to govern the constitutional policy of any fighting organisation like the Congress. Its details will depend on leadership, but its principles are there.

Party's Function

You doubtless expect me to speak about Socialism. As members of the Congress Socialist Party, I wish you to remember, however, that the most important role that we have to play at present is in connection with the freedom movement. It was for this reason that I have examined at length certain problems which happen to be of great immediate importance to that movement. I shall devote the rest of the time I have, to a few remarks regarding our party and its policy and work. You know, the first and main task of the party is to, develop the anti-imperialist movement. There are two aspects of this task, both of which I wish to consider with you. The first relates to our work with the Congress and the other to our work among the masses. The two spheres of work are complementary. Our work within the Congress is governed by the policy of developing it into a true anti-imperialist body. It is not our purpose, as sometimes it has been misunderstood to be, to convert the whole Congress into a full-fledged socialist party.

All we seek to do is so change the content and policy of that organization that it comes truly to represent the masses, having the object of emancipating then both from the foreign power and the native system of exploitation. There are some who ridicule this whole idea. Their view is that the Congress is a bourgeois body with absolutely no chance of being influenced in the direction I have indicated. We do not subscribe to this view. The Congress at present is dominated by upper class interests and its leaders are uncompromisingly opposed to admitted into its objective any Programme aimed at the economic emancipation of the masses. Yet, within the Congress there is a very large body of opinion which would welcome such a programme. Only, this body which had worked under the old leadership has to be convinced that the programme we advocate will not weaken the national struggle by dividing, as they have learnt to think, the nationalist forces. If we seek to influence them and without influencing them no group of pure and brilliant theorists can develop an anti-imperialist movement in this country it is not sufficient to abuse the leadership or to produce learned theses. What is needed is a demonstration in actual practice that our programme is more dynamic and effective. I will take up this point more fully when I come to the second part of our task. So if within the Congress there is a very large anti-imperialist body I believe numerically it is a majority body is it not imperative for a party like ours to work actively within that organization? And, with what object and tactics are we to work? Not to disrupt the Congress, not by denouncing the Congress.

We should work rather with the object of bringing the anti-imperialist elements under our ideological influence through propaganda and work among the masses, so that finally they come to accept a proper anti-imperialist programme. I am not saying that they working in this manner we shall win the right wing to our programme and thus "convert" the Congress. The Congress as it is constituted at present cannot hold together very long. The more successful we are in pushing our programme the manner the day when a split will occur in it. The following will doubtless say that we are disrupting the Congress. But, in reality, it will be a ripening consolidation of anti-imperialist forces. The Congress has faced such splits before and has come out stronger each time. Another split would take it to another, and I expect, the last stage of its anti-imperialist existence. There is another direction in which we must develop the Congress. This concerns its internal organization and constitution. The basis of individual membership on which the Congress is at present organised is very unsatisfactory. It becomes an artificial body, representative not of the masses, but a handful of members.

We must endeavour to change this constitution in such a manner as to make the Congress a direct representative of the people. In my view this can best be done by developing a system of group representation. Members who constitute a primary committee of the Congress should be representatives of class and group organizations They should represent tenants, farmers, labourers, merchants, the professions and so on. The actual details of this plan may be difficult to draw up, but the principle is simple enough, and, to my mind, most just and proper. It should be obvious that such a constitution would remain a paper document till the class and group organisations are actually brought into existence.

The demand for such a constitution would therefore remain unreal and unheeded tilt this is done. It must, therefore, be accompanied by the creation of these organisations. Lest I should be misunderstood, I wish to make it clear that I do not for one moment flatter myself into believing that we are, or shall be, the only political group working towards this consummation I mean the development of an anti-imperialist movement. There are various other socialist groups following different methods and tactics, but basically working for the same end. It is sad to reflect that all of us are not able to work together, but I have no doubt that the efforts of the other groups will have an undoubted share in the ultimate result. Only, if a common line of work was agreed upon, we would be more successful. I must add that I naturally feel that the line that the Congress Socialist Party has been following is the most correct of all the tactics that are being used, and that, having an organic relation with the Congress movement, our efforts are bound to be more fruitful. Had not the radical elements left the Congress in 1929, just on the eve of the great national upheaval of 1930, the radicalisation of the Congress would have gone much further and we would have been much nearer our goal today. This process of development of the anti-imperialist forces that I have mentioned just now, cannot be brought about, as I have already said, by mere ideological propaganda. We must at the same time work among the masses. After all, the anti-imperialist movement will consist not only of ideologues, but of workers, peasants, the impoverished middle classes. To work among these classes, to develop their political consciousness, to organise their economic struggle this is our main and fundamental task. I must admit that we have not been able to make the desirable headway in this direction. However, the nucleus of work has been formed in many provinces. In the labour movement, our task is not so difficult, because there we have only to join hands with other radical groups and strengthen the dynamic labour movement. But in the sphere of peasant work, we have to do pioneering work in most of the provinces. Here in Bengal there has been a certain amount of economic agitation among the peasants and a nucleus night already exist. If it does, your task is made somewhat easier. In Bengal, you have almost a limitless field for activity. Both the peasantry and the working class offer ideal slippers of work. Perhaps nowhere in India is the plight of the peasants so potable as here and perhaps nowhere are the class issues so distinct. The Bengal Congress movement is greatly, dominated by zamindari interests. It is the top layer, however which reflects those interests. The rank and file and the lower strata of leadership are, I have no doubt, opposed to them. But, because they lack a programme and an ideology, they have willy-nilly to follow the present leadership. It will be the task of the Bengal Party to offer the required programme and ideology. It if does so, I have no doubt that it will soon gather around it the great majority of Congress workers of the province and thus pull the Congress movement out of the rut of inaction. In my talks with village Congress workers genuine men with fullest sympathy with our ideals I have found it difficult to explain to them one programme of work among the peasantry. The question I have found most difficult to drive home is how an economic agitation which is naturally aimed immediately against indigenous vested interests can become a force against imperialism. The answer, of course, is that the masses are not directly concerned with imperialism I am using the term here merely in the sense of the foreign power. What they are faced with is a system of economic exploitation which is daily grinding them to poverty. If they, in their millions, will fight any thing, it is this system of exploitation.

But this system is an integral part of imperialism and a fight against it becomes a fight against imperialism itself.

This point can be elaborated greatly and all its various aspects discussed, for instance how does it apply to those parts of the country where the zamindari system does not exist. But I need not go into all that here. As far as Bengal is concerned its application is obvious. To return to the village Congress worker, who I have said has, in most cases, the fullest sympathy with our ideals. It is my experience that it will take something more than an argument, however forceful, to carry conviction with him on this score. He has had no experience with the kind of work we are advocating, though, in provinces like Bihar, Bengal, the U.P., he has ample evidences of class struggle. He has so far worked through ashrams, hospitals, khadi centres. He does not know what an economic approach to the peasant is. But I am sure that if we show him the way he will be sure to follow. I have described to you in brief what the main task of the Party is.

Now I wish to tell you as briefly as possible my idea of its development. It is fulfilling today a dialectic need. And as the situation develops and changes we must adjust our policies accordingly. I do not believe, for instance, that we shall remain, or ought to remain, separate from the other socialist forces in the country. That would not be in the interest of the ideals for which we stand. I firmly believe that unless there is a fusion of the forces which I have mentioned, our common objectives will remain unrealised. I shall therefore warn you against sectionalism and futile controversies and exhort you to develop the greatest possible cooperation with the groups that are, except for minor differences, working for the same objects as ourselves. I shall take this opportunity to appeal to these also to follow a like policy. I do not ask them to give up criticism, nor do I myself forswear it, but I entreat them to work together in the promotion of identical ideals, keeping in mind the day when we shall all come closer and merge into one organisation. I shall not hazard an opinion at present on the nature of that organization, nor indeed, there is an occasion for it now. Now, I wish to take your leave. In concluding, I shall only say that I am fully alive to the difficulties which you have to face in your work in this province. Please remember, however that we cannot expect the other party to make things easy for us. If our methods are elastic we should be able to work under any conditions. I thank you all for giving me your willing attention and hope you will excuse me for having taken so much of your time. A new thesis was presented at the fourth conference of the CSP in 1938. This Thesis, while it reiterates the earlier Thesis, seeks to incorporate the experiences of the past years, particularly of the last year which has been of special significance both in the development of the anti-imperialist movement and in the realisation of socialist unity. This year has witnessed efforts to challenge or confuse the Party's fundamental position and it is therefore desirable to re-state the Party line with greater clarity and precision.

Causes behind Party's Birth

The proper perspective comes more easily when the causes the birth of the Party are recollected. The Congress Socialist Party grew out of the experiences, of the last two national struggles, the world economic crisis and the debacle of the socialist movements in Germany and in, other countries.

Providing New Life to Freedom Struggle

With the collapse of the last Civil Disobedience Movement there came a widespread belief in the necessity of a new orientation of the national movement, a re-definition of its objectives and a revision of its methods.

But the experiences of the two struggles could be properly assessed and adequately utilised only by those who had a theoretical grasp of the forces of our present society. The initiative had therefore to come from those Congressmen who had come under the influence of and had accepted Marxian Socialism. The failure of the Civil Disobedience Movement gave a jolt to and raised a question mark before Congressmen. But the dominant groups in the Congress could only hark back to the revival of constitutional activities or the intensification of constructive work along the familiar channels. Both these methods, useful though they were and are inadequate for developing our struggle which is far too grown them. The Communists, because of their sectarianism, opposition to the national movement and political intolerance mere not in a position to influence the Congress.

The Socialist movements in the West too were still groping their way out of the economic recession and political reaction. The Popular Front was as yet undiscovered. Indian Socialists, in common with Socialists the world over, were confronted with the problem of meeting reaction and marshalling the popular forces. The revitalising of the National Congress was the breaking down of the isolation between the national and the socialist movements and bringing the former increasingly under socialist leadership. It was natural therefore that the organisation that sprang up to meet the needs of the situation should be named the Congress Socialist Party signifying its organic relationship past, present and future with the national movement. Sprung from the National Congress, it desired to develop the national movement by strengthening and broadening the Congress. It approached the task with a confidence and a clarity that spring only from intimate association. That association and that relationship have been the main source of the strength and success of the Party. The task before the Party was to build up a powerful People's Front through the Congress working for direct mass struggle with imperialism. It had to rally together all those who stood for the independence of the country. It had so to clarify the objectives of the struggles as to make increasing sections of the people realise its impact on their lives and problems. It had to develop a method whereby this growing awareness resulted in the strengthening of the Congress.

Anti-Imperialist

Our task within the Congress, according to the Faizpur Thesis, is not only to wean the anti-imperialist elements away from the bourgeois leadership but so to develop and broaden the Congress itself as to transform it into a powerful anti-imperialist front. Such a transformation can come about only when the Party's point of view gains the requisite influence in the counsels of the Congress. Such influence results from intimation in Congress activities. In many provinces, thanks to such active identification, Party members occupy positions of influence and responsibility in the Congress organisation. The Party has further strengthened the Congress by dissolving the opposition of certain Left elements to the Congress and has won their allegiance to it. The Party's approach to the Congress has at last become common to all Left groups. By its analysis of the Congress programme, the Party was able to bring out the weakness of the Congress position and to point the way to future development both ideological and organisational of the Congress. That this influence is far from negligible is borne out by the resolutions of the Congress. Thanks to its actions, constructive work no longer means only social and semi-religious activities, it includes attention to the day-to-day grievances of the people and mass agitation on their basis. Perhaps the Party has failed to take the fullest advantage of this process. The prime consideration before Socialists while working in the Congress should be now what progress the Congress as a whole is making as a result of their efforts. Ideologically, the Congress is travelling Left, but the efforts of this are not yet felt organisationally in its day-to-day work. The transformation of the Congress would follow the removal of this hiatus. The removal of this hiatus depends to a great extent on disarming suspicion and removing hostility between the sections of the Congress. There are doubtless many reasons for the growth of these undesirable tendencies.

The objective causes, such as the attempts of the vested interests to drive a wedge between the two wings of the Congress to gain their hold over it, we cannot remove. One such factor is the irritating over-emphasis on the distinction between Right and Left. By insisting too much and too often on the wings, we run the risk or forgetting the flight of the bird. The alternative leadership that the Party offers must not be understood in a mechanical way. It does not mean a dramatic turnover of opinion. The leadership changes, evolves, with the impact of ideas on realities and with the constant testing of the relation that ideas bear to action and action to realities. This development in leadership, ideology and action is proceeding apace. The Socialist character of the Party, far from hindering such a development hastens it. Its socialist character and perspective have broken the antagonism of certain Left elements to the Congress, have drawn the masses with growing consciousness to the Congress. The experiences of the last 3 years bear irrefutable testimony to that.

Building Up Organisations of Workers and Peasants

The strengthening of the Congress demands besides its development, building up of class organisations of workers and peasants. From its inception the Party has strived to restore unity in the Trade Union Movement and thus lay the basis of lasting strength. That unity is now realised. The Party has built up several new unions, has spread the Trade Union

Movement throughout the country and has strengthened the old unions.

As a result it is the most influential group in the Trade Union Movement today. Gratifying though these facts may be, the Party must take its responsibility for the failure to build up mass unions in the important industrial centres. The Party took pioneer interest in building up the Kisan Sabhas and has been leading the movement ever since. The adoption by the Congress of an agrarian programme more realistically instinct with the economic grievances of the peasants has given an added fillip to the movement. Under the Party's inspiration and guidance the movement is assuming vast proportions and increasing tempo in several provinces. The growth of such a powerful movement based on class consciousness will inevitably provoke conflicts in the national movement, but the Party will ever seek to resolve these conflicts so as to develop the anti-imperialist forces in the country and will never permit their unity to be jeopardised. These organisations, by rousing the class consciousness of the masses, by rallying them on issues that affect them most directly, help to make them politically live and active. They are not rivals, even potentially, of the Congress. They train and bring organised strength to its elbow. The politically conscious elements in these organisations must join the Congress, individually today, and through collective affiliation when it is realised. Their experience and education will prove them a source of strength to the Congress. The more developed elements will turn to socialism and join the Socialist Party. The hostility of certain sections of the Congress will lessen, if not disappear, if this basic relationship is adequately grasped.

Fundamental Perception

It has been asserted ad nauseum that Socialism is not the issue of the day. If by this is meant that the immediate task is the overthrow of imperialism and not the establishment of socialism, it is an obvious and a patent fact that has been axiomatic with us. But if it means and that is what is usually implied that socialism, socialist technique and socialists as such have no role to play in the overthrow of imperialism and the winning of Swaraj, it is demonstrably untrue. Our struggle for freedom is to be developed in the context of the world-wide decline of capitalism, the intensified rivalries of imperialisms, pauperisation of the middle classes and chronic agrarian discontent. These factors cannot be adequately utilized for the development of our movement without socialist perspective and socialist technique. The basic problems of poverty and hunger cannot be solved, even after the severance of the British connection, if our socialist contours remain unchanged. That freedom can scarcely come unless the productive relationships are altered. The success of the freedom movement, therefore, is assured to the extent it adopts the socialist strategy of struggle and a socialist orientation. Once the necessity of socialist propaganda and of the socialist technique of struggle is admitted, a socialist party is definitely indicated, for it is absurd to imagine that socialists can conceive of political action in more marked after the Seventh Congress of the Comintern, the attitude of the Red group towards the Party changed as a result of which, but yet largely on the Party's initiative, it succeeded in establishing friendly relations with them. The "Red" group, in the impact of realities, had to shed its ultra-Leftism and to adopt increasingly the line of the C.S.P. When such adjustment began, the Party in its anxiety for unity opened its doors to the members of the "Red" group with a view to its early merger in the Party. Sub organic unity has not yet been realised because the "Red" group has raised, particularly during the past year, issues that balk such unity. The C.S.P. is a Marxist Socialist Party and its success has been due to its ideological and organisational unity and discipline. The "Reds" desire to loosen these. The C.S.P. according to them, is the growing organisational expression of Left unity and its future lies in its development into a mass party, not with the rigid discipline of a one-class party, but with an organisational structure which corresponds to the unification of the Left forces.

The C.S.P. should further open its doors to all who accept the aim of Socialism. This conception of the C.S.P. strikes at its fundamentals and is contrary to its basic tenets. Such a conception is fraught with dangers and confusion. There is no room for a mass socialist party in the country. Apart from the fact that a mass party today is unlikely to reflect the dominant urge of the people militant nationalism it is unlikely to be of any significance and might even become a confusing factor. The national movement can grow only to the extent that it adopts the socialist technique of national emancipation. It is increasingly adopting it. A steeled and disciplined Socialist Party will have to spread socialist ideas among Congressmen. Already, thanks to the work of the C.S.P., there is a growing realisation that socialism is synonymous with freedom from exploitation and hunger. The national liberation revolution can "grow" into the socialist revolution to the extent that there is such widespread, albeit vague, sympathy for socialism. Socialism is unlikely to follow national liberation quickly enough unless an overwhelming section of the Congress accepts the aim of socialism. The adoption of the socialist technique of struggle for national liberation by the Congress, the acceptance of the aim of socialism increasingly by active anti-imperialists, the early transformation of the national revolution into the socialist revolution ultimately depend upon the existence of a strong, well-disciplined, homogeneous socialist party, such as the C.S.P. is in the process of becoming.

Arrogation of the Role of C.S.P.

The "Red" group seeks to arrogate the role of the C.S.P. exclusively to itself and to turn the C.S.P. into a tertium quid between the Congress and itself. That it desires to turn the C.S.P. into a broader and looser organisation after the fashion of the Congress is further proved from its frequent use of the phrases "to build up", "to develop", that have been used with reference to the Congress.

The C.S.P. cannot tolerate dictation of "development" from an outside, independent group. It cannot play its role and realise its tasks if it thus abdicates its independent initiative to any other group. The conception of the "Red" group is also mischievous from another angle. A mass socialist party is evidently second string to the anti-imperialist bow of the "Reds". They have always entertained certain doubts about the capacity of the Congress to develop into the effective organ of struggle for national liberation. They have not yet finally shed the desire to build up a rival Congress, if need be. The C.S.P. is to be the convenient skeleton for that. Such a conception of the C.S.P. destroys both the national and the socialist basis of the Party. Unity between the two groups on these terms is impossible. Unity can be realised only when the "Red" group abjures its sense of exclusive importance and evinces a desire to build up a single, unified, disciplined socialist party. While the C.S.P. is always anxious, and will ever strive, for such a consummation, it will repel all efforts at diluting its ideology and discipline.

Further Responsibility

The further responsibility are to be envisaged in the context of the Congress in office. To arrest the drift towards constitutionalism, the Party opposed the formation of Congress Ministries. But after they came into existence, the Congress Socialists desire to assist them in running the Congress programme. The Congress programme does not permit concentrating on constitutionalism but is of combating the Constitution and preparing the country for the struggle that is inevitable on the issue of Federation. Our criticism of and cooperation with the Ministries must flow from this standpoint. Advantage should be taken of the Congress being in office expansion of civil liberties, progress socio-economic policies, sympathetic attitude towards mass organisations to obtain a mass basis for Trade Unions and Kisan Sabhas and to broaden and extend the activities and organisation of the Congress. The period of Congress Ministries is the great truce during which the Indian people have to marshal their forces for the final struggle with imperialism. The international situation is becoming tenser. Wars are already raging in two corners of the world.

The intensified imperialist rivalries and the continued decline of capitalism make a world war almost inevitable. Thus, while socialism is not an immediate objective, a socialist party is an immediate necessity and has a decisive role to play. The Socialist Party can play such a part only if it exerts influence in and commands the confidence of the national movement. That postulated intimate relationship with the Congress. It demands the closest participation by its members in Congress activities. The C.S.P. therefore makes Congress membership obligatory on its members. No one who accepts its ideology can remain outside the Congress, for that spells an isolation that ill-serves the national and socialist movements. But this does not mean that the C.S.P. as a party is "within" the Congress. It is an independent political party and it is not affiliated to the Congress. Nevertheless all its members are Congressmen and are bound by Congress discipline. This limitation under which the Party works is in the present situation inescapable, even desirable. It is limitation from which every Socialist, no matter to what independent organisation he belongs, will suffer if he is a Congressman. The limitations under which the C.S.P. works are necessary in the present stage of our struggle and are wholesome both for the national and socialist movements. These limitations, with the growth of its influence, will be a source of strength and not of embarrassment. Is the Party handicapped by its open character ? It is contended by some critics that a legal Socialist Party cannot exist in India today. Such an a priori assertion is ridiculous. There is no reason why the opportunities for open work should be given up and, as experience has shown, these opportunities are considerable. It is romanticism to believe that all socialist work in the country must be done underground. Legal existence must not, of course, become a reason for diluting the Party's stand. The record of the C.S.P. shows that there is no fear of its turning reformist. Apart from the fact that conditions in India are not congenial to reformism, no political party in touch with the masses and with their struggle for freedom can thrive on reformism.

The C.S.P. is the spearhead of the nationalist army. It has intimate contacts with mass movements and is ceaselessly engaged in preparing the masses for direct action. It has shown in the past that it will not curb its activities for the sake of avoiding the hand of the law. The revolutionary or reformist character of a party can be judged from its programme and actions, and by those tests the C.S.P. is the Revolutionary Socialist Party of India.

Predominance of Declassed Intellectuals

The C.S.P., it is contended by some, contains within itself' various socialist trends and is today predominantly petit-bourgeois in composition. The predominance of declassed intellectuals particularly in the higher organs of the Party is not peculiar to the C.S.P. The higher organs of any group in

India today are equally innocent of genuine proletarian elements. The predominance of petit-bourgeois in all the socialist parties of the world is not accidental. In India, it is the expression of the peculiar conditions of the country and the cultural backwardness of our masses.

The pauperisation of the middle classes is making them increasingly radical. The best elements among them naturally turn to socialism. The colonial conditions and their cultural lag that they accentuate make it difficult for proletarian and peasant elements to play an ideologically leading role. The petit-bourgeoisie is not yet completely divorced from the peasants and the working class its intimate contact with them is naturally beneficism of the petit-bourgeois than those they seek to judge. The C.S.P. as a socialist party is a party of the working class. Its tasks are to strengthen the Congress as the effective organ of independence and to prepare the basis for the early, realisation of socialism. For the realisation of the latter task, the C.S.P. welcomes to its fold all socialists who are prepared to give it undivided loyalty and endeavour to make increasing sections of the people socialistically minded. For the realisation of the former task it strives to rally together inside the Congress all those who accept the Party's anti-imperialist platform, which is obviously not a socialist one. Already certain of its items have been accepted by the Congress : The Party strives for its adoption in its entirety. Those who accept the platform, whether socialists or not, constitute today the Left in the Congress. It is necessary to strengthen the Left to weld all such elements closer together inside the Congress under the leadership of the C.S.P. To suggest that the C.S.P. is so to expand as to embrace all the Left elements in the Congress is to divide the Congress organisationally into a Left and a Right.

Such a process would be in obvious violation of our policy to develop the Congress as a whole in order that it may be transformed into a powerful anti-imperialist front. That the C.S.P. is the organisational expression of Left unity is a conception that is fatal to its fundamentals. Left unity, can be integrated and effectively developed only under the leadership of a Socialist Party. If the C.S.P. is the organisational expression of Left unity, it fortiori cannot be that socialist party. It is the Congress, when it adopts the full anti-imperialist programme, that will be the organisational expression of such unity. The C.S.P. endeavours to realiser national unity on the basis of a Left programme a task that only a socialist party can perform.

Desire of Sincere Socialists

Socialist unity is the desire of all sincere Socialists. The Party has strived, from its inception, for its achievement. If unity has not yet been achieved, the responsibility is certainly not of the Congress Socialist Party. The Party faced at the outset the hostility of the Red group which went to the length of describing it as a Left maneuvers of the bourgeoisie. It however refused consistently to join in any such campaign of recrimination.

In fact even in face of such attacks from the groups, the Party negotiated a united front agreement with the "Red" T.U.C. The present thesis seeks to further extend and clarify the two former theses adopted at the previous sessions. It seeks to define the general political tasks of the Party in the light of the experiences and developments of the intervene in period.

Country's Existing Political Condition

The present political situation of our country is determined by the following factors :

(1) The rapidly maturity world war crisis as indicated by the continued war of aggression by fascist

powers against the Spanish people, the renewed offensive of fascist Japan against nationalist China, the consolidation of the war-block of fascist powers against the U.S.S.R., and by the increased war-preparations of imperialist nations especially Britain.

(2) The rise in the volume and the tempo of the anti-imperialist struggle of the masses of our country as shown by the growing number of strikes of workers and students, the growing struggle and organisation of the peasants, by the phenomenal rise in the Congress membership and by the drawing in of the broad strata of the backward masses into the political arena.

(3) The growing need and desire on the part of British imperialism to preserve "the inner peace" in India, to commandeer its resources in men and money for the coming war and for this purpose to effect a solid block with the reactionary vested interests (federation), and to conciliate at its own price a section of Indian nationalist leadership (toleration of ministries, advances to the Congress leadership to join the federation, etc.).

Mighty and Decisive War

In view of this situation, it is quite clear that we are fast approaching a period favourable for mighty and decisive struggle involving the overwhelming majority of our people, for throwing off the yoke of foreign imperialism, for achieving complete independence, establishing a democratic state and guaranteeing to the people their basic economic demands and civil rights and liberties. An occasion favourable for achieving the first decisive advance which alone can open up the possibilities for the free and unhampered economic, political and cultural development of our people and which will eventually open up the path for socialism is facing us.

Developing Political Consciousness

The main political task of our party is to prepare for this struggle, to make it possible and be victorious. We must realise the present opportunities for the organisational consolidation and the broadening of the struggle of the workers and the peasants and develop the political consciousness and initiative of the proletariat and the peasantry. We must strive to build the lower units of the National Congress as the fighting organs of popular struggle against imperialism and its bureaucratic machinery.

The growing mass basis of the National Congress, rising left-ward swing in its lower ranks, makes the task of developing the Congress into a genuine united front of the Indian people for fighting against imperialism both possible and urgent. The Indian National Congress is the principal political mass organisation of this country. It unites within itself diverse elements seeking National liberation. The masses especially the rural masses, see in it the champion of their struggle against imperialist tyranny. All those elements in this country whose interest clasp with the interest of British Imperialism have been increasingly drawn to the I.N.C. A certain measure of unity has been achieved in the process of the development of our struggle for freedom. It is for this reason that the actual programme of the I.N.C. corresponds in a large measure, to the needs of the overwhelming majority of our people. This programme is also appropriate largely to the present stage of our anti-imperialist struggle. The goal of complete independence, the Karachi Declaration of Fundamental Rights, the Agrarian resolutions of the Lucknow Faizpur Congresses, the Election Manifesto of the I.N.C., the Wardha resolution of February 1937 and the

Faizpur resolution on war, do in a broad sense lay down the main immediate objectives of the Indian people as a whole. Besides the peasants, the lower middle, classes and the workers, there are also other elements in the Congress.

The dominant leadership of the Congress, reflecting the interests of the bourgeoisie, a section of landlords and money-lenders, does not consistently draw out and guide the mass activity, does not organise and develop the national struggle of the masses for the redress of their day to day grievances. It does not make an effort in the towns and villages of India with our wider anti-imperialist struggle. On the contrary it uses its dominant position in the Congress to divert these basic struggles of the masses and their anti-imperialist energies into constitutional channels. It seeks to dampen their enthusiasm, instead of developing it. For example, Kisan marches, processions and demonstrations are discouraged, workers' strikes are generally "frowned upon" and everything is done to violate them, students' strike are generally disapproved of. The main obstacle to the transformation of the National Congress into an effective instrument of consistent anti-imperialist struggle, arises from the fact that it functions in a manner which does not develop the initiative of its lower organs, that in practice, undemocratic processes manifest themselves, that the reformist sections of the nationalists (expressing the interests of the bourgeoisie, a section of landlords and money-lenders and other well-to-do-middle classes) successfully impose their own forms and methods of action, their own non-revolutionary ideology on the I.N.C. So that while the programme of the I.N.C. does express the united objectives of the Indian people as a whole, the actual functioning of the Congress machinery at the present and the ways and methods of struggle to achieve the popular objectives are determined in the main by the interests of the bourgeoisie. This contradiction between the programme of the Congress and the actual struggle to realise that programme can be clearly seen when major issues face it. For example, the resolution on the Agrarian question lays down the main outlines of the immediate demands of the peasantry. To realise even these minimum demands intense agitation by the peasants is necessary. These demands cannot be fulfilled except through organising the peasantry for immediate struggle against their oppressors, viz., the landlords, money-lenders, the imperialist bureaucracy. Yet the Congress Right Wing, disapproves of partial struggle of the peasantry, of their processions, marches and demonstrations, it wants to smash the class organisations of the peasantry, it forms open as far as the working class is concerned. The labour programme of the I.N.C. cannot be realised without the organisation and struggle of the working class. Yet general strikes of the workers of Ahmedabad and Kanpur are not only not helped, but the imperialist bureaucracy is allowed by the Congress ministries to use its repressive machinery to imprison and suppress workers' militant activities.

Likewise student strikes for the redress of their legitimate grievances or for the vindication of national honour (National Flag hoisting agitation) are condemned and discouraged. Under the specious slogan of non-violence, imperialist violence is approved of and tried workers in the national movement are allowed to be prosecuted for sedition (Madras and U.P.) under Criminal Law Amendment Act (U.P. and Bombay) For breach of Sec. 144 for C.PC. for preaching class hatred (U.P.), etc. The programme of the I.N.C. is however, quite clear on the question of freedom of speech, organisation and meeting. The rising tide of the anti-imperialist movement, the radicalisation of the masses, the independent struggle of the proletariat an I the peasantry has resulted in the formation of a conscious and organised Left in the I.N.C., of which the

C.S.P. is an expression. This development is to a certain extent reflected also in the leadership of the I.N.C.

Immediate Programme of the Party

The immediate programme put forward by our Party generally corresponds to the programme of the National Congress itself and is in the interest of the overwhelming majority of the Indian people. That is why it can be the basis of the United National Front in the present phase of our struggle. The development of the I.N.C. into the anti-imperialist front of struggle on this basis does not mean the exclusion from it of sections of the capitalists or landlord class who are today in it, as long as these accept the Congress programme and do, not stand in the way of the struggle to achieve this programme.

But this development of the Congress does mean overcoming of the resistance of the reformists and those elements in the Congress who hinder mass struggle whether these struggles are partial struggles for the redress of sectional grievances of the masses or they are struggles for the achievement of our generally democratic rights and liberties. This development means democratisation of the Congress by activising its primary membership and by making the primary Congress Committees the fighting organs of United Front struggles in conjunction with the workers', peasants', students" and youths' organisations. This development means a broadening of the base of the Congress by increasing its membership by forming primary Congress Committees in thousands, and by making these Congress Committees the centres of the united struggles of all the various sections of the masses comprised in that area. This development means the rebuilding of the Congress from bottom upwards. So that through it all the sectional partial struggles of the masses are developed and linked together, and it becomes in a real sense the political expression of our United National struggle for emancipation.

Meerut Thesis

In the Meerut Thesis, the task of building the anti imperialist front is described by the "weaning of the anti-imperialist elements in the Congress away from its present bourgeoisie leadership and to bring them under the influence of revolutionary socialism." The leadership of revolutionary socialism in described in the Faizpur Thesis thus : "The struggle of the Indian masses for freedom will not reach its objective unless the working class is in the vanguard of that struggle. Therefore, it is our task as Socialists to see that it assumes its historic role in the national movement." This must be further clarified.

The process of building the United National Front, while it involves the shifting of the centre of gravity of the leadership from the bourgeoisie to the proletariat does not yet mean the establishment of the leadership of the Proletariat. In the phase of struggle which we visualise in the immediate future the proletariat would come forward as the builder and the initiator of the united front though not yet the exclusive leader. But what is important to grasp is that the task of building the united front, of transforming the Congress, will succeed only in the measure the proletariat comes forward as the builder and the initiator of the process.

Gandhi Continues to be Leading Ideology

In spite of its non-revolutionary character, Gandhism continues to be the leading ideology of the Congress. In its new form of parliamentary reformism it seeks to use the period of Congress ministries to create constitutional illusions about winning complete independence without direct mass action, without a civil disobedience movement. It dominates a considerable section of the masses inside the Congress parading as the practical "anti-imperialist policy" and thus acts as a hindrance to unity and struggle. Its semi-religious principle of non-violence is being freely utilized to curb militant anti-imperialist activities, while paradoxically, there is an acquiescence and even justification by a majority of Right Wing leaders, specially the Congress Ministries, when imperialist violence is used against the rising tide of peasants' and workers' struggle.

Defects and Finally to Unsuccess

Though the C.S.P. and the left generally have made considerable advance inside the Congress and in the independent development of the struggle of the masses, they are not yet in position to influence the basic policy of the Congress to effectively check the reformist tendency which is being imposed upon the forces of our National struggle.

The unsuccess of the C.S.P. and the left in general is due to the following defects in our work :

1. We still continue to work inside the National Congress in the old way mainly as a left opposition. We give the impression of being mere critics of the right wing, not as conscious workers of a positive alternative line, previously thought out.

2. We have not succeeded sufficiently in vitalising the struggle for the fulfilment of the anti-imperialist programme of the Congress by directly linking it up with the independent struggles of the working class and the peasantry.

3. We have failed to take initiative building up United Front between Congress units and workers' and peasants' organisations on issues of partial struggle

and in this way to rebuild the units of the I.N.C. as functioning units of united anti-imperialist struggle.

Sharp Turn towards Proletarianisation

In order to correct these defects, our Party must first of all make a sharp turn towards proletarianisation. Basing ourselves on our day-to-day work in the Trade Union and Kisan Sanghs, on our participation in the independence struggle of the workers and peasants, we must take up the task of raising the political consciousness of the proletariat in town and in the countryside, of creating political trained cadres from among them.

Under the present situation, this task must be done in the closest cooperation with the proletarian groups (Reds) who are seeking united front and collaboration with the C.P.S. with a view to evolving a united Marxist Socialist Party of the working class. The task of building the national front on the basis of the National Congress will succeed in the measure of our Party strikes roots among the proletariat and the peasantry and develops independent political consciousness among them. Our day-to-day work inside the Congress organisation is both agitational and organisational. Our Party must become the focal point for the rallying of all the Congress left forces inside the Congress, who want to convert the Congress into a genuine front of the uncompromising anti-imperialist struggle. We must rally those who want to break with reformism and conciliation with imperialism round the alternative programme of developing mass-struggle to achieve the immediate objective before the country. We must group the left forces inside the Congress on a programme for its democratisation.

This implies giving more initiative to the primary Congress Committees. It will make them functioning bodies for the strengthening and broadening of the United Front between Congress units and other mass organisations, it will make possible through their activity the collective affiliation of workers', peasants', youths' and students' organisations. The consolidation of these forces inside the Congress on this basis is a necessary step for the conversion of the Congress as a whole into a joint front of the entire Indian people for struggle against imperialism.

Organisational Work

Our organisational work inside the Congress must consist in broadening the mass basis of the Congress organisations in towns and villages, by linking these up with worker and peasant struggles and with the Trade Unions and Kisan Sanghs. Through the organisation of the Congress committees and primaries we must seek to mobilise the support and sympathy of all the anti-imperialist elements of our people for the day-to-day struggles of peasants and workers. By our direct participation and leadership of the struggle and organisation of workers and peasants we must convert the Congress units into real champions of the exploited people against bureaucracy.

6

Jay Prakash : Peace and War

"While it is true that I had suggested what is known in international law as 'measure short of war', it is not right to overlook the qualifying conditions and fasten attention only on the final step. Let me remind the reader of the conditions I had set forth. First, I had emphasized that there must be peace and order in India and our Muslim citizens must live without fear and in enjoyment of equal rights with Hindus. As I had said in a later statement, we cannot rush to protect minorities and human rights elsewhere, when we fail to do so at home. Second, I had insisted at Nagpur that though Nehru's friendly approaches had proved infructuous fresh attempts should be made to reach a peaceful solution. "It was only in the even of all peaceful efforts failing and when we had succeeded in keeping peace at home and do injustice to our minorities, that I had suggested what was described as armed intervention. "As it turned out, Nehru's hope was justified, and a peaceful settlement was arrived at.

To oppose that settlement or to sabotage it is to play with fire, for as Nehru has said the alternative is war. War is a frightful affair and no sane person, would rush into it when other avenues of settlement are open. Nor would war necessarily save the Hindus of East Bengal nor help in the rehabilitation of the refugees. "There is a great deal of talk about the honesty of purpose of Pakistan." Will they implement the agreement we are asked on all sides. It occurs to no one to ask if WE will implement it. Judging from the temper of the people of West Bengal and the attitude of its Press, one may well ask that question. "Let us remember that if we implemented the agreement and Pakistan did not, a solution though a tragic solution would yet be available. But if we both failed to do the job no solution could ever be found. A war wrought in a communal climate on both sides would only result in mutual destruction. During the Quit India Movement he was lodged in their Lahore Fort and the Agra Central Jail among with Ram Manohar Lohia. He was released in April 1946, about a year after several Congress leaders were released.

At this point of time he was quite clear in his mind that freedom could not be achieved through negotiations. He once again stated that students, workers and peasants should be mobilised at war footing. He indeed talked about the work at the village level as he realised that millions of people living in the villages were a big force. Not accepting any office after independence, he spent much, of his time for the propagation of the philosophy of Sarvodaya, the good of all. He moved from one region to another and propagated for fundamental changes in our society. For such a change, he argued, the people of India should respect democratic values in order to build a society in which Indian culture should be enshrined.

Detention of Jay Prakash and Its Description

Even though it is now more than two years and two months when the reputed Congress socialist leader Mr. Jay Prakash Narayan, was arrested, yet circumstances under which Mr. Jay Prakash was "captured" by the Punjab Police have remained an unsolved mystery. Circumstances of his arrest, the names of the persons who arrested him as also the place of his arrest have remained a most guarded secret. Mr. Jay Prakash carried a reward of Rs. 10,000 "for his head".' For various reasons the Punjab authorities succeeded in maintaining complete secrecy about Mr. "J. P's" arrest all these long years and even when the Punjab press tried to know the circumstances relating to his captivity, the Punjab authorities persistently refused to divulge any news beyond saying : "He was arrested in the Punjab". The mystery has, however, been partly solved by one of the Punjab security prisoners who was recently released after about two years' detention which be suffered on account of the suspicion of his association with Mr. Jay Prakash .

This security prisoner was detained in the Lahore Fort at the same time when Mr. Jay Prakash was there. It is learnt that "J.P." was arrested in the moving. Frontier Mail on the morning of September 18, 1943, between Amritsar and Lahore. Mr. Jay Prakash was travelling from somewhere on his way to some hill station in the north of the Punjab via Delhi. It appears that the Punjab C.I.D. got information of "J.Ps", journey through the Punjab in all probability from Delhi and made arrangements to catch India's Socialist Leader Number One by surprise when he least expected of being caught. Mr. Jay Prakash had an absolutely comfortable journey all the way till the train reached Amritsar where he got up and took his tea. Hardly had he finished his cup and only a short while before the train moved, there stepped in his compartment one European and two Sikh C.I.D. officers, the European being one of the senior most C.I.D. officials. They were dressed in plain clothes and Mr. "J.P." never doubted that they would be the persons who would arrest him.

These officers did nothing until the train had left Amritsar and while the train was moving between Amritsar and Lahore, a distance of 35 miles the European officer caught hold of Mr. Jay Prakash at the point of his pistol and the two Sikh officers helped their chief in holding up Mr. "J.P." who stood surrounded by men with pistols in their hands while the train was going on at the highest speed. Mr. "Jay Prakash " detrained at Mughalpura a wayside station before Lahore and was then removed to the Lahore Fort where he was detained later on served with a notice in the second week of December 1943, from the Government of India declaring him a State Prisoner. While in detention a very high European official of the Punjab Government and a young Muslim Nawab and knight were allowed to meet Mr. "J.P." once a week in accordance with the provisions contained in Regulation III of 1854. Then long and endless interrogations commenced which lasted for an unknown time. Mr. Jay Prakash was sometime later allowed at his own cost, a copy each of the "Tribune" and the "Statesman". But all news about war in the East, proceedings in the Indian Legislatures, and editorial notes, etc., were clipped off before Mr. "J.P." got the copies of his newspaper.

Details about Dramatic Escape from Jail

Interesting details about the dramatic escape of Comrade Jay Prakash Narayan from the Hazari Bagh Jail (Behar) along with his four associates and the interception of his, now well-known, letters by a C.I.D. official of Deoli Detention Camp, have just come to light, through one of his trusted lieutenants. These stories provide a clear index to the sublime character and passionate patriotism of the hero of the 1942 movement. Feeling an urge within himself that he should not allow himself to stagnate in this fashion, but should resume some contacts with the world outside Deoli Camp, Jay Prakash Narayan, succeeded in hypnotising a subordinate official of a Junior Cadre, attached to the Camp, for sending out instructions to his party men outside for starting work. He wrote down a few letters and planned to send them out through that clerk. The Camp, which was inhabited by about 250 political suspects from all provinces of India, was practically a military Camp, solely in charge of the C.I.D. establishment. It was situated 80 miles from Ajmer and 64 miles from Kotah Junction of B.B. and C.I. Railway. The relatives of the detenus could interview them on two consecutive days. A C.I.D. official knowing different languages spoken in India used to be present at the interviews. In accordance with the plan, a big envelope, containing letters from Comrades Jay Prakash Narayan, Munshi Ahmed Din and Master Mota Singh Anandpuri, was, handed over to that clerk for safe delivery to Mrs. Jay Prakash Narayan, who was waiting outside for the second day interview with her husband. When no acknowledgment, as settled, was received by the sender suspicion grew amongst themselves against the clerk.

Eventually J.P. received an intimation about the non-delivery of the "valuable" documents. When that "official" messenger was caught hold of and threatened with dire consequences, he said that he could not effect the delivery of the packet, owing to the C.I.D. surveillance. He, however, returned that envelope to Jay Prakash Narayan quite intact. Jay Prakash did not sit idle over it. He was keen that his instructions should reach the desired quarters, as he thought that it was psychological moment for carrying out those plans into action. He thought that be could deliver the envelope himself at the time of the interview with his wife who was then summoned telegraphically for an urgent interview. She did not know the errand for which she was being called so suddenly. Jay Prakash tried to pass over the envelope to his wife, from beneath the table, at the time of the interview.

Mr. Bannerjee, the C.I.D. Sub-Inspector from Behar, who was present at the time of interview, on hearing the round, suspected and jumped off his seat. He tried to snatch the envelope but failed. J.P. also could not succeed in destroying the envelope, despite his best efforts. Both grappled with each other. A regular scuffle ensued. The C.I.D. official shouted and invoked the assistance of a military sentinel on duty, with whose help, Jay Prakash was deprived of his "valuable documents," as he called the envelope. Jay Prakash was produced before the Superintendent of the Camp for the breach of the Jail Rules. Lt. Col. Christopher, Superintendent, scolded him for his conduct and ordered that his interviews and letters should be stopped for a couple of months, adding that no further punishment would be awarded to him, if he undertook not to repeat such a thing in future. "I am a professional law-breaker. I do not respect your laws. I am in jail for this very purpose. I have been breaking the laws outside the jail and would not hesitate to break them again, whenever an opportunity occurs. I am prepared for the consequences," was the reply given by Jay Prakash to the warnings of the jail official. Similar punishments were also, awarded to Munshi Ahmed Din and Master Mota Singh Anandpuri.

Private Conference

After a private conference between the various jail officials, it was decided to stick to the punishment already given and forward all the relevant papers, including the document itself, to the Government of India, for further action, if deemed necessary. This incident occurred in July, 1941 and on the 7th October, 1941, some portions from those letters (not the entire text) were released for publication to the papers all over India. This was done, according to the detenus, only to sabotage the threatened hunger-strike, scheduled to take place on the 22nd October, 1941. The detenus in the Camp did not get their copies of the daily newspapers containing the above publication, which caused a flutter in the Camp. Jay Prakash Narayan was summoned by the Superintendent of Jail to his office.

After intimating to him that the Government of India had published his letters, the Superintendent of Jail brought home to him the fact that the publication, in question, had exposed the Communists before their countrymen, adding that there was an apprehension of their wreaking vengeance upon him in some dastardly fashion. Jay Prakash was further intimated that arrangements had been made for shifting him to a separate corner of the Camp, fenced with barbed wires, etc. "I would face all consequences for my honest convictions. I will stick to my post and remain with my friends. I refuse to, be segregated. The letters contain nothing but private instructions to my colleagues for carrying out work outside. I am, prepared for all eventualities". This spirited reply was given by Jay Prakash to the second warning of the jail officials regarding this episode. The daily papers, which had been held back for a couple of days were then delivered to the detenues, who read with keen interest the various comments on the publication of the letters. The Socialist detenues had to commence their hunger strike on the 22nd October and their Communist comrades in, the Camp, on the following day. Mr. S.V. Ghate, Communist leader (Madras) apparently excited by the event stated that they would wash the blot alleged in the letter with their blood, after hunger-strike unto death. The Communists however gave up their hunger-strike after 15 days and soon raised the slogan of "People's War" and thus washed the blot with their action. Jay Prakash Narayan was released from the Agra Central Jail in the evening on April 11, 1946. Dr. Rammanohar Lohia was also released with him. All the inmates of Hazari Bagh Jail, both prisoners and jail-staff were engaged in the celebration of

Deepmala festival and a drama was staged inside the jail premises to mark the occasion.

According to a well planned scheme, all this was being done in one side of the jail, while J.P. and his associates were busy in giving final touches to their plan of quitting the jail, for accelerating work outside. The story of the dramatic escape of Jay Prakash Narayan is still a mystery to millions of his countrymen. Ever since his repatriation to his own province after the abolition of the Deoli Camp, Jay Prakash Narayan was constantly brooding over the idea of organising his and his friends' escape from the Jail, with a view to work for the liberation of his motherland, at his psychological moment in the history of the world. Political prisoners were free to move about in the jail.

The daily counting of prisoners inside the jail was not done in case of political prisoners. They had hit at a plan and decided their course of action. When the entire jail staff was concentrating their attention on the preparations of the stage for the drama, J.P., along with B. Rama Nand Misra (one of the biggest landlords of Bihar and a brother of the Rani of Benares), Comrade Suraj Narayan Singh, Babu Jogindra Shukla and another companion succeeded in escaping from the jail after scaling the big walls with the aid of ropes. As decided beforehand, they were received by a number of comrades at a distance from the jail gates and escorted to a safe place. After staying there for a few hours, they left for their respective places for the fulfilment of their mission. In this connection it will be interesting to note that certain patriotic Indian pilots came to J.P.'s rescue two or three times by carrying him to his destination in the Royal Air Force Planes. Some of these pilots, who were later taken into custody, are still believed to be behind the bars. The climax of this interesting episode was reached when the jail officials came to know of the escape of J.P. and his companions, three days after the actual happening. It so, happened that the Superintendent of the jail had to communicate some orders of the Central Government to J.P. A warder, who was sent to summon him, returned with the news that J.P. was not inside the jail.

The Superintendent of jail treated it as a joke and reprimanded the servant for his impertinence. Another warder, who was then detailed, brought a similar reply. The Superintendent of jail was at his wit's end. He immediately went inside the jail and raised an alarm signal. It transpired that not only J.P. but his four companions were missing from their barracks. A telegraphic report was sent to the Government of India as a result of which both the Superintendent and Deputy Superintendent of jail were suspended. Both of them were prosecuted in a court but were discharged and reinstated. After his escape J.P. roamed about in all the provinces in the country issuing directives to his party regarding the August 1942 movement.

Treatment in Lahore Fort

Jay Prakash Narayan narrated how be was treated in Lahore Fort which he described as Government of India's "torture house." He said that he was kept in a cell for 16 months continuously. He was not allowed to meet or talk to anybody. He was interrogated for about 50 days at a stretch from 12 to 14 hours a day by C.I.D. who had specially been brought from different provinces. During interrogation, he said they poured volleys of abuses at him and the Congress leaders. During the last ten days of interrogation he Was kept awake day and night and was not allowed to move from one place except for going to the latrine. While in the cell he lodged a protest that he should be allowed to exercise in the open. With great difficulty he was given permission, but was kept handcuffed while doing exercise. He again made a protest and threatened to go on hunger-strike if his handcuffs were not removed while exercising. Later on he was transferred from the Lahore Fort. Mr. Jay Prakash denied the reports that he was ever assaulted or made to sit on ice slabs. He met on Saturday, Maulana Abul Kalam Azad, Congress President, Pandit Jawaharlal Nehru, Sardar Vallabhbhai Patel and several other members of the Working Committee. In the evening he paid a visit to the late Shrimati Satyavati Devi's house and enquired about the progress of her memorial.

Failure of Cabinet Mission and Consideration to Start Movement

"If the present negotiations with the Cabinet Mission break down another struggle cannot be avoided," said Jay Prakash Narayan, Congress-socialist leader to an Associated Press of India correspondent in an interview. "I would take all steps to be fully prepared this time," he added. Asked if independence could be achieved through negotiations and constitutional means, the Socialist leader said : "The talks with the Cabinet Mission are not the result of Good-will on the part of British Labour Government. It is the result of the greatest national upheaval since 1857 and also of outside pressure and world situation." Replying to another question Jay Prakash said : "We are on the stage of formulating our party. Congress-Socialist. Party is part of the Congress. We must take stock of the present political situation and then formulate our plans." When asked what was his view about the Communist Party, the Socialist leader said : "I consider the communists to be "Russian fifth Columnists" and as such a perpetual danger to the country irrespective of what policy they may be following at a particular moment."

Jay Prakash accompanied by his wife, Shrimati Prabha Vati, left for Benares 'en route' to Patna.

"J.P.," as the Congress Socialists always love to call Jay Prakash Narayan has for many come to possess a glamour second only to that of Netaji. Both made a firm unshakable resolve to turn the war situation into an opportunity to strike for India's liberation. Both persisted heroically in their endeavour when to others all seemed futile. Both remained loyal to the Congress objective of independence rather than to the programme sanctioned by it for the realization of that objective. Netaji escaped out of India and sought foreign allies for his endeavour. J.P.'s tale of glamorous adventure begins with his escape from prison and his starting secret activity in collaboration with those already 'underground' since August 1942 though it is possible his story also has a chapter running beyond British India to the Nepal border.

Many await an authentic narrative of the jail-breaking and of JP.'s subsequent adventures till his betrayal into the bands of the Punjab police with about the same keenness with which they recently read the stories narrated by Netaji's stay in Kabul as Zia-ud-Din seeking an opportunity to escape to Russia or to the Axis countries. A few perhaps await this authentic narration with more than mere curiosity those suspected or accused by their comrades of complicity in the betrayal for in the Socialist circles, since J.P.'s re-arrest the worst accusation against a comrade has been that there were grounds for suspecting he had a hand in the great betrayal and of course nobody would have truck with Judas. Like Netaji J.P. at first sight is a man who talks little but ponders deeply. Both give one the impression of extraordinary earnestness arising out of grim determination. J.P.'s power lies not in seductive or persuasive radiation : talk it works rather like a silent magic which penetrates much deeper than talk.

A talk with the C.S.P. friends and followers of J.P. often leaves one with the impression that in spite of all their seeming preoccupation with ideologies and theoretical discussion of doctrine and tactics the decisive influence on them has rather been the J.P. radiation. In a display of ideological and dialectical fireworks the Indian Communist often scores against them but I do not think the Communist leadership in India has yet thrown up a personality as radiant and magnetic as J.P.'s or with his penetrative influence. J.P. is cast in the heroic mould. But he has also done and good deal of political thinking. In the C.S.P. thesis and programmes his contribution has ever been outstanding, though these documents have not always been crystal clear have definitely suffered from compromises and confused thought there can be no doubt. J.P's talents for political leadership are of a high order.

In one of his acutest despatches analysing the failure of Wavell's Simla Conference, Preston Grover of the A.P.A. deplored the shortcomings of Indian leadership which was not able to get out of the stereotyped grooves, he also mentioned that many hoped for something better from certain younger leaders and he mentioned Jay Prakash . That must have come as a surprise to many a delightful one for many of my Brother Freebooters. Yes. J.P. is rich in promise for tomorrows India. He was much critical of British rule in India. We are all acquainted with Nazi lies. Dr. Geobbels of gestapo fame was synonymous with lying. But there is also a far subtler and refined tradition of lying imperialist lying, of which the British stories are the brilliant present exponents. The world has been told by them two tremendous lies. The first that Britain holds India down only to educate and train her in the arts of Self-Government and will continue to do so only until such time as she is able properly to look after herself. The second that Britain is prepared to free India immediately if Indians united among themselves.

No greater lies were ever uttered in History. But these are not Ties like those of Goebbles, nor do they come from the mouth of .. Nazi rulers. They have the prestige of ages and tradition, they have the gloss of British culture, they are mouthed by noble lords and aristocrats of wealth. Poetry and literature, learning and science have sanctified them until we witness today the strange spectacle of even the most emancipated British minds failing to transcend their limits. It is an insult to the intelligence of any but a moron to say that imperialisms are founded to train "backward" peoples in the arts of Self-Government. Empires are founded to loot and to rob and to exploit. And the amount of British loot and exploitation in India would stagger anyone for its astronomical figures. British power in India is soaked in violence. It is based on violence. It daily commits the most pitiless forms of violence. It grinds down millions of people and sucks their life blood. While India fights non-violently, the British have only bullets and looting and rape and arson. Before Britain enslaved her, India was a free country. She did not have to learn the art of self-government from anybody. If at that moment the country was torn with wars that was no more evidence of the unfitness of the people to govern themselves, than the much too frequent and far more bloody wars of Europe prove that the continent with its islands, is ready to be taught a lesson in self-government by, let us say, the United States of America.

First to destroy the freedom of a nation and then to claim to train the enslaved in the art of freedom, is such a process of historic perversion that only the master of empire building can venture to father it. And how have the British been training us in the art of self-government? They have been here now for 150 years. In less than that period America after it freed itself from a similar tutorship of the same power, has been able to transform itself from a disunited collection of backward colonies into the mightiest and the most advanced nation of the world. What have the British tutors done to us in a longer period of time. Not more than 10 per cent of the population is literate, not more than 10 per cent of the economic resources of the country have been developed. Even during the last total war one can see what progress the country has made under British tutelage in production for war. This has been so scandalous that the Government of India did not even dare to publish the report of the American Technical Mission, which investigated under Dr. Grady, certain matters of industrial production. So anxious indeed have the British rulers been for our progress, that every little progress-political, economical, educational has been made in the teeth of their opposition and after great agitation and often bitter struggle.

The bitterest struggle of all was fought during 1942. It is commonly supposed that one positive contribution that the British have made to Indian policy is to unify the country, and it is a common lament that they foolishly enough are bent today upon destroying that monument of their noble work. Nothing could be greater folly than this view. Far from creating unity in Indian life the British have always done their best to divide us, to divide Hindus and Muslims, to divide Harijans from other Hindus, to create a Sikh minority, to detach princely India from the rest of the country, to set the princes against the people, to bolster up zamindars into pillars of British rule, to bribe capital and the middle class to turn into enemies of their country. That is in their 150 years' rule they have done all that was possible to bring about a situation in which weakening of British rule was sure to mean chaos and disintegration.

The only unity under British rule is the unity of a dictatorial regime and not a people's or a nation's unity. Such positive unity has been created by the Congress and this unity today is in jeopardy. First of all what justification can a nation have for keeping another nation enslaved just because it is divided? If two brothers fight, is a robber justified in entering their home and taking possession of it? The British are in the position of the robber. Suppose Hindus and Muslims do fight, does that justify the British in marching into our home and occupying it? The plea that if one robber did not take possession of a divided house another would, is an argument that appeals to robber mind alone. No decent man would burgle an unguarded house on the plea that if he did not, another burglar might 4060. But the argument is not even true. The British are not prepared to hand over real power-unity or no unity-into Indian hands. The question of Indian unity has nothing to do with the subject. It has been raised merely to sidetrack the issue.

The real issue is : "Is Britain prepared to liquidate her empire?" The answer of the Cripps mission was a clear no. The same answer was repeated by Mr. Churchill when he announced that he had not assumed the office of the King's First Minister to preside over the liquidation of the Empire. The reply of the : present Labour Government has been the least encouraging. The persistent policy of the British Government particularly its representatives here is to use the Muslim League and other communal elements and the princes to put obstacles in the path of freedom. The British have encouraged and inspired the Muslim League intransigence. The latest instance is the British Government's statement of December 6. Further, the Viceroy and his Political Department have conspired with the Princes in crushing the democratic elements in their enabling the Princes to bar India's way towards an Independent Sovereign Republic. It is strange that while on the one hand, the British are carrying on negotiations with the leaders, on the other hand they are putting new weapons into the hands of the police and' military to crush any movement that they may be faced with.

In Bihar, the adibasis who are a backward people are being recruited in the army on their giving a pledge that they will shoot Congressmen if ordered to. In certain places soldiers are being trained to practice shooting on the Gandhi cap as a target. British just don't mean anything when they say they are ready to leave India. They have created in this country a strong fifth column for them—the Muslim League of Mr. Jinnah and of Khan Bahadurs and the Princes and Dr. Ambedkar. That the British sufficiently rely on this fifth column is clear from the fact that even after years of endless talks and negotiations they have not yet been able to announce their decision to quit India.

The British game at present is to turn our fight for freedom into a domestic fight between the communities. The killings of Bihar, Bengal and Bombay were prompted by the British. The British are using the Muslim League as their tool in their game of divide and rule. It was the British who were the real enemies of the Hindus in Bengal and Muslims in Bihar and by talking of revenge for the happenings in Bengal and Bihar people would be just playing the British game. The Viceroy at the head of Political Department is behind the attempt to crush the Praja Mandals in the native states. All these British attempts to divide and rule in the provinces and to crush peoples' movements in the native states show that Britain is not prepared ever to surrender empire willingly.

The Viceroy gave to the Congress the assurance at the time the Muslim League entered the Interim Government that the League would work in a spirit of common responsibility and would cooperate with the Constituent

Assembly. But the League has not only behaved as the 'King's party' in the Central Government but also refused to cooperate in the task of Constitution making. The demonstration against Pandit Nehru in the tribal areas of the North-West Frontier was engineered by the British Imperialism which made the Muslim League their tool. The Governor of Sind has openly supported the Muslim League party. Every Englishman in India is a Muslim Leaguer, not that he loves but he finds the Leaguer a convenient tool in his hands. This becomes much clear when we pause to consider that neither the Hindu nor the Muslim community stands to gain anything at all by killing each other. The British have everything to gain in this internal turmoil. That has been ever their game. The communal riots, which had occurred in the country, were not communal riots but political riots. The decisions about such riots were not taken in this country but in England. Communalism was the biggest agent of British imperialism in this country. There were several communal organisations in the country of which the Muslim League was the most important. Communalism prevails not only in Muslim League but Hindu Mahasabha and Akali Dal stand on the same footing. They are all black sheep. The British have no power left in themselves and so they are exploiting communalism. They are trying to prolong their stay in India by befriending the Muslim League.

Khan Abdul Ghaffar Khan recently said that every Britisher has become a Muslim Leaguer. This the British are doing because they hope thereby to remain in India longer and to continue to exploit the country. Their game is to convert the fight for freedom into a fight between Muslims and Hindus, so that both Hindus and Muslim should feel a sense of insecurity and beg the British to remain in India for their protection. The British tried this game in Bengal by using the Muslim League as tools to attack their Hindu brethren.

The result of this was that misguided Hindus retaliated in Bihar. This was exactly what the British had planned. They had thought that in this way the Muslims of the Punjab would have retaliated for the Hindu excesses in Bihar and the Hindus of U.P. would have retaliated for the Muslim excesses in the Punjab and so on. They had planned to convert the whole country into one seething mass of shambles. They wanted this fire of communal riots which I characterise as political riots, to spread in the country. They wanted this fire to spread because they thought it will quell the national movement in the country. Fortunately their plan did not work, as saner people in both communities realised what was taking place. But in Bengal and Bihar, Muslims and Hindus were still suspecting their neighbours and even hesitating to go to their mohallas.

The British on the other hand moved about freely in the mohallas of both Hindus and Muslims. Is it not a matter of shame to all of us? The 1942 Movement and the heroic open fights of the Indian National Army have given a new life to people. Today India is more powerful than she was in 1942. The British realise more than ourselves the new India of today. I emphatically declare that if Pandit Nehru and Qaid-e-Azam Jinnah jointly ask Lord Wavell to quit, the latter cannot stay here for more than a single day, but Mr. Jinnah instead of joining Pandit Nehru, supports the British who have made the plight of the Mussalmans worse than even that of the Hindus. We demand from League to fight only for Bengal, Punjab, Sind etc., but they look towards the British and induce them not to quit India. Mr. Jinnah wants his Pakistan. But if he is serious about it, he must fight for it, he must make sacrifices for it, possibly die for it. But, there is the rub : it is exactly these things which Mr. Jinnah and his followers are never prepared to do.

Therefore, Mr. Jinnah shrieks his demand for Pakistan in the face of Mahatma Gandhi. But poor Gandhi is not in possession of Jinnah's sacred homelands. It is the blood-soaked heels of imperialism that possess and trample upon them that defile and desecrate them. The Congress can have no objection if Mr. Jinnah takes his "homelands" from the British. At least a part of India would then be free. But he will not take them, for he is not prepared to pay the price. He therefore wants to get along by blackmailing the Congress. But, in the end it will be the British who will have blackmailed Jinnah, If India is ever partitioned under the auspices of the Mother of Parliaments it would be in the interest of imperialism not to bestow a separate freedom upon the so-called Muslim nation of Hindustan. Ulster does no good to the Irish, but it is a British knife thrust into the very heart of Eire. The League's real politick is the ugly issue of imperialist machination and national treachery. Even Pakistan the Congress is prepared to concede provided the people of Pakistan desire a separate state by the free plebiscite held in a free India. But Mr. Jinnah wants neither mutual settlement nor impartial arbitration. He merely asks Mr. Churchill to stop India from marching on to freedom. That is all that Pakistan means to Mr. Jinnah. The British have ruled over India for a century but it never occurred to Mr. Jinnah to launch direct action against them. Now when his country has reached the threshold of freedom, he is threatening murder, loot and arson. He is angry with the Congress because it has dared to fight the British and has succeeded at last in forming a responsible Provisional Government at the Centre. But I am sure, Mr. Jinnah and Mr. Churchill cannot deflect the course of Indian freedom. The Centre and Provincial Governments must deal firmly with civil disturbances of any anti-social and anti-national character. At the same time these Governments must do everything possible to find out and satisfy all reasonable grievances and aspirations of the Muslims as a community.

The Congress organisation too must ceaselessly attempt to reach Muslims of all classes, particularly the Muslim masses, and explain to them fully its policies and activities. I see no alternative to a war with the British started by the constituent Assembly. I do not fear that such a war will be converted into a civil war though that will be the British game. To the British, even to Lord Pethick-Lawrence, a settlement between the Congress and the League is a settlement between two communities of India. I was amazed to read that statement coming from him. Either be is completely misinformed, or be deliberately says it. There are domestic quarrels in India. But in which country are there no domestic quarrels?

In this country they are promoted and magnified by the British. In order that there should be no quarrel and all communities live in peace and prosperity it was very necessary that there should be no British Raj. As long as the British remained in India there could be no peace. There are two forces in India : First the force of nationalism represented by the Congress, the Trade Union Congress the Students' Congress, Merchants Chambers of Commerce and so on a composite body not based on communities, but either on class interests or national interests. Secondly, the parallel development, very much helped by the British Government, of political forces based on communalism, like the Muslim League, the Scheduled Castes' Federation, Muslim Chambers of Commerce, Muslim Students' Congress, Muslim Trade Unions etc. Ultimately, there could be no compromise between these two.

There might be a temporary settlement but ultimately one of them would have to go under. India's future very much depends on whether the forces of nationalism win, or the forces of communalism win. If the forces of communalism win, it will be a British victory. To me the Muslim League is a British front. The League is in league with Britain. Mr. Jinnah is a deliberate traitor to his country, a Mir Jaffer of the present day. He believes that he can get what he wants from Britain. But Britain is not accustomed to handing over parcels of her Empire to its tools. There is no doubt that after she has made full use of Mr. Jinnah she will throw him into the dust-bin of discarded tools. Let me assert that India is one and undivided and every Indian is free to work anywhere he likes. It had come to my notice that Rulers will refuse to carry on talks with the Negotiation Committee of the Constituent Assembly on the pretext that it was not complete and was merely a toy. It was his reading that the Interim Government and the Constituent Assembly would not come out successful. The former was finished since the day Muslim League joined it. And now if the Princes come into the Constituent Assembly, they will come in not to help making a constitution but wrecking it. Now when we are knocking at the door of freedom we are face to face with two obstacles : Communalism and the States. On the one band British people say that they want to free India and are seeking a proper body to hand over the power and on the other hand they are conspiring with the Viceroy, the Governors and the Political Agents of the States and putting every possible obstacle in the way to freedom. But now we have become powerful enough to wrest administration from their hands within a few months. The repression of the Kak Govt. in Kashmere has been condemned by all and sundry. Due to some difficulties Congress has not been able to send its delegation to this place, but even then the country understands the Kashmere struggle as its own.

This time the fight will not be limited to British India, but the people of the states will also participate in that fight and we in our turn will support their struggle. In this struggle Jammu has lagged behind as it had been propagated that the struggle was carried on by Mussalmans to dethrone the Hindu Ruler. But it is an old trick and we are acquainted with it. I will declare emphatically that Rulers, they may be Hindus or Mussalmans, they are one, are neither Hindus nor Mussalmans. Today Maharaja of Kashmere is being helped by the Nawab of Bhopal. People are misled in the name of religion. Our struggle is of the masses for the establishment of democratic rule in the States. It is everyone's duty to take part in it, In Kashmere there is only one party of the State masses and it is the National Conference, led by Sheikh, Mohammad Abdulla who is rotting behind the prison bars. Jay Prakash Narayan's views about the World War II were expressed by him during 1943 when he was conducting the revolutionary activity from underground. They give an, adequate indication to the nationalist policy regarding the war. The futile controversy about the character of the War still goes on merrily in the backwaters of Indian life. The fifth columnists still insist naturally enough that it is a people's war. And those to whom controversy is the beginning and end of politics get terribly excited about it and argue, with words and sometimes with blows.

But the Indian people have no doubts about the nature of Britain's War and about those of their countrymen who support it. They do not require any longer to be told what fascism is or that this is their own War. British fascism has revealed itself to them in all its horrid brutality in the last year. Those who rot in prison, those who lost their dear ones in the countrywide murder by which the British re-established their "law and order", those whose homes were burnt and looted, whose women dishonoured, those who starve and die like rats on the streets all these people know too well what sort of a people's, war this is. A British general laid the decapitated heads of the Shahzadas of the House of Baber on a tray and sent them to the last Mughal Emperor, the father of the hapless princess as a gift from Queen Victoria. A century and a half later Tottenham boasted to American correspondents that he had bought enough sandalwood to burn the remains of Gandhi. India knows of these deeds and of other black deeds that fill the period from the beginning to the end (for the end i& near) of British rule and she does not need to be told by traitors, masquerading as Marxists, what fascism is. India is opposed to Nazism and Fascism. The Indian National Congress and the Indian Socialist movement, as represented by the All-India Congress Socialist Party, have declared it times without number, that they remain everlastingly opposed to these brutai systems. Before the beginning of the war and before many of the so-called democratic nations had decided to take a stand against Fascism, both Nationalist and Socialist India lined up with Republican Spain and Chiang's Republican China against Germany, Italy and Japan. Had India been free then, she would, no doubt, have played a great part in that international crisis, and it is possible that her intervention might have even prevented this world-war, or at least its spread to Asia. Free India and Free China would be a great guarantee against any aggression, and had these two ancient nations been free to work together, the history of our times might have been differently written. But while we are consistent as total opponents of Fascism, we are also total opponents of Imperialism. We are not prepared to live any longer under its subjection, and we are determined to destroy it root and branch.

At a time particularly when a world war is said to be fought to liberate oppressed peoples, we cannot but fight for our own liberation. We need offer no one any apology nor explanation as to why we long for freedom and why we fight to acquire it. One may perhaps be troubled by the consideration that our fight with the British might weaken the United Nation's was against the Axis. If that is so, the responsibility is not only ours to consider the problem. It is for the United Nations also to give active thought to it. For our part, we do not wish to embarrass or great difficulties for the United Nations. But we cannot help if our war of liberation comes in the way. If it does, it is not our fault, but theirs. They claim to be fighting to restore freedom to humanity : why should the liberation of one-fifth of humanity come in their way? If the United Nations are truly fighting for the aims they profess, the Indian struggle for freedom should not hinder but help them. If it hinders them, it is only proof of the fact that the basis of their war is false, that there is dire discrepancy between their words and deeds, and ideals and practice. Our struggle would, therefore, render an incidental service to the United Nations by forcing them to bring their deeds to accord with their professions, thereby ensuring a Juster Peace. If the British are fighting for a better world, where wealth and opportunity, power and prestige, education and culture, and the good things of life shall be more rationally and equitably distributed, they are going about it the wrong way, if they shoot innocent women and children of India burn and loot houses and try to crush in other fascist ways, the greatest fight for freedom that ever stirred this old Asiatic continent. We do not wish to fight them or harm them, nor do we wish any evil to the British people. We merely wish to fight the empire and destroy it, because it is the enemy of our freedom and happiness and prosperity.

After we are free we shall march shoulder to shoulder with them in an assault on all kinds of oppression and brutality Nazi, imperialist, capitalist. Only then we would build a New World Order. The British must open out their minds and think for themselves. If they continue blindly and meekly to gulp down any propaganda that their rulers feed them with, they would have fought and died in vain, for their children would inherit the same vicious world of tyranny and inequality, poverty and misery,. wars and armaments. So far as India is concerned, I must emphasize that our freedom largely depends upon our own strength and resources. Hopeless inaction which feeds upon the hope of outside help is suicidal politics. No outside help by itself can free us. It is fantastic to believe that Subhas' army, no matter how large, can defeat the Allied armies in India. If any army can defeat them it may possibly be the Japanese. But, if the Japanese defeat the British in India, they would not quietly hand over to us whatever the understanding between Tojo and Subhas. We must be ready in the event of an Axis-Allied clash in India to seize power ourselves. Only if we are ready to make this attempt can outside help, such as Subhas' National Army be of value to us and Tojo be prevented from annexing India. It is difficult to say how far Subhas himself is conscious of this aspect of India's national strategy. This brings me to the question, what should we do when the war enters our doors. British policy has made the average Indian so anti-British that he is prepared if not to welcome the Japanese, at least to remain indifferent to the Anglo-Japanese conflict. This indifference will be our death. We must endeavour to remove it and in its place develop a positive policy of action. In the areas where war is waged or which the Japanese occupy or where they infiltrate, the foreigner's civil rule will weaken or come to an end. In these areas we must establish a Swaraj Government.

In the name of this Government we must appeal to retreating units of the Indian Army to stay behind and become the people's army. From this day we mast prepare to establish such a Government in the Eastern Province which in the course of time might embrace the entire nation. The war has entered its fifth year. The destruction of life and happiness that it has caused can never be repaired. The interests of the common man of both sides demand that the war end immediately. But it cannot be ended by Churchills and Roosevelts, Hitlers and Tojos. Even if they cried halt to the present butchery, it would only be to prepare new and more terrible weapons for more terrible butchery in the future, Allied plans for the post-war world, of which the barest glimpse has been vouchsafed to the common man, picture the same old world of privileged class and national : tyranny, capitalist rivalry and chaos which brought two devastating wars in a generation and will surely bring a third. The war can be truly ended by the common people of the world. But their voice is stifled. Russia which could have become the champion of the common man has herself suppressed him at home and disowned him abroad by truckling to the imperialists and super capitalists of Anglo America. Labour throughout the world has become the camp-follower of the capitalist class and has thus sold its conscience and forfeited its leadership of society and of the new world. In these circumstances India alone actively represents the aspirations and promptings of the disinherited and dispossessed of the Earth. India's fight for freedom is at once anti-imperialist (and therefore also anti-fascist, for imperialism is the parent of fascism) and a drive to end the war through the intervention of the common man.

Neither Allied nor Axis victory is our aim, nor do we pin our hope no either. We work for the defeat both of imperialism and Fascism by the common people of the world and by our struggle we show the way to the ending of wars and the liberation of the black, white and yellow.

Speech at Jamshedpur (Bihar) 1940

"I have been charged with trying to impede the production of munitions and other supplies essential to the efficient prosecution of the War, and with trying to influence the conduct and attitude of the public in a manner prejudicial to the defence of British India and the efficient prosecution of the war. I plead guilty to these charges. "These charges, however, do not constitute a guilt for me but a duty which I discharge, regardless of the consequences. That they also constitute an offence under certain laws of the Foreign Government, established by force in this country, does not concern me. The object of these laws is diametrically opposed to the object of nationalist India, of which I am but a humble representative. That we should come in conflict is only natural. "My country is not party to this War in any manner, for it regards both German Nazism and British Imperialism as evils and enemies. It finds that both the sides in this War are driven by selfish ends of conquest and domination, exploitation and oppression. Great Britain is fighting not to destroy Nazism, which it has nurtured, but to curb a rival, whose might can no longer be allowed to grow unchallenged. It is fighting to maintain its dominant place in the world and to preserve its imperial power and glory. As far as India is concerned, Great Britain is fighting to perpetuate the Indian Empire. "Plainly, India can have no truck with such a War. No Indian can permit the resources of his country to be utilised to buttress up imperialism and to be converted through the processes of the War into the chains of his country's slavery.

The Congress, the only representative voice of nationalist India, has already pointed out this sacred duty to the people of this country. 1, as an humble servant of the Congress, have only tried to fulfil this duty. "The British Government, on the other hand, in utter disregard for Indian opinion, has declared India a belligerent power and is utilising Indian men, money and materials for a war to which we have pledged our uncompromising opposition. This is in the nature of an aggression against India, no less serious in the circumstances than German aggression against Poland. India cannot but resist this aggression. It, therefore, becomes the patriotic duty of every Indian to oppose the attempt of the British Government to use the country's resources for its imperialist end. Thus the charge framed against me of trying to impede the efficient prosecution of the War is only the fulfilment of a patriotic duty. That the British Government should consider, what is a duty for patriotic India to be an offence, only proves further its imperialist character. "Regarding the speech for which I am being prosecuted, I cannot say how far it succeeded in achieving its ends. But nothing would please me more than to learn that it did have some success in impeding the effective prosecution of the War. I shall deem the heaviest punishment well earned if I am found to have succeeded in this. "As for the charge of endangering the defence of British India, I think the irony of it cannot be lost upon us. A slave has no obligation to defend his slave. His only obligation is to destroy his bondage I hope we shall know how to defend ourselves when we have achieved our freedom. "I consider it fortunate that I have been prosecuted for a Jamshedpur speech.

This important industrial centre, which I, consider the most important in the country is peculiarly backward politically and from the point of view of the labour movement. I shall derive some satisfaction in prison, where I expect inevitably to find myself, from the thought that my arrest and incarceration for a speech delivered there has attracted to that city, the notice of the political and labour leaders of my country. It seems scandalous to me that the country's most vital resources should be so wasted in a War to which we are so firmly opposed. And it seems no less scandalous to me that while Labour throughout the country should be reacting vigorously to the conditions created by the War, Jamshedpur Labour should carry on as if nothing extraordinary has happened. May at least, the demand for a war bonus gain some momentum from this prosecution. "Before concluding I should like to add that at least, as an Englishman, you should not misunderstand me. I should make it clear that in impeding prosecution of the War, I have no desire to help Germany or to see Germany victorious. I desire the victory neither of Imperialism nor of Nazism.

Yet, as a Congressman and a Socialist I have nothing but goodwill for the British and German people. If India's opposition to Britain's Imperialist War ensures a Nazi victory, it is for the British people to decide, whether they would have Nazi hegemony or victory with real democracy at home and in India. If the people of Great Britain remove their present rule and denounce imperialism with its capitalist rulers, not only India but the freedom loving people of the whole world would exert themselves to see the defeat of Nazism and the victory of freedom and democracy. In the present circumstances, however, India has no alternative but to fight and end British imperialism. Only in that manner can it contribute to the peace and progress of the world. I am conscious, Sir, that I have made you task easier by this statement. I do not regret it. "In the end I think you for your courtesy and consideration during this trial." He gave vent to his feelings about the Quit India Movement as follows.

The 'Quit India' movement of 1942 had been launched to, rid India of British imperial power, but that struggle did not achieve its end though it released new forces which have taken the country far towards its goal. One of the essential reasons though not the only one, of the outbreak of Great Rebellion was the rise of a belief in the mass mind that the ruling class or power is played out and at the end of its tether. The course of the world war in the months immediately prior to August 1942 had been such that the Indian people had come to believe that the British Empire was crumbling and they had to but deal it a blow for it to totter entirely to the ground. In August 1942 not only did the war situation contribute to the creation of a suitable psychological atmosphere but also the fact that the Congress stood in all its power at the head of the people. The people had faith in their leaders and when the call went forth they responded with confidence and enthusiasm. We really won the first round of the battle in as much as over large territories of the country the civil rule of the British aggressor was completely uprooted. The masses have learnt from experience that the imposing edifice of the police and magistracy and law courts which goes by the name of British Raj is bent a house of cards when they hurt against either their collective power. This lesson is not likely to be forgotten and it constitutes the starting point for the next offensive. Let me mention a very significant incident about the August Movement, namely, the strike by the police at Jamshedpur. The authorities were alarmed and sent out British soldiers, to control the situation. Some arrests were also made, but care was taken by the authorities not to give sufficient publicity and importance to the incident. It was a matter of pride that a tyrannical and loyal department like the police could also co-operate with the freedom struggle. I hope that when the time comes, the police all over would show the same spirit. What happened in 1942 in this country does not often happen in any country always. It was a rare event, but it was not fully utilised. If we had to make the British quit, our leaders should have pointed out to us the method of achieving that object. On the one hand we gave a challenge to the British Government, on the other no programme was placed before us. Except Pandit Jawaharlal Nehru, no leader gave a thought to the problem or admitted the mistake. They only tried to defend themselves by arguing that they had vested the leadership of the Congress in Gandhiji. But it was their duty to give us the lead. Their argument is without substance. Was that the proper attitude at the time of revolution? Was it an act of wisdom? They should have formulated a programme. I cannot accept the argument that our High Command knows everything and that we need not think and prepare for the struggle. About forty thousand persons lost their lives during the August Movement.

The leaders are responsible for that great sacrifice of human lives. The people did not know how to conduct the fight. They were in dark and now the leaders find fault with those who showed light to the people. It was their duty to show the light. We are charged with having defied non-violence. I have as much faith in non-violence as Maulana Azad, Maulana Azad has much faith in violence as I have. I understand Mahatmaji's non-violence. I bow before it. But since I do not possess that much soul-force, I think it easy to fight with guns. And after all, what does Congress want? Did not Maulana Azad say once that if a National Government was established only with limited political power he would fight with guns against the Japanese? Are not Japanese lives human lives? Are only British lives human lives, so that to use arms against them is to defy non-violence? The Congress itself expressed its willingness to defy nonviolence on two occasions since 1942. In my opinion, non violence is being utilized and exploited for power politics. I feel I must say a few words about the noise the British authorities have made about the violence committed in the course of the Revolution. There was some violence indeed under extreme provocation, but it was remarkably little as compared with the magnitude of the rising and the staggering manifestation of individual and collective non-violence.

It is not realised, perhaps, that thousands of British and Indian employees of the foreign power were for some days literally at the mercy of the masses, who took compassion of their foes and spared them their lives and property. And what of the cool, sublime courage of those thousands of young and old who received the enemy's bullets on their chests with the Rag of revolution in their hands and "*Inqlab Zindabad*" on their lips. Have the British a word of praise for this courage? Some controversy has been going on about the question whether the 1942 struggle was started by the Congress and whether it could be called a Congress movement. It had been claimed by some, who went in 1943 so far as to suggest that a rump A.I.C.C. should meet to withdraw the August Resolution, that since Gandhiji and Congress leaders were arrested before they could make a formal declaration of war, 1942 struggle was not a Congress struggle at all.

According to the logic of this argument no struggle, if the British were to arrest the leaders in time, could ever have the formal authority and sanction of the Congress. What is it that those who deny the authority of the Congress to the struggle would desire to have happened on the 9th of August after the cowardly attack on our leaders? What do they think was the desire of Mahatma Gandhi and the Working Committee in the event of their arrest? Would the detractors of the struggle have been happy if there had been no reaction to the arrest of the leaders, if the country had calmly bowed its head before the imperialist jack-boot? Or was it expected that only protest meetings should have been held demanding the release of arrested leaders (as was advocated by certain erstwhile Revolutionaries), and when they were not released, further meetings should have been held, till the audience became too disgusted to attend, after which the co-protestants" could have gone to sleep with a clear conscience. If this be so, where was the sense of that brave resolution and those brave words that were poured forth from the lips of the greatest in the land at the Bombay A.I.C.C? If on the other hand this be not so, and if the people were expected to rise in answer to the British offensive, if, indeed, the arrest of the leaders was a signal for a mass struggle, then where is the grace and fairness in decrying the present struggle as uncongress and un-authorised? When you are on the war path, it is foolish to expect the enemy to allow you the leisure to complete all the formalities required by a peace-time constitution. It therefore appears to me to be mean and cowardly to attempt to show that the National struggle that started on that 9th of August, 1942, had not the authority and sanction of the Congress. It is a different matter when we turn to the question whether the programme of that struggle was authorised by Gandhiji or the Working Committee.

Here we are in the realm of facts and not principles, and political ethics. And about the facts there is no dispute. It is well know that the Working Committee had not prepared a plan of action but merely requested Gandhiji to assume command of the struggle. Gandhiji in his turn had also no plan of action. He had sketched the merest outlines in his address to the A.I.C.C. That outline and his articles in the Harijan were all that the people had before them and they formed the basis of that detailed programme which was prepared by those Congressmen who were left behind, and who hastily met in Bombay to lay foundations of that "illegal" Congress organization. There was no room for murder in that programme, nor for any form of violence to the person. If murders were committed in India as they were, 99 percent of them were acts of the British fascists and hooligans and not more than one per cent were of an infuriated and sorely tried people. Creation of deadlock and paralysing and dislocation of British rule by all non-violent means was the sheet anchor of that programme and "go to the fullest extent under Ahimsa" the star to steer it by. While it is true that there were some who in the name of non-violence attempted to disown certain parts of the programme, which they had themselves sanctioned previously and which even such a high authority as Shree Kishorelal Mashruwala did not have the heart to condemn or ask the people to desist from, there is no doubt that the conscious basis of the programme which the Congress organizations followed since August 1942 was nonviolence, as interpreted by the people in authority during that period. They who prepared the programme have never disowned the responsibility. But that as it may, to fasten the August programme on Gandhiji is a piece of perjury of which only the British ruling class can be capable. Magnificent was the battle which India gave to the enemy in 1942.

Nothing like it had ever happened before in this our long suffering and suppressed country. The Rebellion, no doubt, was suppressed for the comment. But I hope, you will agree with me that it had been suppressed only for the moment. This should cause us no surprise. As a matter of fact, had the very first assault been successful and had it completely crushed imperialism, that in reality would have been a matter of surprise. The very fact that the enemy himself admitted that the Rebellion came pretty near destroying his power, shows bow successful was the first phase of our National Revolution. And how was the first phase suppressed? Was it the Military power of the enemy, his unmitigated reign of goondaism, looting, arson and murder that did the job? No. It is wrong to consider the "Revolt" as having been "suppressed". The history of all Revolutions shows that a Revolution is not an event. It is a phase, a social process. And during the evolution of a revolution, tides and ebbs are normal. Our Revolution went through the period of low water, so soon rather than to higher heights and from victory to victory not because the superior physical force of the Imperialist aggressors intervened, but because of two important reasons. Firstly there was no efficient organisation of the national revolutionary forces that could function and give effective lead to the mighty forces that were released. The Congress, though a great organisation, was not tuned to the pitch to which revolution was to rise. The lack of organisation was so considerable that even important congressmen were not aware of the progress of the Revolt, and till late in course of the rising it remained a matter of debate in accordance with the Congress programme. In the same connection should be mentioned the regrettable fact that quite a considerable number of influential Congressmen failed to attune their mental attitude to the spirit of this "last fight for freedom".

The earnestness, the urgency, the determination that marked the attitude of leaders like Mahatma Gandhi, Dr. Rajendra Prasad or Sardar Patel failed to reflect in the minds and hearts of all Congress leaders. Secondly, after the first phase of the Rising was over there was no further programme placed before the people. After, they had completely destroyed the British Raj in their areas, the people considered their task fulfilled, and went back to their homes not knowing what more to do. Nor was it their fault. The failure was ours, we should have supplied them with a programme for the next phase. When this was not done, the Revolt came to a standstill and the phase of the ebb began. This situation was created many days before the British soldiers arrived in sufficient numbers to push back yet further the receding ranks of the revolt. What programme should have been placed before the people in the second phase? The answer is suggested by the nature of revolutions. A revolution is not only a destructive process, it is at the same time a great constructive force. No revolution could succeed if it only destroyed. If it should survive, it must create an authority to replace the one it has destroyed. Our Revolution too having accomplished over large territories of the country the negative task of destruction, called for a positive programme.

The people who destroyed the objects and means of administration of the foreign power and drove away its agents should have set up in their areas their own units of Revolutionary Government and created their own police and militia. Had this been done it would have released such an unprecedented volume of energy and opened up such a vast field for constructive work that the waves of the Revolution would have mounted higher and higher till if the rising was countrywide the imperialist power had been broken and the people had seized supreme authority throughout the land. The lack of efficient organisation and of a complete programme of National Revolution : these were two causes of the, downward course of the first phase of the Revolution. The movement of 1942 had revolutionised the spirit of the Country. Enthusiasm, courage and the desire to be free were, present in an abundant measure. But that was not enough. What we needed was organisation. Let me cite the instance of Ballia district in the 1942 days to stress the value of organisation. In that district, British power had ceased to exist for a few days. The people were really free and the district authorities were in a way prisoners of the people. But only a few days later a contingent of three hundred soldiers not only restored British power but committed excesses which led to complete demoralisation. Leaders had toured the district and paid tribute to its heroic deeds. What Ballia did as a district was done by the province of Bihar as a whole. But no where were the people able to retain the acquired power for long. I would undertake a tour of Ballia to find out the cause of the defeat of the people by a small force. The mistakes that had been made should not be repeated. The British Cabinet Mission proposals do not deliver freedom to India but enable the British Government to play the mediator between the Congress and the Muslim League. The British have created the so-called differences and they are still trying to exploit them. The Muslim League may have a large following among

Muslims of India today, but the League is still the ally and friend of the British. The Cabinet Mission, is asking the Congress to swallow its principles and compromise with the League leader who in 1942 unashamedly declared that 'Quit India' Movement was not against the British but against the Muslims to perpetuate Hindu domination. How could the Congress settle with such a leader? I feel confident that the Congress can break the League's hold on the Muslims by its going direct to the Muslim masses. Instead of making this direct approach we are trying to negotiate with the leader of the Muslim League whom we know to be the friend of our enemies. I feel the acceptance of the Constituent Assembly scheme also foreshadows danger. The Constituent Assembly proposed by the British is far from our original idea which was given to us by our leader Pandit Nehru. This Constituent Assembly is the creation of the British and it can never bring us the freedom that we have been fighting for. The British Government may promise to accept the constitution drawn up by the Constituent Assembly but then the British Government themselves will pull the wires in such a manner as not to allow us to frame a constitution that we all desire for a free and independent India.

Whenever a difference of opinion arises between the Congress and the League in the Constituent Assembly, and differences are bound to arise, then we have to go to the British Government for a solution. And do you think we can , expect fair play from the British in such a situation? If on the contrary the Constituent Assembly is the outcome of the strength of the people we can solve all our difficulties by an appeal to our people. The only thing we can do is to tell the British Government that we do not want such a restricted and curbed Constituent Assembly. We shall weaken ourselves, if we were to accept the British Government's proposals. The acceptance of offices in the provinces has weakened us considerably. If we accept these proposals, we shall further weaken ourselves. The course of negotiations adopted by the Working Committee in my opinion has not led us to our goal. Why then should we not abandon such negotiations and prepare for another struggle? There is only one way open to us and that is to strengthen the Congress organisation and when we are sure of our own inherent strength start a fight with the British Government, compel them to quit India and make them understand that they have to transfer power and that can be done only by negotiating with the Congress. The complete overthrow of imperialism should be our objective and we must keep this steadfastly in view. There can be no compromise on this issue. Either we win or we lose. And lose we shall not. Not only because we are determined ceaselessly to work for victory, but also because powerful world forces are drawing the doom of imperialism and fascism ever nearer and nearer. I do not believe that the formal results of the last war would settle the fate of the world.

War is a strange alchemist, and in its hidden chambers are such forces and powers brewed and distilled that they tear down the plans of the victorious and vanquished alike. No peace-conference at the end of the World War I decided that four mighty Empires of Europe and Asia should fall into dust the Russian, the German, the Austrian and Ottoman. Nor, was the Russian, the German, the Turkish revolutions decreed by Lloyd George, Clemenceau or Wilson. Throughout the world where men are fighting, dying and suffering, the alchemist is at work, just as be is in India where he already let loose a mighty social upheaval in 1942. It is force such as we represent that will determine the future of the world. Can we doubt that revolutionary forces are stirring everywhere? Can we believe that millions of people are undergoing unutterable suffering without a thought for the future? Can we believe that millions are satisfied with the lies that their rulers daily feed them with? No, it cannot be so. Having therefore definitely fixed our vision on the goal of total victory, we have to march ahead. What concretely must we do? What does a general do when he loses or wins a battle? He consolidates and prepares for the next battle. Rommel stopped at El Alamein after his great victory to consolidate and prepare. Alexander too prepared and he turned his serious defeat into a resounding victory. Ours was not even a defeat. We really won the first round of the fight in as much as over large territories of the country the civil rule of the British aggressor was completely uprooted. We are told the British are quitting India. I saw no signs of it in my recent tour in the Punjab and in Kashmere. I saw no signs of it in the way the League has been brought into the Interim Government. The Congress is supposed to be, helping the British to pack their bedding but it looks as if the British during their 200 years in India, have collected so much that the bedding takes years to pack. I don't think British are going to quit India willingly. They will have to be forced to do so. I think it is a dis-service to the country to dull it with false hopes. Granting for a moment that there is possibility of freedom being achieved through the Constituent Assembly, I still hold that it is the duty of the Congress leaders to keep the people ready for direct action in the event of the expectations not being fulfilled. Let them have the alternative string of the bow ready also.

The British are prepared for all eventualities. We should also be prepared for all eventualities. Let not their mistake of 1942 (unpreparedness on the part of India) be repeated. We had then taken a momentous decision but people who were unprepared did not know what to do. Supposing tomorrow the Congress finds that after getting the Muslim League and the Princes into the Constituent Assembly and for the purpose of keeping them in, they have to, make impossible compromises, the Congress may have to come out, once again to the people, would they like the Indian people to be found unprepared once again? There are only two ways of settling the Indian problem, one way is the way of peaceful settlement and the other the method of revolution. I myself prefer a peaceful settlement. Even the British are bound to gain far more by that method than if the Indian question is settled by a revolution. But it seems to me that a peaceful settlement is possible only if India would give up her claim to full freedom. I am convinced in the event of a revolutionary outbreak there will be no civil war. In fact revolution seems to me to be an effective remedy against the dangers of a civil war which in my opinion is after all the result of a mad cry for loaves and fishes. The present Constituent Assembly is not a true Constituent Assembly as it was not brought into being by the people themselves but by the British Government. The method of its composition and other details were set by a foreign Government. Such an Assembly, therefore, cannot be a sovereign body formed by a free people. The present situation is one of transition and rapid change.

Congressmen have decided to sit in the British-sponsored Constituent Assembly. An interim government under the British Viceroy is functioning. This government however, cannot be a free government of a free country till the Viceroy and the British armed forces and other British personnel quit India. To beg that this government be allowed to function as a free government is to beg the question. Those who have he power to hand over power at their pleasure, have also the power to take it back at their pleasure. Therefore, let us not be duped by the talk of the interim government being "in effect" the government of a free India. Could then the so-called Constituent Assembly bring us freedom? In other words, could that Assembly declare India an independent republic and enforce that declaration? Could it, for instance, appoint a provisional government and force the Viceroy to hand over all power to it and quit India? Could the Provisional Government pack off all British soldiers and military and civil officers to Britain? Could that government tear up the strangle-hold of British finance over this country? Could the Constituent Assembly dissolve itself and empower the free Provisional Government, after the British had quit, to convene a real Constituent Assembly elected by the people oil the basis of unrestricted adult suffrage? Could the proposed Constituent Assembly take all these steps, everyone of which is essential to lead India to full freedom and democracy? It would be a grave folly to suppose that in the existing circumstances and with the present co-relation of forces it could ever be possible for the present Constituent Assembly to take any of these steps and achieve any of these objectives.

But even if we were to suppose for a moment that the Assembly could make this attempt, the British would be certain to bar its way. Then if the Assembly were sincere and honest it would have to accept the British challenge and invoke its mass sanctions in order to enforce its will. The Viceroy who would have called the Assembly to begin with would then step in and order its dissolution. Thus an all-out war of independence would ensue out of which should emerge a real Constituent Assembly of the people and a free, democratic and united Republic of India. The Constituent Assembly, however, is not very likely to follow these steps.

Aware of what Pandit Nehru has described as the compulsion of facts, i.e., aware of the limitations of its sovereignty, aware of its weaknesses, aware of the British stooges and enemies of freedom and democracy in its ranks, aware of the presence of the British Army and British Viceroy aware of all this and more, the Constituent Assembly might choose to tread what I am sure is going to be described as the path of realism. In other words the Assembly might decide to make compromise after compromise producing in the end neither freedom, nor democracy, nor national unity. So, the nation, thwarted and disillusioned, would have to turn once again to the path from which it is being misled today the path of revolutionary action, the path of resistance and struggle, the straight but difficult path of freedom. Thus we see that in either case, i.e., whether the Constituent Assembly "succeeds" or whether it fights and "fails" a struggle for freedom is inevitable. Anyone who has a correct appreciation of the present co-relation of forces in this country should not find it difficult to accept this conclusion.

Today, it is still possible for British imperialism to face us with the "compulsion of facts". Till this compulsion is removed by revolutionary action, freedom would be an illusion. Nor can any one expect to change the facts of the present situation by argument, concession and diplomatic finesse. We therefore reach the conclusion and it will bear repetition that the struggle for freedom does not cease with the acceptance of the British constitutional proposals. That struggle will continue. In fact, the character and scope of that struggle will become deeper and wider. To the struggle for liberty will be added the struggle for national unity and bread. The struggle for national unity is bound to acquire a special importance with the acceptance of the British proposals. Secondly, the impleading constitutional changes are bound to bring to the fore, economic and class issues. The form of Swaraj, the question, "Swaraj for whom?" will no longer remain academic or remote questions, but will become matters of immediate and urgent importance demanding immediate answers and affecting all our politics not theoretically but practically. That is the struggle for bread, always an integral part of the struggle for freedom, will move up to the front line and acquire an importance no less than any, other. I should make it clear that these are not three separate struggles, but aspects or parts of one common struggle of the people. At different stages, one or the other aspect receives, greater or less emphasis, but as the present constitutional plans develop, all these are likely to assume equal importance. As matters stand, the common struggle of the people would have to be waged in the context of a Constituent Assembly, possibly an interim government, and later on in the context of a Union government, Group and Provincial governments. The Congress, of which we are a part, seems likely to be associated with all these developments.

As such, it seems certain that the Congress struggle for liberty, unity and bread will be conducted, if at all, through constitutional and state machinery. Already the Congress is being converted into a parliamentary party. If this process goes on to its logical conclusion, there can be little doubt that the Congress must fail of achieve much success in this three-fold struggle. A constitutional and administrative machinery might be of use in certain circumstances but situated as we are, the people's struggle must be carried on mainly outside the Legislatures and the portals of Government departments. To carry on this struggle is our job today-the job of all fighters for freedom. Where we failed in 1942, we would succeed now and succeed in making the British quit. I can tell you that British will not quit India unless they are pushed out. His views on revolution were as follows :

Congress leaders have been giving the impression that freedom is round the corner. I entirely agree that freedom is round the corner but let me emphasize that before we achiever freedom an all-out struggle is necessary. The obstacles put in our path cannot he removed except by a revolutionary struggle, unless of course, we compromise on principles. A revolution has therefore become inevitable. If tomorrow the Muslim League and the princes enter the

Constituent Assembly, they would start pulling wires under instructions from the British. I have been against an understanding with the British Government from the very start. But when the interim Government was formed some people thought that India had been put on the path of freedom. Subsequent events, however, belied the expectations. When the British Government gave its latest interpretation about the enforcement of the decisions of the Constituent Assembly the last hope vanished. If the British Government did not accept the decisions of the Constituent Assembly then there would be no way open for India except to fight for freedom. I welcome Pandit Nehru's resolution moved in the Constituent Assembly. If the leaders keep this ideal, the Constituent Assembly will.... become the front for the future struggle. When the Constituent Assembly has prepared a constitution for free India, and the British refuse to accept it for the whole country, the President of the Assembly will ask the Viceroy to quit India. This will be a signal for the struggle. It will be struggle between a free India and the British imperialism. This revolutionary struggle which is inevitable to come would be much more extensive than the 1942 movement. There is no question of the constitution framed by the Constituent Assembly being approved by the British Parliament. We should not ask or wait for their approval, but go ahead with our decisions and enforce them. In the enforcement of those decisions, I visualise a conflict with the British if in the meanwhile, we do not give up the fundamentals. How shall we wage this struggle? By terrorism? By sporadic violence? By fratricide? By dacoities? By incendiarism Obviously no. At the present moment the only manner in which we can wage this struggle is by forgoing mass sanctions.

The creation of mass sanctions includes first, the psychological preparation of the masses for a struggle, second, the building up of organizations of the masses, such as peasant and labour unions, volunteer crops, student and youth organizations, village republics and weavers co-operative and myriad other organizations which would help in different ways to develop the collective strength and consciousness of the people. To all this must be added the overall task of strengthening and vitalising the Congress organisation and renewing and extending its effective contacts with the people. A full picture of the task of creating mass sanctions, in so far as it relates to the present phase of our struggle, is laid out below in the section dealing with our programme. Here let me illustrate my meaning of the term "mass sanctions" in the context of national unity. National unity cannot be imposed from above. It must be based on unity at the bottom. Such unity can be brought about, or at least a considerable success be gained in the task, by patient political work among the Muslims, by the development of economic or class organisations, such as labour unions, Kisan Sabhas, 'Weavers' co-operatives, by social reform among the Hindus by encouraging common cultural and recreational activities, by strengthening those forces in Society that by their very nature work for national unity, such as the need for a strong frontier, the need for a coordinated plan of economic development, the need for a common economic system, the need for a common medium of speech, etc., and in many other ways. The first requirement, I need hardly stress, is for every freedom fighter to be completely free from communal or caste prejudice or arrogance, and to practise in his personal life the principle of the equality of all human beings. The mass sanctions for national unity are particular weak at the moment. Their development is a foremost priority on the list of our present tasks. Lest there should be misunderstanding I must point out that the work of developing mass Sanctions cannot be split into compartments and Sections for each objective created separately from the others.

The political, economic and social sanctions overlap, interpenetrate and supplement each other and form part of one broad movement of the people. Whereas in our previous fights with the British, our programme had been to fill the jails, in the coming fight we are not fill the jails. We have strength enough to arrest our enemies. We should put into prison all those who are the enemies of the revolution. This I admit is not an ordinary task. If the fight followed the disagreement of the British. Government with the decisions of the Constituent Assembly then our fight would be on a very high plan in the eyes of the people of the world, The Premiers could at once order some magistrates and police officials to arrest the Governors and other anti-India officials and put them into prison. If we start making preparations now we would be completely ready within a few months. I want you to start preparations in such a way that when the bugle for the fight was sounded the people should be able to begin the work simultaneously and to end the British Raj at once every sign of it. We should at once capture all Government offices an& establish people's Raj there with the help of those officials who would be willing to work for the new Government. All pro-British officials be driven out and new officials appointed in their place. The new Government should start collecting taxes to carry on the new administration. It should also recruit police force and army and equip them all imaginable weapons including guns made by local iron-smiths. You will say that it is a difficult task. I must say, however, that it would be an easy task because I know the hollowness of the British Government. If you can bring about such a revolution, in the whole country it would be beyond the power of the British to reconquer the country. With the commencement of the revolution there should be a countrywide strike. If such a fight continued for three months the British Government would end all over the country for ever and the world would not merely watch the events in India. The coming struggle is going to be on the lines of the 1942 movement. All college and school students must come out and participate in the fight. All mills, factories and other places must go on strike. No one should go to the jails, but on the other hand arrest the Governors, the collectors and all,' those who sided with the British Government.

Every 'thana', 'tehsil' and district should be occupied and people's Raj established. If the fight continued for three months, they could easily defeat the British Government in this country. The British Government is on its last legs and it is time to strike. I ask the students to keep the coming struggle in the forefront and adjust their decisions accordingly. The final struggle for freedom is not going to be a child's play, but a fierce and grim fight, much more fiercer than the 1857 and 1942 struggles. We would not only have to sacrifice in thousands, but in lakhs. Our slogan should be "Do or Die." By a struggle in India, we have so far understood the filling up of jails. What I mean by proposing the arrest of Governors is to debunk that idea. We have left that stage behind. At a certain stage, jail-going is necessary when the people are crowed down and so on. We had a leader who put self-respect in us, by giving us the programme of jail-going. But we have left such a stage behind. In the next struggle, if anybody has to go to jail, it will be the other party and not us. In a conflict, naturally the British will put us in jail in some places, and we will put them in jail in others. For instance, if there was an uprising in a particular district and the collector there decided to go over to the side of the revolutionaries, he would administer the district on behalf of the revolutionaries. If not, he would try to arrest the revolutionaries while the revolutionaries would try to get him arrested. But the arrest of Governors is not the main programme. The main programme is the rising of the people general strikes and so on. It will be a struggle not like the old struggles a slave India fighting for freedom but a free India fighting to protect her freedom from aggressors. In that case, there is no question of jail-going and instead of our being put into jail, those who come in our way whether they are Governors or British-officials or Indian officials will have to be dealt with. Something parallel to the American revolution. The whole countryside, where the British type of Nazi Hell wag let loose in 1942, is seething with the most intense discontent, anger and thirst for revenge.

The people have merely to understand that powerful preparations are afoot to, take courage again and to enter the plans and schemes of the next offensive, with active, coordinated and disciplined work, it will be wholly favourable for the next assault. The question of the next offensive is linked up with the question of the positive task of the Revolution i.e., the establishment of the units of the Revolutionary Governments. With later question is bound up the question of violence and maintained armed forces. They must strengthen their organization and carry ceaseless war unto the enemy. No suffering, no sacrifice should be counted too great, no controversy, no temptation, no false hope should deflect our course. All avenues of struggle are open to us. Whatever be our faiths and creeds, whatever our methods and weapons, our course is clear. Every fighter for freedom is free to choose his own method. Those who believe in similar methods should work together as a disciplined group. And the least that those who follow a different path should do is not to come in the way of one another and waste their energies in mutual recrimination. Where "Do or Die" is the mantram of action, there is no room for recrimination whatever. We must offer resistance to the British power in every shape or form possible, in accordance with whatever creed or programme we believe in. I would call this our minimum programme for the present : organisation, propaganda, overt resistance. In addition to, this we have the whole wide field of preparation : our work among students and labour must continue, our contacts with the Army and the services must be maintained and developed, our preparations for dislocation must go on. A rising of the nature of that of the 9th of August, but on a bigger scale and better organized and directed, should be our goal. Our every effort should take us a step nearer that goal. Fighters have therefore the job their most important job in the circumstances to create feelings of resentment and anger in the needy and starving and to turn those feelings against the foreign power which is at bottom responsible for all this misery. Let the hungry create a situation in which normal British administration becomes impossible. Let us tell them not only tell but help them to do it to seize food where they can get it.

In the rural areas we should prevent grains from being sent out and distribute stocks through village panchayats or similar agencies (taking care to keep away from Government or pro-Government bodies'. Fighters, organised as guerillas, should seize grain from Government depots and similar places and distribute them among the needy. Forcible seizure by Government of crops should be resisted. In the cities and towns too the passivity and despair of the hungry and needy should be turned into resentment and anger and given concrete, active shape of demonstration and direct action. I want people to be prepared to sacrifice their lives for freedom-We die every year in lakhs due to hunger and disease. Is it not good that we should die as brave men for the freedom of our country and the coming generations? I am of the opinion that the revolution which I have outlined is not against the Congress ideal of Ahimsa as the Congress had already agreed during the war to the filling of Germans and the Japanese in return for a mere National Government in Delhi under a British Viceroy. And as for the British how are they concerned with what weapons we choose to fight them with? Have they pledged non-violence if the rebels adhere to it? Did they not shoot down thousands of our non-violent soldiers in 1942. Whatever weapons we use the British have only bullets for us and looting and rape and arson. So let them keep quiet as to how we fight them, it is our business entirely to decide that. I should add that I have no hesitation in admitting that non-violence of the brave, if practised on a sufficiently large scale, would make violence unnecessary, but where such nonviolence is absent, I should not allow cowardice, clothed in Shastric subtleties, to block the development of the revolution and lead to its failure. With the implication of the last phase of the revolution clear in our minds, we have to prepare, organise, train and discipline our forces. In everything we do, we have constantly to bear in mind that ours is not to be merely a conspiratorial action. It is total revolt of the masses that is our objective. So, along with our immense technical work, we must do intensive work among the masses-peasants in the villages and the workers in the factories, mines, railways, and elsewhere.

We must do ceaseless propaganda among them and help them in their present difficulties, organise them to fight for their present demands, recruit from that selected soldiers for our various activities and train them technically and politically. With training a few may succeed where thousands failed before. In every fiska and taluka, and thana, in every considerable factory and workshop or other industrial centres, we must have a band of militants, mentally and materially equipped for the next rising. Then there is our work in the Indian Army and the Services. There is agitational and demonstrative work. There is work in the schools and colleges and in the market place. There is the work in the Native States and on the frontiers of India. It is not possible for me here to describe our preparations more concretely. Let it suffice to say that there is tremendous work to be done and work for every one. Much is being done at present, but vastly more remains to be done.

7

Jay Prakash and His Total Revolution

Jay Prakash Narayan came out of the influence of Marxism and propagated his philosophy of socialism, which for him was only solution to the problems of India. During second phase he devoted himself to the cause of Sarvodaya and became Jeevandani. Between 1970-72 he made effort to end the influence of Naxalwad in Bihar. Because of his endevours in 1972 as many as 400 dacoits of Chambal Valley decided to surrender before him. They promised to live as peaceful and good citizens of India. He was however, not satisfied with several policies of Congress government then headed by Prime Minister Smt. Indira Gandhi and in 1974 he gave the slogan of Total Revolution. With a view to achieve his objective he organised demonstrations and setup students committees and held public meetings. Due to his activities, which had good response from the masses. On 26th June, 1975 internal emergency was declared and he was put behind the bars, where he remained till emergency was lifted in 1977.

Concept of Total Revolution

On June 5, 1974 J.P. gave a call of Total Revolution at Patna. The whole idea was to bring about a complete change in the existing structures of Indian society. He was of the view that power could not be transferred to the people through military strength or violence because after bringing changes military does not involve the people in the formation of policies and programmes. According to his total revolution, which covered seven areas, the number of which could increase or decrease, could bring real changes in many ways. It could result in cultural creativity, moral autonomy and spiritual liberation.

His Total Revolution was combination of seven revolutions namely social, economic, political, cultural, ideological or intellectual, educational and spiritual. This number could increase or decrease as well e.g. economic revolution could be split into agricultural, industrial and technological revolutions. Similarly intellectual revolution could be split into scientific and philosophical. Likewise spiritual revolution also could be part of cultural revolution.

The concept of Total Revolution had wide implications. It aimed at total transformation of both man and society. It has been viewed differently by different people.

In the economic sphere Total Revolution aimed at reducing grossly disproportionate inequalities in socio-economic fields. It also aimed at saving the villages from urban exploiters and transfer of land ownership to the villages for solving the problem of inequality centering round land ownership. It also wanted that public co-operation pattern in industries should be made more popular and everyone must be provided need-based wages with guarantee of full employment. Effective checks should be put on price rise. The manufacture of consumer goods for domestic use should be only in the small rural industries. Workers should be considered as the trustees of large industrial establishments and the basic principle should be social ownership. In the industry similarly the idea of self-government should be developed. Rural based industries should be developed and strengthened and for the purpose massive and integrated programme may be developed. There should be real linkage between the prices of agricultural and industrial products. Planning should be not from above to down below.

Political Revolution

In the political field it was provided that the candidates for the elected bodies should be selected by the peoples committees and the people should be consulted for the objective. Both the army and the police need not obey those orders of the government which aimed at killing the innocent or were manifestly illegal or tried to subvert democratic culture of our society. Governmental processes should be based on discussions and there should be detailed law against defection. For selecting candidates there should be combination of majority vote and list system. The system of recall of elected legislators who have lost the confidence of the people, should be introduced. Everyone who holds high posts whether elected or otherwise should periodically declare assets and none should hold any political office for more than two terms.

Social Revolution

In the social sphere revolution aimed at ending irrational and illogical customs, conventions and practices. The system of inter-caste marriages should be encouraged. Existing caste system should be replaced by one caste i.e. human caste.

Educational Revolution

In intellectual, moral, educational and spiritual fields Total Revolution aimed at avoiding violence and desired that educational and economic planning should go hand in hand. With a view to promote good life some moral and ideal standards acceptable to all should be developed. Universities should be freed from nepotism and should also become pure centres of teaching, training and research. Only those should be permitted to pursue higher education who have academic orientation. Co-operation in every sphere of life should be encouraged. Consistent attempts should be made to develop good habits in the minds of the people. Science should be humanised and spirit of tolerance to admire the viewpoint of others should be developed. Power to oppose oppression and tyranny should be developed and so should be love for liberty and self-determination.

His Line of Action

In his programme of action he did not favour the use of violence, which according to him brought changes in the elites and not in the lot of the masses. He favoured the policy of Gandhian Satyagraha. He however, said that once goals were fixed there could be no dogmatism about the means provided goals and values were kept in view. On the ground of experience the means could be changed as well. He favoured persuasion and where required the policy of non-cooperation could also be used. All bureaucratic pressures should be countered effectively and vigorously by the people. Youth and student power should be fully mobilised because that can go a long way in bringing Total Revolution. He favoured civil disobedience and civil resistance and also direct takeover of the management and running of the enterprises. For him in bringing Total Revolution strikes were important method.

Critical Assessment of Concept of Total Revolution

J.P.'s concept of Total Revolution was a good synthesis of socialist dynamism and rural realism which J.P. developed during second phase of evolution of political development. It was a detailed concept and had many dimensions. It was intended to bringing radical changes not by violent means but with the help of persuasion. It had lofty ideal of reducing both poverty and craze for power. It wanted social control over means of production and distribution. It also aimed to ending social stagnation and use youth and student energies in constructive channels. It touched most significant problem of rural reconstruction on the one hand and checking of urban exploiters of rural masses on the other. It wanted to push to remote comers casteism and communalism which were chronic problems of Indian society and great obstacles in the way of bringing social harmony. It also wanted that by distribution of land to the cultivators not only production would increase but land thirst of several would also be satisfied. But unfortunately his concept of Total Revolution was viewed differently and before it could hold ground J.P. was arrested in 1975 and released in 1977 after remaining in jail for about 19 months because of declaration of internal emergency. During these 19 months no agitations were allowed and the concept did not draw much attention.

After lifting of internal emergency J.P. organised some non-Congress (I) political parties which formed Janata Government at the Centre, after 1977 elections. It was crowning success of his attempts, but soon he realised that his endeavours were not to give fruit for long because of internal bickering of constituents of Janata Party. He would have tried to unite them again, but he himself fell ill and died in 1979 as a frustrated man.

8

Jay Prakash Narayan : An Overview

Jay Prakash Narayan along with Vinoba Bhave believed in a partyless democracy and felt that the present system of election was very defective. He wanted to introduce morality in democracy. He also believed in the system of decentralization and Panchayati Raj. He also wanted to change the method of election so that Government really became a majority Government. He also did not favour the idea of large scale industrialization but on the other hand suggested minimising the wants so that there was village autonomy. He gave philosophy of total revolution and for that he gave exhaustive scheme as well.

J.P. Narayan, was born in 1902 and educated in the U.S.A. It was here that he came in contact with many socialists and practically went under the influence of Marxism. It was also during his stay over there that he studied M.N. Roy, another revolutionary of India, who had escaped to the U.S.A. to save himself from arrest and was influenced by his virtual

Marxian philosophy. For quite sometime he remained under the influence of Marxism but as the time passed he began to lose faith in that mainly because it denied individual freedom and stood for party regimentation. In 1934 he founded Indian Socialist Party in which subsequently he also admitted the Communists. However, finding them not very sincere to socialist doctrines he turned them out and thus saved his party from infiltration. In 1940 Jay Prakash Narayan openly denounced Popular Front of the Communists and in 1942 he actively participated in the revolutionary movement. He got virtual name and fame in 1942 during Quit India Movement. He remained in jail for four years and once he even managed to escape from Hazari Bagh Central Jail. In 1946 along with other socialists he planned for a mass revolution. In 1953 he initiated talks with Jawaharlal Nehru for increased co-operation between the Congress and the Socialists which made some head way. First Phase of J.Ps Thoughts. Jay Prakash Narayan, commonly known as J.P. was a patriot who during first phase which spread between 1929-1953 thought in terms of socialism for solving India's socio-economic and political problems. He considered socialism as a way of reconstructing Indian economy. According to him present socio-economic inequality in India was primarily because of disproportionate ownership and control of means of production. He has said that for country's development was essential that institutions which create hurdles on the way of development of man should be removed. In 1934 All India Congress Socialist Party came out with its 15-point programme which had J.P's ideology.

In the programme which had J.P's ideology it was proposed that all power should be transferred to producing masses and that economic life of the country should be developed, controlled and planned by the state. All key industries should be socialised and foreign trade should be monopolised by the state. It provided that public debt of India should be repudiated and state should not make any distinction on sex basis. In production and distribution stress should be laid on co-operative system and landlordism and similar other institutions of exploitations should be abolished without payment of any compensation. State should not make any distinction on the basis of caste, community, creed or religion. In the programme it was provided that the system of adult franchise on functional basis should be introduced and land should be distributed to the peasants ; every one should be given land according to his need and each one should work according to his capacity and lastly the right to work should be recognised. He had proposed complete separation of India from British imperialism and that debts of peasants and workers should be liquidated. He proposed that the producing masses should have all political and economic power and land should be given to the tillers. Jay Prakash Narayan also proposed abolition of landlordism in every form. According to J.P. objectives of socialism can be achieved by socialisation of means of production. He also stood for reduction of land revenue.

In 1940 J.P. submitted a draft resolution to the Ram Garh Congress, in which he advocated collective ownership and control of all large scale production and urged the Congress to stand for nationalisation of heavy transport, shipping, mining and heavy industries. In his draft resolution he proposed that in free India nation will work for peace between nations and there will be total rejection of armaments. Attempts will also be made to have excellent friendly relations with neighbouring states. The state will guarantee full individual and civil liberty and shall not discriminate in any manner between the citizens of the nation. The political and economic organisation of the state shall be based on the principle of social justice and economic freedom. The village shall be made self-governing units, to the extent feasible. The land laws of the country will be drastically reformed on the principle that land should belong to the actual cultivator. The interests of the poor and down-trodden shall be respected. In state controlled industries workers shall be represented on the management. In Indian states there shall be complete democratic government. J.P. believed that village should be made self-governing unit. He stood for co-operative farming. He wanted to end the exploitation of the tillers and liquidation of all agrarian debts. He favoured agrarian reconstruction.

In J.P's philosophy India's problems can be solved when village is reconstructed. He stood for Gramraj. In 1946 he gave his scheme of constructive work for Gramraj. In that he suggested that in the villages cultural centres should be opened and problems of health and sanitation should be solved keeping problems of each village in view. Attention should be paid for quick redressal of grievances and removal of untouchability. Other items which needed attention included co-operative marketing, setting of grain banks and prohibition.

Jay Prakash put his 14 points programme. In 1953 J.P. put forth fourteen-point scheme for increasing co-operation between Congress and PSP of Jay Prakash Narayan. Though no compromise could be reached, yet his scheme indicated his thinking. In the scheme he suggested that Constitution should be so amended that in that guarantees given to princes and civil servants are ended second chambers are abolished and all those articles of the Constitution which stand on the way of bringing social changes are removed. He wanted that administrative reforms at all levels should be introduced, corruption cases should be summarily dealt with and legal procedure should be suitably reformed. J.P. wanted that administrative map of India should be redrawn taking language, economic and administrative factors into view. Administrative costs should be drastically reduced and in order to remove economic inequality and exploitation, land should be redistributed. State should not deal with individual peasants but with them through their groups in a group or panchayat. Rural economy should be transformed to co-operative economy and fragmentation of land should be checked. Suitable steps should be taken for consolidation of land holdings. All evictions from lands should be immediately stopped. In his scheme J.P. proposed that waste lands should be recarnated and all banks and insurance companies should be nationalised. State trading should also be progressively developed and selected number of plants in different industries should be owned and run by the state or co-operatives. Unions should become socially responsible agencies, coals and other minings should be nationalised and in state enterprises workers should be associated with management. Areas of activities between large and small scale industries should be demarcated and salaries of highly paid officials should be brought down. He wanted that spirit of swadeshi should be promoted. During this phase of life he thoroughly stood for developing India on socialist principles. He laid stress on increased agricultural production and wanted to bring social revolution. He denounced both national and international communism because it denied civil liberties. He did not contribute to both state controlled system of education and its complete control over national economy.

Sarvodaya of Jay Prakash

J.P. in 1954, resigned from the Socialist Party, then known as P.S.P., and became Jeewan Dani for Sarvodaya Movement and devoted himself to the cause of bringing about a new society in India in which there would be no exploitation and decentralization of authority would be the basic principle. He was very closely related to Vinoba Bhave in his Bhoodan Movement. He wanted to have a new society which he termed as Sarvodaya. In 1974 he gave the concept of Total Revolution, which had mass appeal. In 1975 internal emergency was declared in the country and he was jailed. In 1977 elections were held in India and due to his efforts anti-Congress forces could form Janata Party which snatched power from the ruling Congress and formed Government at the Centre and also in several States. To his dismay these disintegrated in 1979. He fell ill and died in October of that year.

J.P. loved Marxism his love for it did not last long. He developed differences with that for many reasons. He did not support atrocities of Russian Bolshevik Party on the one hand and authoritarian regimentation of Russian Communism on the other. He also did not like Communist approach towards national freedom being launched under Gandhiji. They denounced it as bourgeoisie and Gandhiji as Indian bourgeoisie. He percepted that Communists in India were tools of Moscow. He condemned their loyalties towards Russia than to India. He was opposed to Lenin's colonial policy. Though he developed differences with Marxism yet he could not go very near Congress approach. He believed that Congress could not provide real socialist programme to the country and conduct the fight for independence in a more revolutionary manner with the result that he formed Congress Socialist Party with the help of some disillusioned Congressmen. Throughout first phase of his political life he propagated socialist ideas, a mention about it has already been made. Towards Sarvodaya (Second Phase). J.P. stood for bringing socialism in India but after some years he realised that it could not take mankind towards freedom, equality, brotherhood and peace. At Bodh Gaya Sarvodaya Sammelan held in 1953 he was convinced that unless Socialism was transferred into Sarvodaya, people could not go near the objectives of freedom, equality and brotherhood. He then completely broke away from Communism and proceeded towards Sarvodaya.

The idea of Sarvodaya was first adopted by Gandhiji from Ruskins 'Unto the Last'. According to Gandhiji he himself realised a sort of inner happiness when he got this idea. Sarvodaya meant collective welfare in which also was individual's own welfare and that there was always respect for work and that all kinds of jobs were respectable. In addition to this, it also meant that simple living and high thinking was true life and there should be universal development for all sections of society. According to Vinoba Bhave, "Self-sacrifice is the very foundation of the Sarvodaya which preaches the emerging of oneself in the good of all." On the whole both Jay Prakash Narayan and Vinoba Bhave believed that Sarvodaya is a moral programme and line of action and that it should be a useful instrument for collective welfare. In addition to that, Sarvodaya is an indication of a political revolution by peaceful means through free and frank expression of ideas. It has been said, "Ideally such a structure would replace entirely the compulsion in the State of individual initiative and voluntary organisation, it is a sort of enlightened anarchy." In the economic field Sarvodaya stands for decentralization of authority and that the means of production as well as distribution shall be controlled and managed by the society.

In Sarvodaya society there will be co-operative system of production both in the industry as well as agriculture. There will also be village autonomy. In the words of Gandhiji, "Society based on non-violence can only comprise of groups settled in villages in which voluntary co-operation is the condition of dignified and peaceful existence. In Sarvodaya society there would be partyless democracy and as such the evil influence of present party system would eliminate."

A Sarvodaya worker was required to spin daily and use the cloth spun by himself. As far as feasible he should use goods produced by cottage and small scale industries. He should try to use cow milk and should clean latrines or do other work concerning to cleanliness of the village at least once a month. Where there are feasibilities of introducing fundamental system of education he should try to introduce that. He should also try to learn at least one of the regional languages of India. Not only that but he should be an ideal non-violent person with a sense of self-confidence and belief in power of the masses. He should also try to promote unity among different religions and sections of the society and should boycott caste system and discourage the use of intoxicating goods. He should also promote female education and try to spread the idea that both men and women are equal. He should also try to spread regional languages and provincial cultures so that none of them realised neglected. He should aim at bringing about economic equality, growth of agriculture, help in the unity of labourers and uplifting the poor. He should serve the lepers and protect cows.

The Society which shall thus be established under Sarvodaya Samaj will he free from coercive centralized authority and shall be more or less a loose federation comprising of self-governing autonomous villages. Every village or unit shall be self-sufficient and believe in the system of economic decentralization. In Sarvodaya society there was to be no parliament of the kind which we at present have and those who came to power were not be the rulers but servants of the society. He believed that State shall be unnecessary in Sarvodaya society, and as far as feasible the authority of the State will considerably be reduced. In his view State does not help in the development of individual facalties but on the other hand is an unhealthy check even on individual's healthy activities. He, therefore, realised that there was no requirement to load government with various punitive weapons and authorities in actual practice hampered individual progress. He realised that in Sarvodaya society there shall be no party system and the people shall sit together to decide their own affairs. They will not require representatives to speak and talk on their behalf but on the other hand shall get opportunity to express their own ideas themselves. He was intended that in Sarvodaya society consciousness among the people should be created and there should be real Lok Neeti instead of Raj Neeti. In other words in Sarvodaya society there shall not be party or power politics but only authority shall flow from the people themselves who will work in a sense and spirit of serving the people rather than of governing over them. Jay Prakash Narayan believed that conflicts always arise in a society because of various reasons but in his opinion solution to such problems did not lie in equipping the government with more punitive powers but in creating awakening and consciousness among the masses so that they could adjust themselves in a better and reasonable way.

In his early life Jay Prakash Narayan was a serious student of Marxism. 1929 when Indian National Congress declared complete independence as the objective of its national struggle. Jay Prakash then bade farewell to his Marxist ideology and actively participated in the civil disobedience movement launched by Mahatma Gandhi. He, however, wanted to introduce socialism in the Congress with the result that he founded the Congress Socialist Party which was later reliable for giving socio-economic programme both to the party and also the country, he seriously studied Gandhi an philosophy and was convinced that spiritual foundation was required for a lasting peace. Besides that, he started to realise the value of individual freedom, equality and brotherhood which were in practice missing from Communism. A turning point, however, came with Vinoba's coming in the field. His starting of the Bhoodan Movement and getting a donation of 100 acres of land from Shri Ram Chandra Reddy changed the very course of his philosophy. He started to appreciate the significance and importance of the methods which he realised could bring about an economic revolution in the country, if seriously implemented. He found in Bhoodan Movement a fair, better and effective alternative to Communist revolution which provided for snatching of land by forceful methods.

According to him Gandhism taught us the method of Satyagraha which brought freedom to India and that Bhoodan and Gramdan Movement was bound to bring economic revolution and make our political freedom a reality. He was also inspired by the idea of Lok Neeti instead of Raj Neeti as expounded by Vinobaji. Steadily he was also convinced about the desirability of cottage industries and the system of democratic decentralization. He also wanted to change the face of India by introducing village autonomy and raising the down-trodden and the poor who form a huge majority of Indian population. In his view Bhoodan and Gramdan movements are constructive techniques and easy as well as practicable solution to India's problems. The outcome of all this was that he later decided to leave P.S.P. and join Bhoodan Movement. "I became at this time, and still am, an ardent believer, like Gandhiji, in the maxim that Government was the best that governed the least."

Politically, he believed that dawn of a new society for all, irrespective of caste and status, would emerge under Sarvodaya. His significant political ideas are as under :

Jay Prakash Narayan was a very great supporter of democracy and favoured democratic institutions. For him, democracy was both a creed and a way of life and that nothing beyond democracy could satisfy him. He was believer of individual freedom which could best be achieved only in democracy. He was however, not satisfied with the present democratic system which he felt was highly defective. In his opinion present system was highly centralized with the result that the people could not take any active part in the proper functioning of democratic institutions. The control of party bosses is so rigid that individual is practically ignored. He also realised that parliamentary system, in its present form, has a very narrow base because in that the authority starts from above rather from down below. It has thus an inverted structure which cannot last long. He also condemned democracy because legislative bodies which governed the name of majority were in fact minority Governments. In real practice minority rules over the majority. Not only this but the decisions arrived at by the majority party are not unanimous.

Similarly even in the Cabinet decisions are not arrived at unanimously and only a few powerful persons carry others with them. All this explicitly shows that the majority is ruled by the minority. He also felt that in our present parliamentary democracy the institution of party system is very unhealthy. It had practically denied liberty to the individuals. Party bosses try to dominate their members. There is an on going and continuous struggle for supremacy which divides the rank and file and also promotes insincerity. He has denounced democracy also because he finds that in it there is much unnecessary waste of national money.

Jay Prakash Narayan was also pained to see that in our modern democracies those who could speak well irrespective of any other consideration managed to come to power. He was also pained to find that in order to win the elections all healthy and unhealthy practices were being used. Even casteism and communalism which is not to be legally used in elections, is used to win the election. He, therefore, very strongly condemned the present system of parliamentary democracy.

In his view a democracy in its true sense must have spiritual basis and that can only be feasible when the people practising it start to believe in truth. They should also truly follow non-violence and should be ready to face all oppressions and high-handedness with courage and boldness. They should love liberty and believe in the spirit of not only toleration and co-operation. A true democrat should also be ready to willingly discharge his duties and liabilities. He should be a believer in human equality. There should be belief in the decentralization of authority. The power should flow from down to above and not flow from above to down below. He also believed that in true democracy there should be the system of decentralization of authority.

In Spite of all his reservations for parliamentary democracy, be had still hopes that it could deliver the goods. In it, there is every possibility of maximum decentralisation of authority. Again it is the system which can establish links and co-ordination between industry and agriculture.

Jay Prakash realised that the introduction of party system in our present political set-up had degenerated democracy. The present day system encourages party politics and divides the nation. He, therefore, realised that the whole system should be changed. There should be a partyless democracy. His suggestion was that in each village there should be a Gram Mandal or a Conference consisting of elected representatives of the village, one atleast from each family.

Such a Mandal should meet monthly to decide all pending issues of the village.

There should be no need and necessity of electing representatives to speak on behalf of the people but the people themselves will express their feelings and approach. Each Mandal then in turn will become an electoral college to send representatives to the legislatures. The whole arrangement shall be of the kind and nature that the authority will go down from villages to the legislatures and thus real democracy will be established. He has suggested that our cabinet should not be formed on the ground of party system but these should be partyless cabinets which should enlist capable and intelligent persons from all political parties.

During second phase of his political development he tried to reconstruct Indian polity. He suggested that the defects of modern democracies which required to be removed include corruption, expensive elections, centralisation of authority and partisanship attitude of political parties. Masses should be mobilised for active participation in democratic processes. There should be work-oriented education and that legitimate demands of the masses should also be met.

Other suggestions made by him comprise differentiation in the names of political system, checking of authoritarian domination, involvement of all adults in the political system, promotion of social collaboration, Gramdan, administrative efficiency, formation of Shanti Sena, undertaking of rural reconstruction programme and more autonomy for states. He wanted that our present day democratic setup should be based on ancient Indian values. He also wanted that our whole system should be above all castes, creeds and religions so that all Indians without any other consideration could participate in that. According to him in real democracy there should be rule of law. He also laid stress on moral values. He considered democracy not only a form of government but also a creed and way of life. It should be made to operate in a way that all get social and economic justice, there is equality of opportunity and also balanced development of industry and agriculture. He believed that political and economic democracies could not be separated from each other.

Panchayati Raj and Jay Prakash . According to Jay Prakash Narayan real solution to our political problems laid in the introduction of Panchayati Raj system is our body politic. As the authority is not decentralized among the millions in our villages, nothing concrete can come out. The proposal given by him was that in each village there should be Gram Sabha. The Sabha shall comprise all adult men and women living in the village and shall have the power to discuss about life and problems of the village. Gram Panchayat shall be the executive organ of this Sabha.

Subsequently there shall be Zila Parishads and Block Samitis at the higher level. Block Samitis shall cover the villages falling in one block and few blocks combined together shall form Zilas and these Zilas in turns constitute the State and country. Jay Prakash Narayan fully well realized the difficulties which could arise in the establishment of Gram Sabha or Gram Conference. Such difficulties can possibly because of family which are common in our villages. In addition to this, he also realized that caste system could also be one of the reasons for its not very successful working. He realised that if proper and effective steps are taken, there can no reason to think that all difficulties and complications which can come in the way of proper and successful working of Panchayati Raj can not be overcome. One of the methods suggested by him in this regard, was that the people should be given proper education. As far as possible family feuds and party system should not be allowed to interfere in the

Gram Panchayats and Gram Sabhas. These Sabhas should be given some effective powers and real authority should be given to the Sabhas so that these could effectively exert themselves. He also suggested that the Sabhas should be given sufficient economic resources and authority to control civil servants working under their jurisdiction. As far as feasible the Sabhas and Panchayats should have a non-political character and there should be no intervention from the high ups in the sphere of their jurisdiction. Jay Prakash felt that if the system was introduced in the villages a new life was bound to come in the country. In his view such a system was bound to bring consciousness among the people and they shall refuse by the city people. In other words indirectly cities shall also be suitably improved.

Jay Prakash Narayan believed in the socialisation of means of production and distribution. He also believed in the nationalization of industries and suggested that economic resources should. He placed at the disposal of the nation rather than any individual. He also suggested reduction of land revenue and also limitations on expenditure.

He favoured collective ownership and control of all large scale industries. He made suggestion that such heavy industries, as transport, mining or shipping should forthwith be nationalized. He, however, believed that co-operative effort alone could bring about balance between agriculture and industry. He wanted to have economic rehabilitation of the poor and the down-trodden. He also believed in agrarian reconstruction. He was a great supporter of co-operative farming. In his philosophy there was very close relationship between culture and economics as the culture of a nation was reflected by economic conditions of its people. He realised that economic conditions of the country should be such that every individual got equality of opportunity and was given some minimum economic standard. Jay Prakash Narayan was a socialist of the first order. He tried to awaken the youth of India by telling them to remember the role which they played during Quit India Movement and gave them a call to re-unite themselves to perform that constructive duty. His system of democratic decentralization and Panchayati Raj and that of adopting democracy in its new form, if properly adopted, can bring a new outlook in India.

BIBLIOGRAPHY

Bhargava, G.S. : *Leaders of the Left*, Bombay, 1951.

Bhasin, Prem : *Socialism in India*, New Delhi, 1968.

Bhattacharjea, Ajit : *Jayaprakash Narayan*, New Delhi, 1975.

Bimal Prasad : *Gandhi, Nehru and J.P.*, Delhi, 1985.

Durga Das : *India From Curzon to Nehru and After*, London, 1969.

Ghose, Shankar : *Socialism, Democracy and Nationalism in India*, New Delhi, 1973.

Gupta, Ram Chandra ; *J.P. : From Marxism to Total Revolution*, New Delhi, 1981.

Lal, Lakshmi Narain : *Jayaprakash-Rebel Extraordinary*, New Delhi, 1975.

Limaye, Madhu : *Evolution of the Socialist Party*, Hyderabad, 1968.

Lohia, Rammanohar: *Marx, Gandhi and Socialism*, Hyderabad. 1963.

Mehta, Asoka : *Democratic Socialism*, Bombay, 1963.

Narain, Brij : *Indian Socialism*, Lahore, 1937.

Narayan, Jayaprakash : *Congress Socialist Party (Hindi)*, Patna, Samta Prakashan, 1946.—From Socialism to Sarvodaya (Statement on his leaving the Party), Akhil Bharat Sarva Seva Sangh, Publication, 1959.

Narayan, Jayaprakash : *In the Labour Front*, Patna, 1942.

Nehru, Jawaharlal : *An Autobiography*, Bombay, 1962.

Rao, V.K.R.V. : *Indian Socialism : Retrospect and Prospect*, New Delhi, 1982.

Sharma, M.L. : *Gandhi As a Socialist*, New Delhi, 1980.

INDEX